The Edinburgh Companion to James Hogg

Edinburgh Companions to Scottish Literature

Series Editors: Ian Brown and Thomas Owen Clancy

Titles in the series include:

The Edinburgh Companion to Robert Burns
Edited by Gerard Carruthers
978 0 7486 3648 8 (hardback)
978 0 7486 3649 5 (paperback)

*The Edinburgh Companion to Twentieth-
Century Scottish Literature*
Edited by Ian Brown and Alan Riach
978 0 7486 3693 8 (hardback)
978 0 7486 3694 5 (paperback)

*The Edinburgh Companion to Contemporary
Scottish Poetry*
Edited by Matt McGuire and Colin
Nicholson
978 0 7486 3625 9 (hardback)
978 0 7486 3626 6 (paperback)

The Edinburgh Companion to Muriel Spark
Edited by Michael Gardiner and Willy
Maley
978 0 7486 3768 3 (hardback)
978 0 7486 3769 0 (paperback)

*The Edinburgh Companion to Robert Louis
Stevenson*
Edited by Penny Fielding
978 0 7486 3554 2 (hardback)
978 0 7486 3555 9 (paperback)

The Edinburgh Companion to Irvine Welsh
Edited by Berthold Schoene
978 0 7486 3917 5 (hardback)
978 0 7486 3918 2 (paperback)

The Edinburgh Companion to James Kelman
Edited by Scott Hames
978 0 7486 3963 2 (hardback)
978 0 7486 3964 9 (paperback)

*The Edinburgh Companion to Scottish
Romanticism*
Edited by Murray Pittock
978 0 7486 3845 1 (hardback)
978 0 7486 3846 8 (paperback)

The Edinburgh Companion to Scottish Drama
Edited by Ian Brown
978 0 7486 4108 6 (hardback)
978 0 7486 4107 9 (paperback)

The Edinburgh Companion to Sir Walter Scott
Edited by Fiona Robertson
978 0 7486 4130 7 (hardback)
978 0 7486 4129 1 (paperback)

*The Edinburgh Companion to Hugh
MacDiarmid*
Edited by Scott Lyall and Margery Palmer
McCulloch
978 0 7486 4190 1 (hardback)
978 0 7486 4189 5 (paperback)

The Edinburgh Companion to James Hogg
Edited by Ian Duncan and Douglas Mack
978 0 7486 4124 6 (hardback)
978 0 7486 4123 9 (paperback)

*The Edinburgh Companion to Scottish
Literature 1400–1650*
Edited by Nicola Royan
978 0 7486 4391 2 (hardback)
978 0 7486 4390 5 (paperback)

*The Edinburgh Companion to Scottish
Women's Writing*
Edited by Glenda Norquay
978 0 7486 4432 2 (hardback)
978 0 7486 4431 5 (paperback)

*The Edinburgh Companion to Scottish
Traditional Literatures*
Edited by Sarah Dunnigan and Suzanne
Gilbert
978 0 7486 4540 4 (hardback)
978 0 7486 4539 8 (paperback)

The Edinburgh Companion to Liz Lochhead
Edited by Anne Varty
978 0 7486 5472 7 (hardback)
978 0 7486 5471 0 (paperback)

Visit the Edinburgh Companions to Scottish Literature website at
www.euppublishing.com/series/ecsl

The Edinburgh Companion to James Hogg

Edited by Ian Duncan and Douglas S. Mack

EDINBURGH
University Press

© in this edition Edinburgh University Press, 2012
© in the individual contributions is retained by the authors

Edinburgh University Press Ltd
22 George Square, Edinburgh

www.euppublishing.com

Typeset in 10.5/12.5 Adobe Goudy
by Servis Filmsetting Ltd, Stockport, Cheshire, and
printed and bound in Great Britain by
CPI Group (UK) Ltd, Croydon, CR0 4YY

A CIP record for this book is available from the British Library

ISBN 978 0 7486 4124 6 (hardback)
ISBN 978 0 7486 4123 9 (paperback)
ISBN 978 0 7486 5514 4 (webready PDF)
ISBN 978 0 7486 5516 8 (epub)
ISBN 978 0 7486 5515 1 (Amazon ebook)

The right of the contributors
to be identified as author of this work
has been asserted in accordance with
the Copyright, Designs and Patents Act 1988.

Contents

Figures

Acknowledgements

Ian Duncan thanks Lauren Naturale and Monica Soare for their assistance in preparing the volume for press, and Ian Brown, joint series editor of *The Edinburgh Companions to Scottish Literature*, for his encouragement and patience.

Douglas S. Mack, dean of Hogg studies and co-editor of the *Edinburgh Companion to James Hogg*, died at the end of 2009, while the volume was in preparation. It is dedicated to his memory.

Series Editors' Preface

The fourth tranche of the *Companions* series marks in its own way the underlying themes of the series as whole: Scottish literature is multivalent, multilingual and vibrant. Each volume also reflects the series ethos: to challenge, set new perspectives and work towards defining differences of canon in Scottish literature. Such definition of difference must always be sensitive and each volume in the 2012 tranche shows not only the confidence of up-to-date, leading-edge scholarship, but the flexibility of nuanced thought that has developed in Scottish literary studies in recent years. A tranche which balances a volume on women's writing with volumes on two major male writers subverts, even on the most superficial reading, any version of an older tradition which depended on a canon based on 'great' writers, mostly, if not exclusively, male. In approaching Scott and Hogg contributors have demonstrated fresh thinking and re-contextualised their work, opening them to new insights and enjoyment, while the authors in the volume on *Women's Writing* reinterpret and re-organise the very structures of thought through which we experience the writing explored.

Scott, often in the past taken to represent a stuffy old-fashioned male-dominated literary canon, is revisited, reassessed and brought to our minds anew. One is reminded of the remark of the great European scholar Martin Esslin to one of the series editors that Scott was the greatest artist in any artform of the nineteenth century. Such a statement may embody the generalising attitudes of an older generation, but Esslin's argument was based not just on Scott's range and innovations, but on the importance of his influence on his successors, not just in literature but in other arts. Hogg meantime has often previously suffered by comparison with Scott, misunderstood and misread in ways the *Hogg* volume makes clear as it demystifies past perceptions and opens new vistas on his work's scope. The *Scottish Women's Writing* volume completes a trio of innovative *Companions* in its range of disparate viewpoints. Avoiding easy categories or theories, these demonstrate with rigour and vigour that, though in some genres, like drama, women's writing has had a difficult time historically, it has, not least in the Gaelic tradition, always played a crucial role. The volume rightly and lucidly interrogates any system of classification that obscures this insight. The 2012 tranche as a whole continues the *Companions* series project of reviewing and renewing the way we read and enjoy the rich diversity of Scottish literature

Ian Brown
Thomas Owen Clancy

Brief Biography of James Hogg

James Hogg was born in November 1770 at Ettrickhall farm, in the valley of Ettrick, Selkirkshire, to Robert Hogg, a tenant farmer and former shepherd, and Margaret Laidlaw. His father's bankruptcy terminated James's formal schooling when he was six years old; over the next dozen years he did menial farm labour, borrowing books to further his education. Employed as a shepherd from 1788, Hogg acquired a local reputation as a poet and songwriter. His first poem, 'Mistakes of a Night', appeared in the *Scots Magazine* in 1790, and his first, self-published book, *Scottish Pastorals*, followed in 1801. In 1802 Hogg met Walter Scott, whom he assisted with the third volume of *Minstrelsy of the Scottish Border* (1803). Scott helped Hogg publish his own book of original ballads, *The Mountain Bard*, in 1807.

After a failed farming venture Hogg began his literary career in earnest in Edinburgh in 1810, writing and editing a short-lived weekly magazine, *The Spy*. Hogg's breakthrough came with his poetic miscellany *The Queen's Wake* (1813), which was widely and favourably reviewed, went through several editions, and made him famous. Hogg became involved with the rising publisher William Blackwood and helped launch *Blackwood's Edinburgh Magazine* in 1817. Although their friendship was often strained – and twice broken by serious quarrels – it would prove the most important professional association of Hogg's career. In 1818 Hogg published his first collection of prose tales, *The Brownie of Bodsbeck*, with Blackwood; subsequent prose fiction titles came out with other publishers, including Oliver and Boyd (*Winter Evening Tales*, 1820) and Longman (the experimental novels, *The Three Perils of Man*, 1822; *The Three Perils of Woman*, 1823; and *The Private Memoirs and Confessions of a Justified Sinner*, 1824). John Wilson, Hogg's friend and de facto editor of *Blackwood's Magazine*, savagely lampooned Hogg's literary ambitions in 1821 and 1823; Wilson's reviews, though extreme, were symptomatic of a mounting resistance on the part of the Edinburgh literary establishment to Hogg's forays into metropolitan genres such as the historical novel and epic. (Hogg's essay in the latter, *Queen Hynde*, was mutilated in the press in 1824.) A fictionalised version of Hogg, the 'Shepherd', became a popular mainstay of the satirical series 'Noctes Ambrosianae', written mainly by Wilson and published in *Blackwood's* from 1822. Throughout the late 1820s Hogg found his public persona increasingly usurped by Wilson's comic invention.

Hogg enjoyed a sustaining family life, having married Margaret Phillips, who would bear him seven children, in 1820; but money troubles encroached. Although the Duke of Buccleuch had granted him rent-free lease of a cottage at Altrive Lake, Hogg took on an expensive farm at Mount Benger in 1821. In 1830, deeply in debt, he lost the Mount Benger lease and went back to Altrive. Hogg continued to enjoy popular success with his magazine tales, poems and songs. In 1832 he visited London and found himself lionised. Attempts to bring out a collected edition of his fiction foundered in the economic turbulence of the early 1830s. Late works (1834) range from a volume of *Lay Sermons* to the *Familiar Anecdotes of Sir Walter Scott*, which stirred up a minor scandal. Hogg died of liver failure on 21 November 1835, and was buried in Ettrick kirkyard.

Introduction: Hogg and his Worlds

Ian Duncan

I

'Having appeared as a poet, and a speculative farmer besides, no one would now employ me as a shepherd', James Hogg recalled in his 'Memoir of the Author's Life': 'therefore, in February 1810, in utter desperation, I took my plaid about my shoulders, and marched away to Edinburgh, determined, since no better could be, to push my fortune as a literary man'.[1] Edinburgh in 1810 was a literary boomtown – one of the thriving centres of what Pascale Casanova has called 'international literary space' in the early nineteenth century.[2] The ascendant genres of an industrialising, empire-wide print market – periodicals and fiction – were being reinvented here, in the former capital of the Scottish Enlightenment. Walter Scott, whom Hogg had helped to gather ballads for *Minstrelsy of the Scottish Border* in 1802, was establishing himself as the dominant presence on the scene: Scotland's cultural viceroy. The founding of *The Edinburgh Review* (1802) and the craze for Scott's metrical romances (*The Lay of the Last Minstrel*, 1805; *Marmion*, 1808; *The Lady of the Lake*, 1810) energised a publishing and reviewing industry that was beginning to rival London's, and would be further boosted by Scott's Waverley Novels (from 1814) and *Blackwood's Edinburgh Magazine* (from 1817). This hothouse of literary innovation was stratified by emergent as well as traditional hierarchies of class and rank. Scott, the critics of the *Edinburgh Review*, and Hogg's friends at *Blackwood's*, John Gibson Lockhart and John Wilson, were all gentlemen, university educated and trained in the city's elite legal profession. Hogg was a former shepherd and failed farmer.

Hogg made much of his rural origins, and much was made of them by critics, not always to his advantage. Born and raised in Ettrick, he kept his household, raised a family, and continued farming there, even as he paid regular, extended visits to Edinburgh. As Valentina Bold and Suzanne Gilbert show in the first chapter in this *Companion*, Hogg cherished his roots in traditionary culture, and kept open the imaginative channels between them and his literary work. A consummate 'sentimental' poet, in Schiller's formulation, he knew how to play

1

the part of a naive one for urban audiences.[3] Although he had been publishing poems since the 1790s, Hogg made his official literary debut as 'the Ettrick Shepherd', the successor of the 'heaven-taught ploughman' Robert Burns, in a Highland tour serialised in the *Scots Magazine* (1802–3) and a volume of original ballads, *The Mountain Bard* (1807). Despite experiments with other personae ('Mr Spy', the shifty editor of a weekly magazine; 'J. H. Craig of Douglas, Esq.', a genteel author of 'dramatic tales') the Ettrick Shepherd would be the label that stuck, throughout the Victorian era and afterwards.

In his lifetime Hogg was most acclaimed for his romantic ballad miscellany *The Queen's Wake* (1813), and especially for two poems in it, the dream vision 'Kilmeny' and the black-comic fabliau 'The Witch of Fife', as well as for the dozens of songs, tales and sketches he contributed to periodicals, above all to *Blackwood's Edinburgh Magazine*, with which he was indelibly associated. In the 1820s a fantastic avatar of Hogg, the 'Shepherd', became current in the pages of *Blackwood's*, in the satirical symposium series 'Noctes Ambrosianae'. Uncouth, uproarious, tenderhearted, an irrepressible fount of comic and pathetic ditties, folk wisdom and boozy slapstick, this hugely popular rendition of Hogg as rural genius (and Tory cultural mascot) was mainly the work of his professed friend, the de facto editor of *Blackwood's*, John Wilson.[4] It effectively replaced Hogg, the struggling author, in the public eye for the remainder of the century.

The vogue for the Shepherd accompanied a stiffening resistance on the part of the Edinburgh literary establishment to Hogg's attempts to rise beyond his rustic-bard persona. The 'peasant poet', patronised by the great and good, was a familiar figure in the Romantic-period literary field, as Sharon Alker and Holly Faith Nelson show in Chapter 6; Hogg affronted decorum by refusing either to stick to the role or to perish when he ventured outside it. The shadow of the client–patron relation would vex his friendship with Scott, whose lead he followed from ballad imitation to metrical romance and national historical novel.[5] Reviewers rebuffed the fierce energy with which Hogg reimagined metropolitan genres, accusing him of boorishness and 'indelicacy'. Variously commercial and ideological currents of this disquiet ruffled his dealings with publishers, which Peter Garside discusses in Chapter 2; while Suzanne Gilbert traces the sometimes flowery, more often stony path of Hogg's nineteenth-century critical reception.

More than a century would pass before James Hogg and the Ettrick Shepherd could be disentangled. The decisive event, by most reckonings, was André Gide's discovery of *The Private Memoirs and Confessions of a Justified Sinner* in the 1940s (Gide's influential introduction to the Cresset Press edition of *Confessions* appeared in the same year, 1947, that he was awarded the Nobel Prize). 'James Hogg' makes a cameo appearance in the closing pages of the novel, playing the role of an authentic Ettrick Shepherd, who refuses – growling thorny dialect – to assist a party of literary gentlemen in their quest for the relics of the eponymous sinner. At a stroke Hogg reclaims his pastoral persona from the *Blackwood's* wits and divorces it from the invisible, alienated author of *Confessions of a Justified Sinner* – a story so 'replete with horrors' (he later wrote) that 'after I had written it I durst not venture to put my name to it'.[6] Hogg's horror story became readable, at last, in the aesthetic lens of late modernism. He returned to view as the author of a single, miraculous masterpiece, a cult classic and *roman maudit*, the most sophisticated as well as most unsettling entry in a nineteenth-century tradition of fables of demonic temptation, perverse criminality and psychic doubling (from Hoffmann, Poe and Gogol to Dostoevsky, Stevenson and Wilde).

Gide's advocacy paved the way for Louis Simpson's critical reconsideration of Hogg in 1962 and John Carey's edition of *Confessions of a Justified Sinner* for Oxford English Novels in 1969, which gave the work canonical status and impelled a wave of further critical revaluations. Focusing, inevitably, on the *Confessions*, these began to call attention to Hogg's wider achievement – making claims, at first, for the originality and power of his prose fiction. Douglas Gifford's 1976 monograph, *James Hogg*, flanked by his 1972 edition of *The Three Perils of Man* and Douglas Mack's 1976 edition of *The Brownie of Bodsbeck*, effectively turned upside-down the nineteenth-century account of Hogg's achievement, replacing the lyric folk-poet with the 'dark', proto-postmodern novelist. The project of ongoing reassessment, carried out by Mack, David Groves, Gillian Hughes, and other scholars through the 1970s and 1980s, achieved institutional consolidation in the form of a James Hogg Society (founded in 1981), which sponsors a regular series of conferences, and (from 1990) an annual scholarly journal, *Studies in Hogg and his World*. (This is currently the only journal devoted to topics in Scottish Romanticism, which says something about Hogg's centrality to a renewed interest in the field.) Hogg's full return to visibility began in earnest in the mid-1990s, however, with the appearance of the first three volumes (*The Shepherd's Calendar*, *The Three Perils of Woman*, and *A Queer Book*) of a scholarly edition, the Stirling/ South Carolina Edition of the Collected Works of James Hogg, published by Edinburgh University Press. Some of these works, bowdlerised and otherwise disfigured in the press in his lifetime, are appearing for the first time as Hogg originally wrote them. The present *Edinburgh Companion to James Hogg* joins a critical revival that is bringing the entirety of one of the most remarkable achievements of European literary Romanticism into public view.

II

The new collected edition is revealing a Hogg who wrote in a wider variety of literary forms than almost any contemporary. It seems as though he would

try his hand at anything, from the pastoral genres of song, ballad and folk-
tale that made him famous to that quintessentially urban, modern form,
the magazine or miscellany, and its constituent parts, the review, sketch,
anecdote and satirical squib. While Hogg excelled at the shorter lyric and
ballad-based forms showcased in his early collections *The Mountain Bard* and
The Forest Minstrel, his attempts at the book-length narrative verse genres of
British Romanticism are characterised by a bold, sometimes bizarre experimentalism, as Fiona Wilson shows in Chapter 11, on Hogg's poetry. Besides
the anthology of ballad-revival styles that comprises *The Queen's Wake*, these
include a legendary-historical romance in Spenserian stanzas (*Mador of the
Moor*), a cosmological vision-poem (*The Pilgrims of the Sun*), and a post-*Fingal*
Caledonian epic in six books (*Queen Hynde*).[7]

Bold and Gilbert bring out the complexity of Hogg's engagement with –
and refashioning of – oral traditional genres in his poetry and fiction; while
Kirsteen McCue emphasises the professionalism, as well as versatility, with
which Hogg adapted his talents to the salon requirements of art-song, as
well as varieties of popular song. Meiko O'Halloran attends to an especially
neglected corner of Hogg's oeuvre, his essays in the drama (potentially one
of the most lucrative literary ventures of the day, she reminds us). Besides
the 'dramatic tales', or national history plays, discussed by O'Halloran,
these included a pastoral comedy along the lines of (but grittier than) Allan
Ramsay's *The Gentle Shepherd* and even a masque for George IV's 1822 visit
to Edinburgh (its venue relocated from the court to the street), brought back
to light in Douglas Mack's recent edition of *The Bush Aboon Traquair and The
Royal Jubilee*.[8]

Graham Tulloch discusses Hogg's novels in terms of the different sub-
genres and publication formats of a still-emergent literary form, from the
historical romance (*The Three Perils of Man*) and national domestic tale (*The
Three Perils of Woman*) in three volumes to the one-volume novel of psychological obsession and fatality (*The Private Memoirs and Confessions of a Justified
Sinner*), something of a Blackwood's specialty in the early 1820s.[9] Writing
for magazines, Hogg had developed an expertise in shorter fictional forms,
evident in the novella-length works included in his collections *The Brownie
of Bodsbeck* and *Winter Evening Tales*, such that (Tulloch argues) he found a
truly congenial vehicle in the single-volume format of *Confessions of a Justified
Sinner*. *Confessions* rehearses a further, dizzying fission into its constituent
narratives and discourses, only this time the formal disintegration bears the
logic of a fully thematised intention. John Plotz explores the brilliant variety
and virtuosity of Hogg's exercises in the short fiction forms generated in
the Romantic-period expansion of periodical publishing. He issues a timely
caution against not only the long-standing tendency among literary historians
to favour the novel as the teleological form of prose fiction, but the concomi-

tant evaluation of a particular paradigm of the short story – formally unified, intensive, 'finished' – as the novel's antithetical complement. Instead, Plotz bids us appreciate the mixed, ragged, unresolved aesthetic of Hogg's writing, as it resists closure into the settled forms preferred by later criticism.

Hogg wrote in other genres and formats, which (for reasons of space) are not given systematic coverage here: satirical burlesque (the notorious 'Translation from an Ancient Chaldee Manuscript', drafted by Hogg and enlarged by Wilson and Lockhart for the relaunch of *Blackwood's Edinburgh Magazine* in September 1817), parody (*The Poetic Mirror*, with its dead-on impressions of Byron, Scott, Southey, Wordsworth and Coleridge), memoir (of himself, of Scott), antiquarian collection (the two-volume *Jacobite Relics of Scotland*), moral essay (*Lay Sermons*), and farming treatise (*The Shepherd's Guide*, a husbandry manual that remained authoritative well after Hogg's death). As Bold and Gilbert emphasise, Hogg continued to write about Ettrick, in poems and tales (*The Mountain Bard, The Shepherd's Calendar*), in quasi-fictional ethnographic sketches (the *Blackwood's* series of 'Tales and Anecdotes of Pastoral Life'), and in analytic and meditative essays on the historical transformations of rural society, from his 1823 *Blackwood's* review of Lord Napier's *Treatise on Practical Store-Farming* to a late article in the *Quarterly Journal of Agriculture* (1831–2).[10] His accounts of his periodic visits to the Highlands display the Borderer's keen interest in a region that had acquired a specific literary gravity by the early nineteenth century, thanks to James Macpherson's 'Ossian' poems, Scott, and a booming tourist industry; H. B. de Groot, in Chapter 5, tracks the spillover of Hogg's Highland journeys into his poems and fiction.

Monthly and weekly magazines, a dominant publication format by the early 1820s, fostered this variety of literary forms, and Hogg's achievement cannot be understood without reference to them. While his association with *Blackwood's* remained paramount,[11] Hogg contributed to a wide range of periodicals (including newspapers), as Gillian Hughes shows in Chapter 3, and they comprised a strand of his career scarcely less important than his ventures in book-based genres. In his last years Hogg was taken up by both *Chambers's* and *Fraser's*, ascendant in the early 1830s, and he adapted readily to the gift-book-style annuals that became fashionable in the late 1820s; while research by Janette Currie has uncovered Hogg's popularity in the American periodical press.[12]

Recent scholarship has begun to reorientate our view of the early nineteenth-century literary field around the unprecedented expansion of print markets across the North Atlantic world, with the consequent diversification of formats and genres encouraging the revival and reconditioning of old forms as well as the invention of new ones.[13] This emerging account allows us to see, more clearly than before, Hogg as working at the centre of what we have grown used to calling 'Romanticism', rather than fumbling at its margin. Hogg's standing will likewise gain from the ongoing shift of critical attention from the genres conventionally favoured in the literary historiography of Romanticism, such as the 'greater Romantic lyric' and (latterly) the novel, to phenomena such as the ballad revival, the rise of the tale, and the proliferation of periodicals, in all of which he plays an exemplary rather than eccentric part.[14] Finally, Gillian Hughes's recent three-volume edition of Hogg's letters exhibits his mastery of a major eighteenth- and nineteenth-century genre that flourished alongside the circuits of print. There is scarcely a better place for readers to savour Hogg's versatility and skill, as he shapes his persona to different correspondents and situations. Hogg writes himself across the plot of his own life as a complex, rounded, fully professional as well as domestic man – a far cry from the naive shepherd of the 'Noctes' or the victimised, self-divided figure of some more recent commentary.

III

Gillian Hughes's recent biography evokes Hogg's career 'between worlds' while emphasising the fullness of his achievement:

> Hogg's life took place between worlds, that of the labouring-class community into which he had been born and that of the professional literary men where his talent and determination placed him. He was born into a traditional oral culture and lived to see the beginnings of a mass culture, of a widening franchise and cheap penny papers. He told of ancient superstitions and social customs by means of the latest developments in print culture and publishing, and died only shortly before the age of photography . . . His writing was the natural expression of this double vision, with its multiple viewpoints and rapid and unpredictable shifts of tone.[15]

If a single quality or concept could characterise that achievement, it might be *experiment*, with all that term's connotations of unevenness, roughness, oddness, partial success and even occasional failure, as well as originality, novelty, audacity and discovery: in short, an aesthetic energy that expresses itself in the unsettling, recombination and disruption of form rather than in its resolution or perfection. The acknowledged masterpieces of the period, from *Lyrical Ballads* to *Waverley* and *Frankenstein*, self-consciously offered themselves to the public as experiments; their own success and subsequent familiarity has made them look like natural features of a literary landscape. In this experimental impulse, sharpened by his outsider status, we can identify Hogg's 'Romanticism'.[16]

Hogg's experiments register, first, at the level of style. His sheer virtuosity in writing vernacular Scots, from imitations of popular song to the differentiation among Border dialects in tales such as 'Love Adventures of Mr. George Cochrane', can seduce the reader into mistaking the effects of art for those of nature – and certainly Hogg's own strategic claims upon the persona of untaught rustic bard have encouraged the misperception.[17] *The Poetic Mirror* shows off Hogg's skill in the literary verse styles of the day (unforgettably in his out-take from *The Recluse*, 'The Stranger'). Hogg's late, aptly-titled collection *A Queer Book* (1832) features poetic exercises in what he called his 'ancient stile': a prototype, quarried from the makars and other elder poets, of Hugh MacDiarmid's 'synthetic Scots', and a strong example of the 'distressed' technique that Susan Stewart has analysed in the ballad revival and other Romantic refashionings of pre-modern genres.[18] Hogg's 'distressings' can be entertainingly grotesque, as in 'The Witch of Fife', or alienating and unintelligible, as in 'The Harper's Song' in *Mador of the Moor*, or charming, as in his self-parody for *The Poetic Mirror*, 'The Gude Greye Katt'. In his novels and tales, amplifying cues given by Scott, Hogg mixes literary and other print-media styles, languages and registers (such as the charter parody in *Confessions of a Justified Sinner*) with passages of vernacular storytelling that may expand to take over the entire work. Nothing on this scale, or of this quality, had been attempted before in British prose fiction, although Burns's 'Tam o' Shanter' inaugurates the practice in verse. When Scott inserts a Scots-narrated 'folk' episode into one of his novels ('Wandering Willie's Tale', in *Redgauntlet*), he is imitating Hogg.

More broadly, the experimental principle reproduces itself as a formal heterogeneity – what David Duff has called 'rough-mixing'[19] – internal to particular works, especially extended works. The picaresque fictional autobiography 'Renowned Adventures of Basil Lee' replicates, in a kind of fractal logic, the miscellaneous character of the collection in which it appears: *Winter Evening Tales*. Dispatching its feckless protagonist through pastoral misadventures in the Borders, anti-heroic exploits in the American War of Independence, ghost-hunting on the Isle of Lewis, and farcical imbroglios in the Edinburgh marriage market, it noisily shifts the gears of genre along the way, affronting the smooth ideological and aesthetic resolutions of 'nation' and 'history'.[20] Hogg's attempts at multi-volume, novel-magnitude works of fiction in the early 1820s retain this miscellaneous internal structuration, as Tulloch's essay shows. *The Three Perils of Woman* presents itself as a 'series of domestic Scottish tales' rather than as a novel or even a 'national tale', dispersing its narrative through successive 'circles' that tumble catastrophically backwards and downwards from the 1820s to 1745 (the matter of *Waverley*), undoing the literary-historical development (from national tale to historical novel) written into that progressive chronology.[21] Two of Hogg's late stories thematise 'rough-mixing' with their outrageous reinventions of pastoral as inter-species idyll – with great apes (in 'The Pongos') and polar bears (in 'The

Surpassing Adventures of Allan Gordon') instead of sheep and collie-dogs
– in a wild burlesque of fashionable genres of colonial adventure and arctic
exploration.[22]

Not just styles and forms, then, but discourses, themes and topoi. A cluster
of essays in this *Companion*, by Alker and Nelson, Mack, McCracken-Flesher,
and Mergenthal, attends to the various ways in which Hogg writes against
the ideological frameworks – of rank or class, religion, politics, nationality, sexuality and gender – that structured public and domestic life in the
period, and that it was literature's implicit task to reproduce. As Mack in
particular insists, Hogg kept faith with his rural Presbyterian upbringing as
a critical bulwark against polite codes that were often alien to him. Other
commentators have read a more resolutely negative, even demonic energy in
his imaginative play – 'antinomian' in the creative-destructive sense championed by his contemporary, William Blake. Hogg's attachment to traditional
idioms and materials (a topic of reflection in his 1815 poem 'Superstition')
nourished, rather than inhibited, his fascination with contemporary scientific developments. No other Romantic-era author was more attuned to the
advanced, even heterodox, discoveries and debates that were stirring in post-
Enlightenment Edinburgh. Scholars have begun to explore Hogg's interest
in optical technology (including the magic lantern and kaleidoscope) and
medical science, especially with regards to extreme physiological and mental
states, including galvanism, phrenology, apparition sightings, and modes of
unconscious cerebration.[23]

All the components of what Hughes calls Hogg's 'double vision'– the
fluctuations of tone and viewpoint, the miscellany or anthology of genres,
cultural registers from the theological and folkloric to the scientific, the
movement across rural and urban settings ('the west', Edinburgh, the Scottish
Borders) – are put to work in *The Private Memoirs and Confessions of a Justified
Sinner*, which remains unique among Hogg's book-length works for its formal
symmetry and balance. Hogg forges an explosively tense equipoise out of the
work's heterogeneous constituents by making heterogeneity itself, recon-
ceived as internal division, its theme. All culturally sanctioned totalities or
unities – religion, nation, family, self – are held together by the antagonistic
energy of opposed internal principles. The novel generates a psychic and
symbolic force-field from which the reader, any less than the work's characters, narrators, or author, may not emerge unscathed. Hogg's masterpiece
sank out of sight for a hundred years after it was first published, in 1824.
Nearly two hundred years later, it exerts an imaginative hold that grows ever
more compelling, as we see in the recent proliferation of critical approaches
(Penny Fielding's topic in Chapter 15) as well as creative imitations and
adaptations by current authors (the topic of Hughes's closing chapter). James
Hogg, our contemporary: at last we are catching up with him.

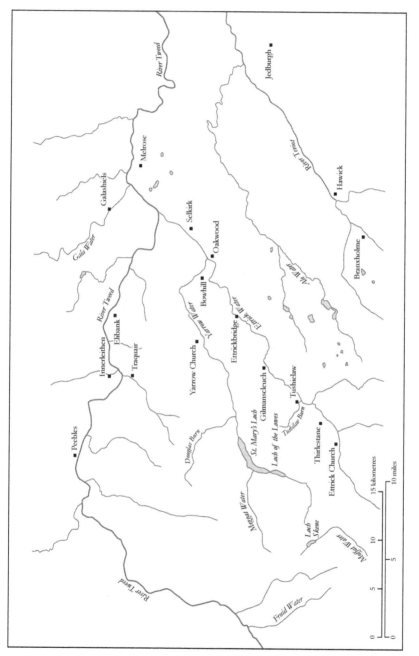

Figure 1 Ettrick and Yarrow

CHAPTER ONE

Hogg, Ettrick, and Oral Tradition

Valentina Bold and Suzanne Gilbert

James Hogg's work is embedded in the oral traditions of Selkirkshire and, specifically, in those of the Ettrick valley and its environs. This chapter explores the interface between Hogg's knowledge of, and familiarity and fondness for, traditional cultural practices and ways of communication. Hogg's attitude to traditional culture was ambivalent, partly because of his desire for personal and economic success; his reliability as a source on folk culture has been questioned in the past, and reassessed. What cannot be questioned is that all his writing draws on a rich seam of song, beliefs, and anecdotes from Ettrick. Moreover, Hogg himself has entered into the traditional culture of Scotland in a literary way, through his (active and passive) inclusion in the 'Noctes Ambrosianae' series of *Blackwood's*, and into the oral traditions of Selkirkshire. All these aspects are considered, making reference to a variety of literary sources, and to Ettrick-made field recordings from the 1980s.

Ettrick life, c.1770–1830[1]

Hogg spent most of his life in the isolated, neighbouring valleys of Ettrick and Yarrow, within the region traditionally known as Ettrick Forest. This 'assemblage of hills'[2] is intersected by *hopes* (small valleys, enclosed by hills) and two major rivers: Ettrick and Yarrow. St Mary's Loch, about three miles long, lies to the East, with the smaller Loch of the Lowes beyond. During the Middle Ages, the Forest was a favoured royal hunting ground; from 1324 to 1455 it was governed by the Douglas family, almost as personal property. Crown hunting rights were protected, and it was administered by forest law.[3] Hogg draws on this medieval background for tales such as 'The Hunt of Eildon' (1818) and 'The Profligate Princes' (1817). The Borders was a buffer zone during frequent wars with neighbours to the south, and a general atmosphere of unrest was compounded by raids, feuds, murder, cattle and sheep stealing, at least until the late sixteenth century (sheep stealing into the nineteenth century). The Covenanting period provided a dramatic interlude, which was long remembered.

In Hogg's lifetime the valleys were inaccessible. During the winter, the valleys could be cut off for months by snow. Locals often ignored the roads, which were useless in poor weather, and took direct routes – in the *Brownie of Bodsbeck*, Jasper and Catherine travel to Dunse Castle, 'over hill and dale, as a shepherd always does, who hates the *wimples*, as he calls them, of a turnpike. He takes such a line as an eagle would take, or a flock of wild geese'.[4] The only substantial bridges were at Ettrickbridge and Deuchar but there were smaller bridges, such as the one crossing Altrive Lake above Eldinhope. Hogg's wife's fall over this bridge in November 1833[5] probably inspired Julia Mackenzie's fall in *Tales of the Wars of Montrose*.

Then (as now), the area was sparsely populated. In 1790 the population of Yarrow and Ettrick was estimated respectively at 1230 (584 male, 646 female) and 470 (222 male, 248 female).[6] The Scotts of Buccleuch held 75 per cent of the land, and the main economic activity was sheep farming. The land was poorly suited to arable farming, with a few subsistence crops: barley, oats, pease, turnips, potatoes.[7]

This was a period of dramatic agricultural change. Arable land and pasture were increasingly separated, and ploughed fields subdivided. Enclosure progressed on both – substantial stone walls being built on farms nearest to Selkirk; hurdles or nets in other places. Some improvements were enforced by landowners. On the Buccleuch estates, for instance, crop rotation was regulated in the 1778 conditions of lease. Large-scale tree planting was carried out – 2000 acres of woods were planted in Selkirkshire, including one hundred of natural wood (oak, ash, birch and hazel), most on the Buccleuch estates as well as at Torwoodlee, Yair and Hanginshaw in Yarrow, with recent planting often enclosed by dykes, to prevent sheep from eating the trees. Drainage and fertilisation techniques were improved on arable land and pasture; and several watered meadows were created.[8]

Agricultural life was harsh, with labourers working from 6 a.m. to 6 p.m. in the summer, with an hour each off for breakfast and at midday. Wages were low – by the 1790s male farm servants earned £6–7; females £3 10s. to £4 a year; day labourers 8*d.* a day and skilled workers 15–20s. per day. The previously communal lifestyle changed as new equipment was introduced. Instead of groups of both genders using sickles in bandwins (bands of reapers) at harvest times, the introduction of the scythe meant smaller teams with the active role performed by men; the two-horse swing plough ended the need for large ploughing teams and again men were in command with women increasingly relegated to 'menial tasks such as weeding and hoeing (in company with children), gathering and stacking'.[9]

Local enthusiasts such as Lord Napier ensured that emerging ideas entered the Forest. Circulating libraries at Hawick and Selkirk played a major role along with new agricultural societies – such as the Hawick and Kelso

Agricultural Society, and the Pastoral Society of Selkirkshire (founded 1818; after 1906 the Yarrow and Ettrick Pastoral Society) whose members included Lord Napier and Walter Scott.[10] Hogg was President of the smaller Crookwelcome Club, in Yarrow and Ettrick, founded in 1801; it valued the crops and livestock of the Forest, and held hearty dinners – on one occasion twelve members shared seven bottles of whisky made into toddy.[11]

Traditional expressive culture remained relatively unchanged until the agricultural revolution of the late eighteenth century. The coming of widespread literacy, at approximately the same period, did change local attitudes towards traditional culture: oral history, for instance, was no longer treated with the same respect when written accounts were available. Nevertheless, a wide range of expressive culture was performed in a variety of contexts. There were spontaneous performances of proverbs and anecdotes, as they suited immediate occasions; premeditated song and tale sessions in the public context of the inn and the home. Evenings, especially in winter, were passed with a mixture of song, story and conversation. No doubt, as now, performance styles were as varied as the performers, providing a resource for Hogg to adapt in his own narratives, in poetry and prose.

The Ettrick Bard

Into this traditional culture Hogg was born in 1770, the second of four sons of Robert Hogg, a small tenant farmer, and Margaret Laidlaw. Although hard farm work governed his early life, the young Hogg showed an appetite for reading and a talent for expression, no doubt inspired by the singers and storytellers within his family. As Elaine Petrie has observed, Hogg's family was steeped and skilled in song, singing, and ballad-making.[12] His maternal grandfather William Laidlaw (Will o' Phaup) was a tradition-bearer of renown who passed on his repertoire to his children Margaret (Hogg's mother) and William (Hogg's uncle). As he grew up, Hogg was also in contact with good singers on his father's side of the family, including his cousins Thomas and Frank Hogg. The letters of Margaret's oldest son William reveal the function of ballads in her day-to-day life: '[O]ur mother to keep us boys quiet would often tell us tales of kings, giants, knights, fairies, kelpies, brownies [. . .] These tales arrested our attention, and filled our minds with the most dreadful apprehensions.' William describes the songs and tales as being sung 'in a plaintive, melancholy air' and their influence on his brother James's mind as 'altogether unperceived at the time, and perhaps indescribable now'.[13]

Hogg's earliest compositions were songs. Having obtained a fiddle at age fourteen, he developed a regional reputation as a songwriter and singer, becoming known as 'Jamie the poeter'. Like Burns and others before him, he appropriated traditional tunes to which he joined his own words;[14] and some of these, such as 'The Mistakes of a Night', found their way into the *Scots Magazine*. But it was Walter Scott's drive to collect ballads for the *Minstrelsy of the Scottish Border* (1802–3) that suggested new connections between the world of Ettrick and a new world of literary pursuit. Scott had been travelling throughout the Borders countryside in search of these ancient narrative songs. '[I]n defiance of mountains, rivers, and bogs, damp and dry, we have penetrated the very recesses of Ettrick Forest', he wrote to a friend: 'I have [. . .] returned *loaded* with the treasures of oral tradition.'[15] Hogg assisted Scott with locating traditional material for the *Minstrelsy*, ultimately providing variants of eleven ballads and directing him to many others known by family members.[16] The best known of these is his mother's ballad of 'Auld Maitland', not for the song itself but for the anecdote that became associated with it, of Hogg's mother rebuking Scott when he visited her to obtain the ballad:

> there war never ane o' my sangs prentit till ye prentit them yoursel', an' ye hae spoilt them awthegither. They were made for singing an' no for reading; but ye hae broken the charm now, an' they'll never be sung mair. An' the worst thing of a', they're nouther right spell'd nor right setten down.[17]

Hogg wrote his account many years after the event it describes. His retrospective and strategic deployment of the anecdote, which was published in 1829, 1832 and 1834, critiques the antiquarian endeavour as a whole: for its printing of what had been transmitted orally over centuries, for hastening what was perceived as the inevitable death of oral tradition, and for not even transcribing the material correctly.[18]

In later life Hogg lamented the loss of traditional expression and practices, as in the essay 'On the Changes in the Habits, Amusements, and Condition of the Scottish Peasantry', published in the *Quarterly Journal of Agriculture* in the early 1830s: 'On looking back, the first great falling off is in song. This, to me, is not only astonishing, but unaccountable. [. . .] Where are those melting strains now? Gone, and for ever!' For this he blames Scott:

> The publication of the Border Minstrelsy had a singular and unexpected effect in this respect. These songs had floated down on the stream of oral tradition, from generation to generation, and were regarded as a precious treasure belonging to the country; but when Mr Scott's work appeared their arcanum was laid open, and a deadening blow was inflicted on our rural literature and principal enjoyment by the very means adopted for their preservation.[19]

By this time Hogg had come to distrust the antiquarian search for the 'real', original object of antiquity and the seeming disdain for practitioners of living tradition.

Hogg's construction was representative of the culture in which he was raised, and which he sought to protect. His perspective might be aligned with Ruth Finnegan's definition of tradition, not as an antique object or antiquated practice, 'not as a piece of dead baggage from the past but [. . .] something constantly in change and continually needing to be actively renewed'.[20] Or in John Miles Foley's words, tradition is 'not a static and unreactive monolith' but 'a dynamic and processual force',[21] created and perpetuated, and best understood, by its practitioners in the community; it invokes 'a context that is enormously larger and more echoic than the text or work itself, that brings the lifeblood of generations of poems and performances to the individual performance or text'.[22] Hogg's project was concerned with the wider question of cultural difference and friction, and his use of oral tradition was part of a larger strategy. Beyond self-promotion, he sought to protect the traditional culture which he believed was under assault in the contemporary drive to modernity.

Poetry

Hogg's strategic deployment of tradition is evident throughout his career, in every genre; and given his roots in songs and ballads, it is understandable that his poetry would draw heavily on this cultural legacy. Hogg's self-presentation as a 'mountain bard', assuming that prophetic voice in the title of his book, marks a crucial distinction from Scott's 'minstrelsy', characterised as 'relics' of an ancient group of courtly poets introduced by an antiquarian editor. In *The Mountain Bard* (1807) Hogg's role is as a modern bard of his native region, whose intimate personal knowledge of oral tradition qualifies him to continue the ballad tradition of which Scott is merely a collector. 'I confess', he wrote, 'that I was not satisfied with many of [Scott's] imitations of the ancients. I immediately chose a number of traditional facts, and set about imitating the different manners of the ancients myself.' Accordingly, the first section of *The Mountain Bard* is headed 'Ballads, in Imitation of the Ancients', a clear echo of the section of the *Minstrelsy* entitled 'Imitations of the Ancient Ballads'.[23] Implicit in his assertion is an argument for the distinctiveness of oral art forms, which only someone steeped in the tradition can authentically translate.

As a mountain bard, Hogg adopts the role of spokesman for the people of Ettrick, and he invites comparison with the recent manifestations of bardic poetry in the work of Robert Burns, and in James Macpherson's Ossian poems. *The Mountain Bard* opens with an epigraph that invokes Macpherson's 'Songs of Selma' in calling for 'tales of other times' to be renewed.[24] Hogg draws upon many ballad narratives: for example, 'Sir David Graeme' expands the brief, grim, evocative narrative of 'Twa Corbies'. Hogg recycles songs and ballad narratives in many of his poems, heavily in *Mador of the Moor* (1816), where songs such as 'Waly, Waly, Gin Love Be Bonny' and 'Charlie is My Darling' are quoted extensively and the story alludes to motifs from 'The Maid and the Palmer' and 'The Cruel Mother'. The poem's recurring motif of disguise and revelation is underscored by Hogg's allusions to another traditional ballad family, including 'The Jolly Beggar' and 'The Gaberlunzie Man'.[25] 'Kilmeny', from *The Queen's Wake* (1813), invokes a number of ballads, among them the fairy abduction narrative of 'Thomas the Rhymer', in its lament that 'Kilmeny on earth was never mair seen'.[26]

The Queen's Wake features a song contest in which bards from across Scotland (and one from Italy) compete for the harp of Mary Queen of Scots. The significance of traditional continuity is underscored in the narrative links between the songs, as in the commentary that follows the song of the aristocratic Highland bard Gardyn, whose harp 'of wonderous frame' is engraved with 'his lineage and his name', and who ultimately wins first prize. Hogg praises 'many a song of wonderous power', still 'Well known in cot and green-wood bower, / Wherever swells the shepherd's reed / On Yarrow's banks and braes of Tweed'.[27] However, as Douglas S. Mack argues, Hogg complicates the received, antiquarian account of an aristocratic practice by 'envisaging rival aristocratic and non-aristocratic versions of the traditional bardic culture of pre-Union Scotland'.[28] The Bard of Ettrick, who wins a 'consolation prize', 'turns out to be the embodiment of an ancient oral popular culture that speaks in and through those eloquent and powerful songs of the people, the traditional oral ballads of the Scottish Borders'.[29]

Queen Hynde (1824) draws structurally on Ossianic epic, conceived as having deep roots in traditional Gaelic culture, in order to trace a similar vision of pre-Union bardship in the Highlands. Hynde's palace of Selma derives from the Selma of *Fingal*; the poem is divided into six books, like *Fingal*; and both poems narrate the defeat of invading Norsemen by a Scots-Irish alliance.[30] And yet the poem insists on modernity. The epic past is framed by the Ettrick Shepherd's contemporary addresses to the Maids of Dunedin, in which he at once exhorts his audience (figured as female readers of sentimental novels) to empathise with the beleaguered Queen Hynde and makes fun of them:

> Maids of Dunedin, in despair
> Will ye not weep and rend your hair?
> Ye who in these o'erpolished times,
> Can shed the tear o'er woeful rhymes;
> O'er plot of novel sore repine,
> And cry for hapless heroine.[31]

Instead of containing traditional narrative in scenarios of impotent heroism, elegy, or melancholy, Hogg unleashes it – exuberantly, energetically, unabashedly – into the present.

Prose

Hogg made rich use of Ettrick tradition in his prose, while exploring new narrative forms. *The Shepherd's Guide* (1807) is an evocative resource on husbandry and country life; *The Shepherd's Calendar*, first published in *Blackwood's Edinburgh Magazine* (1823–8), explores agricultural practices, social lives, and related beliefs in the medium of fiction. Together, they offer a wealth of subtle commentary on everyday concerns in Ettrick. Life for the shepherd was unremitting: going round the hill twice a day, or three, if the sheep were prone to casting (awalding, or falling on their backs). His collie dog was indispensable: 'a shepherd may be a very able, trusty, and good shepherd without a sweetheart [. . .] But what is he without his dog?'[32] There were compensations – socialising at harvest and clipping (shearing) time in mid-June, 'every young shepherd's sweetheart [. . .] helping him to clip, or holding the ewes by the hind legs to make them lie easy'.[33] Otherwise, it was relentless: transporting animals for September sheep sales; smearing (treating fleece with tar and grease to protect it against parasites) in late October and, in late November, putting tups (rams) to ewes (ten days later to the gimmers, young ewes); in the spring, lambing. Harsh winter weather was the bane of the sheep farmer, as shown in the 'Storms' sequence.[34] In 1772, snow lay from mid-December to mid-April; the sheep were so weakened they could not be moved to lower, safer pastures.[35] The worst storm Hogg ever saw occurred on 24 January 1794, blowing 'with peculiar violence' between Crawford-Moor and the Border. Seventeen shepherds died; 'one farmer alone, Thomas Beattie, lost 72 scores and many others in the same quarter from 30 to 40 scores'.[36] Unlike today, with transportable block feeds, entire flocks could be lost over a winter, as happened to Hogg in 1808.[37]

Until the foundation of the Gamgee and Dick veterinary colleges in the 1840s, and the availability of commercial treatments, remedies were passed on by self-taught experts, drawing on resources to hand, including foodstuffs and plants. Hogg is often critical of contemporary husbandry. Regarding lambing (around 10–20 April in Ettrick), he condemns pulling wool away from the ewe's udder (thought to assist suckling) as unnecessary and cruel.[38] He rejects the practice, too, of milking ewes after weanings, to make cheese (alluded to in Jane Elliot's 'The Lament for Flodden'). This was becoming less common as farmers, like Hogg, realised it weakened the ewes.[39] Hogg is sensitive to animals' feelings too, such as the 'fondness' shown by ewes to lambs, even the 'spare' (orphaned or twin) lambs they accept, wearing a dead infant's skin.[40]

Hogg thought deeply about how to diagnose and treat varieties of illness. For instance, he identifies four types of the braxy, an intestinal illness which affected hogs or young sheep, and suggests specific cures for them: for water braxy, bleeding; for the others, forcing the sheep to run to heat up, then bathing them with warm water for eight to ten minutes, before injecting water gruel and water, or another softener.[41] Hogg also inserts anecdotes, such as one about a shepherd who thought his sheep were dying when they had been afflicted by the 'staggers', a non-fatal ailment in which they fall into fits after feeding on broom, and cut the throats of four before his master stopped him: 'his master asked him, in a rage, "How would you like, if people were always to cut your throat when you are drunk?"'[42] Hogg's standard cure is gruesome: using an awl or large corking pin to pierce the softened skull if water had settled there or, if the skull felt soft at the forehead, 'thrusting a stiff-sharpened wire up each nostril, until it stops against the upper part of the skull'.[43] Doing this, Hogg boasts, he had 'cured many a sheep to different owners'.

There are traces of a peculiarly Ettrick ethos in the central tale of *The Brownie of Bodsbeck* (1818). Set in the neighbourhood of Chapelhope and Riskenhope farms, 'The Brownie' mixes traditional and written histories with supernatural legend. The elusive hero John Brown hides out on Chapelhope with his broken band of followers. A convoluted plot revolves around the interpretation of Brown's presence as a supernatural 'brownie', and the persecution of the farmer, Laidlaw, and his family for sheltering Covenanters. In Hogg's lifetime the period was clearly recalled: leading Covenanters had preached locally, and Ettrick suffered royalist depredation, in the 1640s and during the 'Killing Times'. Hogg's depiction gives vent to emotive folk memories – take, for instance, the initially comic and then harrowing encounter between John Hoy of Mucrah and 'Bloody Clavers'. Clavers refuses to believe Hoy's evidently innocent testimony and issues the order: 'Burn him on the cheek, cut off his ears, and do not part with him till he pay you down a fine of two hundred marks.'[44]

Hogg claims the authority of tradition for his tales, insisting that they were well known in contemporary Ettrick. The 'Brownie' himself takes after his namesake in Scottish tradition: 'a wee bit hurklin crile of an unearthly thing, as shrinkit an' wan as he had been lien seven years i' the grave'.[45] Although there is a logical explanation – Brown was horribly wounded at Bothwell Bridge – he performs tasks around Chapelhope farm, based on the traditional creature's attributes: harvesting corn overnight, smearing the sheep. The mistress, Maron Laidlaw, is annoyed because she has given the Brownie his 'accustomed wages' yet he has not left the toun.

'The Brownie' was first published with two additional Ettrick tales, 'The Wool-gatherer' and 'The Hunt of Eildon', which represent a real and living landscape, integrating people and place. 'The Wool-gatherer', set in the nineteenth century, draws on ballad and märchen conventions and Ramsay's *Gentle Shepherd*. 'The Hunt of Eildon', from 'ancient' times, combines supernatural and religious elements from Borders traditions with literary precedents like *A Midsummer Night's Dream*, and draws a macabre yet comic link between traditional enchantments and modern urban life. The heroine and her lover are transformed into moorfowl on Teviotdale, where they live in harmony, 'till last year, that Wauchope shot the hens'; people in Edinburgh then ate them, giving rise to a proverb: 'When any one is in a querulous or peevish humour, they say, – "He has got a wing of Wauchope's moor-hen."'[46] The cock, however, survives, and might be transformed back, to give an account of the last two centuries.

The Brownie of Bodsbeck offers a sequence of tales of transformations, deceptions and revelations of identity, drawing on traditional motifs (brownies, magical shapeshifting, the overcoming of difficulties in love). It is, equally, a series of 'hunts' (for religion, identity, love and sex) through different periods, 'modern' and 'ancient', unified upon a Borders topography and the traditions and experiences of its inhabitants. The whole collection resembles an episodic, traditional oral storytelling session, privileging local and lowly, community and religious interests, and alternating humorous, horrific and morally resonant episodes, in a thematically-linked structure which Hogg would develop further in *The Three Perils of Man* (1822).

Hogg's background in oral tradition, along with his interest in modern life, informs *The Private Memoirs and Confessions of a Justified Sinner* (1824).[47] Traditional beliefs are pervasive, especially around the demonic figure of Gil-Martin. He is initially thought to be an exotic Eastern prince; people cannot remember his name. Like the devil in traditional culture, he walks with stiff joints; towards the end of the novel he comes to resemble Milton's Satan. Hogg skilfully suggests that, while Gil-Martin might be the devil, he might, equally, be a figment of the characters', the narrators', and even the reader's imagination. Moreover, in his exploration of doubling – the pairing of Wringhim with Gil-Martin; the opposition of characters like the Laird of Dalcastle and Wringhim senior; or the possibility that Wringhim junior is, himself, a divided personality – Hogg recalls the traditional (ballad as well as epic) narrative techniques discussed by Axel Olrik in 'Epic Laws of Folk Narrative'.[48] Karl Miller's characterisation of *Confessions* as 'a tall tale' draws attention to its roots in oral idiom and local knowledge, as well as its appeal to an audience adept in these modes of discourse.[49]

Hogg in Ettrick Tradition

The implication of such an audience in his writing may explain the affection with which Hogg is still held in Ettrick. Local historian Thomas Craig-Brown firmly anchored the poet in his particular landscapes: 'the mountains and the valleys of the Forest inspired his song, her legends gave form to his poems'; in return this 'hereditary freeman of the Forest' left 'her fields greener where he trod, her gloamings lovelier and more glamorous'.[50] The 'Blanket Preaching' of 1935, 150 years after Hogg's birth, issued a similar encomium; without Hogg, 'Yarrow would not be the Yarrow we know, nor Ettrick the Ettrick'.[51]

First-hand memories persisted. Early examples include an account in the *Border Magazine* of the elderly Mrs Fletcher, who recited Hogg's poetry and 'had more than once seen the Ettrick Shepherd on a Fair Day in Selkirk with his collies at his heel, a lass on each arm, and a kindly joke for every one he met'.[52] Such recollections have lasted in oral circulation to the present.[53] To those with closest links to Hogg, like the late Tibbie Shaw, formerly of Tibbie Shiel's Inn, Hogg was 'every bit as famous as Burns' and, like Burns, a man who appreciated drink and women. Shiel's descendants, the Mitchell family at Henderland, possessed a letter to Shiels in which Hogg claims to have often faced the cutty stool (or stool of repentance, where fornicators had to sit in front of the congregation). Hogg as a great lover has proved a persistent image, as can be seen in the (albeit humorous) observation from the late Walter Barrie, who lived in Hogg's farmhouse at Eldinhope: 'We get a lot of people claiming to be descendants [. . .] [from] New Zealand, Australia, Canada, the States. Some of them probably *will* be, but no *all* of them can be.'

Hogg is, however, treated with rather more respect than the familiar 'Rabbie'. He is 'James Hogg' or 'Hogg' and, while failings are acknowledged, the people of Yarrow and Ettrick know enough about farming to be sympathetic. Although Mrs Shaw noted that: 'he never made good in farming [. . .] his thoughts were aye on verse and song', in contrast, Barrie told me: 'he'd be a good enough practical farmer [. . .] brought up to it [. . .] as a young chap he worked among sheep [. . .] His father was a shepherd, and that counts for a lot [. . .] You pick up a lot from your father.' The Barries and the Mitchells, having considered Hogg's *Shepherd's Guide*, conclude that Hogg's knowledge of sheep diseases was as effective as his period allowed.

The people of Ettrick are well informed about the work. The late James Mitchell's grandfather preserved a copy of the 1794 *Scots Magazine*, suggesting that the authorship of 'The Mistakes of a Night' was known locally before it was literary knowledge. Walter Barrie was aware of Hogg's use of Ettrick traditions, from his work with Scott to the novels: 'He embroidered a lot of these stories: used them in his essays and writings, the *Brownie of Bodsbeck* and the Covenanters and [. . .] the *Justified Sinner* [. . .] about the body bein' dug up where three lairds' lands meet by the three cairns'. Barrie was well aware of the literary traditions, agreeing with the verdict (recorded by R. P. Gillies) that while Hogg was plagued with innumerable visitors, he was always a gentleman. However, Barrie added: '*He* says in, one o' his letters that when they *drew* the plan [of Eldinhope], they wanted a' the reek to come out o' one lum! So that folk wouldna ken if he was in or not, and they wouldnae come in! [. . .] but he was hospitable, I think.'

A group of anecdotes focuses on Tibbie Shiel's perceptions of Hogg. Tibbie's oft-quoted remark, 'Aye, Hogg was a gey sensible man, for all the nonsense he wrat', is well known in Ettrick, as is a printed anecdote about a severely hung-over Hogg asking Tibbie to 'bring in the loch' for him to drink. Other traditions only survive orally, for instance Mrs Shaw's, about how Tibbie had a specially designed settle/bed: when Hogg was drunk she could open a door at the back of the settle and tip the poet into a box bed behind. Mrs Shaw recalls several unrecorded humorous tales from her grandfather. In one, Hogg went out onto the hills on a particularly foggy day: it was so dense he filled his pipe with fog. Such a tale could be applied to anyone, but it is significant local anecdotes accrue around Hogg. They place him firmly in his Ettrick setting.

Helped by visual icons – the Hogg statue at the head of St Mary's Loch, the Ettrickhall Memorial – Hogg's personality is epitomised in local relics such the curling stone Tibbie Shaw possessed, or the plaid in Bowhill museum, which stand witness to a working participation in Forest life. Hogg's watch was retained in the Mitchell family, presented to Shiel for the care she gave the poet in his decline, creating a bond between him and her descendants. Manuscripts, including the Crookwelcome Book, the Selkirkshire Agricultural Society books, and the letter to Tibbie Shiel, are treasured heirlooms, testifying to a shared heritage with Hogg. These, backed by oral and literary traditions, show the very high esteem in which Hogg is held, both as a writer and as a man of Ettrick.

Following the formal dinners in Hogg's honour, in 1832 in London and in 1834 in Peebles, public dinners have been held for Hogg at Yarrow on the centenary of his birth (8 December 1871) and at Tibbie Shiel's, with Mrs Shaw as guest of honour, on the 150th anniversary of his death (1985). The traditional Burns menu was replaced with an Ettrick variation: 'muttons and greens [. . .] and clootie dumpling', along with celebrations in words and in music. As James Mitchell recalled, 'A said that if anybody ga'ing oot o this establishment *tonight* doesnae see the faires floatin round his *pedestal* they hadnae enjoyed themselves! A think quite a few of them saw them!'

CHAPTER TWO

Hogg and the Book Trade

Peter Garside

Hogg's struggle to establish himself as a writer is perhaps most vividly illustrated in his dealings with the book trade. While it is possible to figure the relationship in largely oppositional terms, there can be little doubt that Hogg's development as an author was not only made possible but also shaped by contemporary publishing conditions. In his first emergence from local celebrity in an oral culture to the recognised authorship of printed books Hogg benefited from two established kinds of support, already available to later eighteenth-century working-class writers: in the form of patronage, and through publication by the subscription method, whereby sponsors from the general public vouched to purchase copies of a book on publication. Determined to surmount the elements of dependency inherent in both systems, Hogg in his middle career set out to achieve independence as a professional writer in a commercial situation. Here his ambitions were supported by an especially buoyant moment in publishing history, with Edinburgh in the 1810s and 1820s achieving the status of a major metropolitan literary centre, not least as the home of two of the most fashionable literary products of the day, the long narrative poem and the upmarket 'Scotch novel'. At the same time, Hogg's social background and lack of financial clout often left him in a vulnerable position, mystified by the complex methods of author remuneration, subject to disapproval on the grounds of indecorousness, or diminished as an imitator belonging to the second rank. Always alive to the latest advances in production and marketing, Hogg in his later career found a number of alternative outlets, with a new willingness to engage directly with the London trade in the 1830s. His last years are also marked by a determination to assemble hitherto scattered materials in collected form, emulating the kind of canonical status being claimed in their own time by other writers of the period, such as Walter Scott.

While contributions to periodicals provided the most obvious vehicle for an unknown author writing in Scots at the turn of the century, the relationship was essentially of an 'amateur' nature, as Gillian Hughes outlines more fully in Chapter 3. Hogg's sense of the superiority of the book, as a means of drawing together a body of material and asserting a fuller authorial identity, seems to have been well developed at an early stage. Hogg's first printed book, *Scottish Pastorals* (1801), in following this path, tends to show the process of publication in its simplest and most unmediated form. According to his 'Memoir of the Author's Life', Hogg entered into the project having delivered sheep to market in Edinburgh, writing out some of his poems from memory and engaging 'a person to print at my expense'.[1] The printer involved was John Taylor, essentially a stationer, whose premises are described as 'opposite Buchts [i.e. sheep-pens]' in the Edinburgh Grassmarket. Taylor's other publications were chiefly chapbooks, a low-status form which Hogg's 62-page pamphlet in some respects resembles, and any kind of retail sale is likely to have come directly from his shop. Hogg's own accounts suggest that much of the impression ended up with himself, for distribution among a not very large circle of personal acquaintances, some of whom showed signs of discontent, one complaint being that Hogg had elevated his social standing in allowing the self-description 'Tenant in Ettrick' to be used in its promotion. Although there are indications that he received some sort of proofs, Hogg was also embarrassed by the large number of misprints in the text, and showed little desire to reclaim the title for his oeuvre in later life. Perhaps worst of all, in retrospect, was the entanglement of the ingénue poet in a kind of vanity publication: 'I knew no more about publishing than the man of the moon; and the only motive that influenced me was the gratification of my vanity by seeing my works in print.'[2]

Hogg learned another salutary lesson through his experiences with his patriotic song *Donald Macdonald*, which enjoyed a runaway success early in the nineteenth century. Surviving copies of the sixpenny broadside sheet, published in Edinburgh by the music specialist John Hamilton, carry the ascription 'Written by James Hog [sic]'; but in his 'Memoir' and elsewhere Hogg complains of having received no public credit or other personal reward. One outcome was a rapid dissemination in unauthorised print form, in chapbooks and musical miscellanies, which proliferated even as Hogg sought to reclaim the piece in his own collections. Another loss of control lay in a widespread return of the song to the oral world, but without the personal association that applied in his native Ettrick. In later accounts, Hogg gives several instances of its free-floating existence as witnessed by himself, including an attempt to lay claim to the piece after a performance in a Lancaster theatre, leading to him being regarded as 'a half-crazed Scots pedlar'.[3]

If Robert Burns was an important talismanic figure for Hogg in creative terms, Scott represented an essential conduit to the mainstream book trade and the world of polite letters in Edinburgh. According to Hogg's later accounts of his 'First Interview' with Scott – an event which most probably took place in early Autumn 1802 – the recently appointed Sheriff of

Selkirkshire, in pursuit of ballads to complete his *Minstrelsy of the Scottish Border* (1802–3), finds a vital oral culture in Ettrick and natural genius in Hogg's own person, with Hogg's mother unleashing her famous put-down over ballads being meant for singing and not printing. There is evidence that Hogg had already met Scott at least once before this confrontation, and that it was the latter's status as a published author that impressed him as much as anything: a letter from Hogg to Scott dated 30 June (1802) singles out the *Minstrelsy* as 'the first book I ever perused which was written by a person I had seen and conversed with'.[4] Another letter to Scott, written immediately in the wake of the Ettrick interview, shows an eagerness to continue the relationship, with Hogg proffering one of his songs for inclusion among the modern 'Imitations' in the forthcoming third volume of the *Minstrelsy*.[5] It must have been with some disappointment that he noted his exclusion in favour of more socially elevated contacts of Scott when he received a presentation set in April 1803. Still undeterred, Hogg went on to propose to Scott an edition of his songs, in terms that suggest a fairly immediate transference, aided by Scott's mediation, from local fame to status as a published author:

> I have lately taken it into my head to publish a copy of all my own songs which I can collect [. . .] I have as many of my own songs beside me, which are certainly not the worst of my productions, as will make above an hundred pages closs [sic] printed, and about two hundred printed as the minstrelsy is. [. . .] The first thing that suggested it was their extraordinary repute in Ettrick.[6]

The earliest manifestation of this, *The Mountain Bard* of 1807, provided Hogg with his first full encounter with the perilous terrain lying between the conception and the achievement of a successful published work. Dedicated to Scott and containing the first version of Hogg's 'Memoir' in the form of an Epistle to him, the project fell awkwardly between the one-off subscription volume that Scott had primarily in mind and the independent breakthrough to literary recognition that Hogg craved. Hogg's unsettled position, and his eventual need to resort to service as a shepherd in Nithsdale, left him increasingly dependent on Scott, whose ideas on the contents sometimes differed substantially, for seeing the work through the press. Scott's invisible hand can be sensed in Hogg's attempt to negotiate terms with the publisher Archibald Constable in March 1806, with Constable advocating an edition of 1000, comprising 750 copies for retail sale and 250 on larger paper for subscribers. The terms over remuneration seem to have been less precise, however, and Hogg appears to have been left scrambling to collect payments from his subscribers, while to some degree remaining dependent on Constable's say-so in determining any settlement for the commercial sale. In the event, according to the 'Memoir', Constable made an addition to the proceeds Hogg received

from the subscription. The amount was swollen further by outright payment
of £86 for his agricultural treatise *The Shepherd's Guide*, published the same
year, allowing Hogg's establishment as a tenant farmer, which from Scott's
vantage point might well have seemed an advantageous terminus in his
publishing career.[7]

A radical change in Hogg's relationship with the book trade was heralded
by his determination early in 1810 – following his failure as a tenant farmer
– to move to Edinburgh permanently in an effort 'to push my fortune as a
literary man'.[8] To an outsider this ambition must have looked foolhardy at
best, and it would be difficult to find another instance of barriers being surmounted successfully from such a low starting point. In the intervening years,
however, Hogg had built up relationships with a number of people engaged
in literary activity in Edinburgh, including the schoolmaster James Gray,
as well as a more practical kind of patron in John Grieve, a fellow native of
Ettrick and a successful hat merchant. Hogg was also entering the Scottish
metropolis at an especially buoyant time. Recent successes against the French
in the Peninsular War, where Highland troops had played a prominent part,
encouraged a wave of patriotic feeling, with a fresh confidence in Scotland's
role in the larger British enterprise. The Edinburgh publishing industry also
stood on the cusp of a new kind of success, Constable having ventured 1000
guineas to purchase the copyright of Scott's *Marmion* (1808), and with the
author's next poem, *The Lady of the Lake*, about to cause a sensation on its
issue in May 1810.

This context probably helped encourage Constable to take on *The Forest
Minstrel* (1810), consisting mainly of songs by Hogg, the bulk of which had
failed to find a home in *The Mountain Bard*. No records for this publication
have apparently survived, but the 'Memoir' suggests a direct approach by
Hogg, and a primarily commercial arrangement, with Constable offering to
print 1000 copies on a 'half profits' basis (whereby the author and publisher
shared the proceeds after production costs had been deducted). Manufactured
to look like a companion piece to *The Mountain Bard*, and lacking the accom-
panying musical notations found in more prestigious song collections of the
period, *The Forest Minstrel* met with scant critical attention, and was a commercial failure. In his 'Memoir' Hogg suggests that embarrassment prevented
him from inquiring about remuneration, and it is not unlikely that the experience left him feeling helpless in the face of the mystifying procedures of the
publishing industry. A determination to cut through this web is evident in his
next major venture, *The Spy* (1810–11), where, after an unsuccessful quest for
an Edinburgh publisher to front his periodical, Hogg for a while effectively
fell back on employing a printer directly.

It was after the failure of *The Spy* that Hogg achieved his one unmitigated
literary success with *The Queen's Wake* (1813), a brilliant arrangement of

shorter pieces which rose on the high tide of the popularity of the long narrative poem, ostensibly going through six editions in as many years, and placing Hogg for while on a level close to Scott and Byron. In seeking terms, Hogg again approached Constable, who offered £100 for each impression of 1000 copies, though with the proviso that he secure 200 subscribers beforehand to cover costs. By now Hogg had had enough of the business of soliciting subscriptions, as well as waiting on Constable, and it was probably the less condescending terms offered that encouraged his turn to George Goldie, a relative newcomer to the trade, whom Hogg knew through the Forum debating club. Goldie's headquarters were in Princes Street, where he also ran a circulating library, making him one of the first booksellers to be centred in the fashionable New Town. To Hogg's delight the work proved an immediate success among readers in Edinburgh, with two editions apparently cleared in the year of publication, allowing him to report the commissioning of a third edition 'which is to be more than twice as large as both the other two'.[9]

Closer examination, however, shows a more chequered publication history, with Hogg in the process showing new acumen in dealing with the trade, but also experiencing fresh kinds of disappointment. The first and second editions of the work were in reality tranches of the same impression, with the second bearing a replacement title page and an 'Advertisement' vouching the work to be 'truly the production of *James Hogg*, a common Shepherd'. Sales within the first year of publication then can barely have exceeded 1000, with Hogg hardly achieving a Byronic standing among his own countrymen. Nor is there evidence of any significant penetration in London, Hogg observing to Byron that 'in England it is scarcely as yet known'.[10] Worse still were rumours of Goldie's financial instability, leading Hogg to turn again to Constable, who nevertheless ceded the right to publish the third edition to Goldie. Goldie's eventual failure, which resulted in unsold copies being placed in the hands of trustees, led to acrimonious personal accusations, but can be seen more broadly as symptomatic of a much wider crisis in the Edinburgh book trade during 1813–14. By an unexpected turn of events, Hogg then suddenly found himself in an advantageous position. This came as a result of the sequestered copies being purchased by William Blackwood, then an up-and-coming Edinburgh bookseller based in the Old Town opposite the university. Since 1811 Blackwood had enjoyed the agency of John Murray's publications in Scotland, with the result that on its eventual appearance the fourth edition (actually the reclaimed part of the third) carried the prestigious joint imprint of Blackwood and Murray. A further uplift was given by the eventual appearance of Francis Jeffrey's review of the work in the *Edinburgh Review* for November 1814. For once the kind of advantages enjoyed by front-rank authors in the Regency period, including sizeable advances and the power to play publishers against each other, might have seemed to be heading Hogg's way.

In the immediately succeeding years Hogg noticeably failed to capital-
ise on this situation, and the delayed 'fifth' and 'sixth' editions (1819) of
the *Queen's Wake*, actually one printing in different sizes, return to the
old pattern of combining a subscription and retail sale. A good deal of the
1821 version of Hogg's 'Memoir' is devoted to finding causes for his frus-
tration at the hands of the trade, these ranging from moral disapproval by
the Edinburgh 'blue-stockings' to an over-reliance of publishers on literary
advisers, themselves prone to regard him as 'an intruder in the paths of literature'.[11] Undeniably Hogg suffered through various forms of snobbery, and
more especially a heightened sense of the importance of decorum in polite
publishing. His impecunious position also placed him at a disadvantage when
attempting to secure transparent returns, at a time when all but a few authors
were meant either to sell copyright cheaply or wait patiently for any payment
until editions cleared. One especially telling instance of Hogg's vulnerability
in such respects is found in the decision of John Murray to remove his name
as a primary publisher from his following poem *The Pilgrims of the Sun* (1815),
scuppering any chances of a renewed nationwide success.

Hogg's resilience is again in evidence in his turn to the novel as an alternative genre, which was to dominate his output during the early 1820s, and
involved him in relationships with a variety of publishers, generally in a more
open commercial situation. While the main part of his output coincided
with a brief golden age in the production of fiction in Scotland, his active
interest in this mode can be taken back to plans for a collection of 'Rural and
Traditionary Tales of Scotland', as proposed to Constable in two letters of
1813. The first of these, dated 20 May, proposed a pseudonymous publication
(by J. H. Craig of Douglas Esq.), in two octavo or four duodecimo volumes,
with Constable purchasing at least one of the editions, so that 'he may have
an interest in furthering it to the utmost of his power'.[12] Constable failed
to respond to Hogg's satisfaction, and another letter of 12 July, proposing
a gentler testing of the market with just one volume, begged for a definite
answer in writing: 'Do not send word for me to *come and speak with you* for
a quiet word with you is impossible.'[13] Constable's reasons for not taking up
the offer can only be guessed at, but it is worth bearing in mind that at that
point he had no track record as a publisher of fiction, the more obvious port
of call then being Manners & Miller, the Edinburgh publishers of Elizabeth
Hamilton's *Cottagers of Glenburnie* (1808) and Mary Brunton's *Self-Control*
(1811), although their specialism in the polite evangelical mode would have
made them singularly unsuitable for what Hogg had in mind.

The project next surfaces in an approach to William Blackwood late in
1816, followed by a formal letter on 4 January 1817 offering the copyright of
a first edition of 'Cottage Winter Nights' at £63 7s. a volume.[14] Blackwood's
own star had risen rapidly in recent years, with a move to fashionable

headquarters in the New Town, and a first taste of the fruits of handling a best-selling title through his management, in partnership with Murray, of Scott's fourth work of fiction, *Tales of My Landlord* (1816). A preoccupation with Scott probably helps explain Blackwood's tardiness in proceeding, and may well have helped determine changes to the lead story in the eventual publication of the collection as *The Brownie of Bodsbeck; and Other Tales* (1818). Negotiations resumed in December 1817, with Hogg attempting to up the asking price to 100 guineas a volume, but also offering half profits as an alternative, the latter method being finally adopted in agreement with John Murray, who took two-thirds of the 1500 copies. The *Brownie* was published in May 1818, alongside Susan Ferrier's first novel, *Marriage* (1818), which was also co-published by Blackwood and Murray in a similar impression.

Early sales indicate an equivalent success, with 500 or more copies cleared in the first month, but by October Hogg was receiving rumours of a serious decline in sales. This is reflected in publishing accounts which reveal that in the vital first year of publication less than a thousand were cleared, with sales thereafter reduced to a trickle, terminating in a remaindering of the last copies. In his post-mortem Hogg contended that the work's progress had been deliberately impeded: 'I know that The Brownie *should have gone through more editions than either one or two.*'[15] Although he pointed a finger particularly at William Gifford, Murray's literary adviser, it is not unlikely that Murray himself, alarmed at the anti-aristocratic tendencies in the main tale and other alleged crudities, was proactive in obscuring the title's presence among his publications. Matters were worsened by the increasing hostility between Blackwood and Murray, resulting in a termination of their relationship in 1819, one effect of which was to leave Hogg floundering in a seemingly obsessive pursuit of a £50 settlement from Murray on account of his share of author's profits.[16]

With his suspicions about Blackwood mounting, Hogg turned for his next work of fiction to the Edinburgh firm of Oliver & Boyd. Having sounded out George Boyd previously, and smarting still over the intangibility of half profits on the *Brownie*, his formal letter of 2 August 1819 offered an edition of 1500 in two extensive volumes for £100: half payable immediately by a bill at four months, the remainder on publication by a longer bill payable at twelve months.[17] Oliver & Boyd had only managed two novels to date, though in the 1820s they were to become the third largest producers of new fiction in Scotland, after Blackwood and Constable. Unlike the two latter, the constituent partners had emerged from the more 'artisan' side of the trade, Thomas Oliver having worked as a printer and George Boyd as a book-binder. At the centre of the firm's activities from the 1810s were its wholesale operations, and the house's records show a willingness to discount generously in order to move stock. These qualities were shared by its London partners, Whittaker &

Co., themselves considerable publishers of fiction. Such factors help explain the moderate but real success achieved by *Winter Evening Tales* (1820), the original impression selling out within almost five months, and Hogg being asked to name a price for a second edition of 1000 copies. Sensing himself, for once, in a strong bargaining position, Hogg requested a clear one-sixth of the retail price: a way of calculating which in some ways anticipates the modern royalty system. A reputation for making immoderate claims, combined with demands for the reprinting of earlier works, may both have played a part in the sudden refusal in June 1821 to take on the 'Border Romance' (*Three Perils of Man*), on which Hogg pinned such high hopes. A long imploring letter to Scott, on 26 June, offered another possible cause in quoting from Boyd's letter of refusal: 'it is of that cast that must draw down comparisons with the romances of the author of Waverly [*sic*] and manifestly to its disadvantage these being made the criterion of judging of merit'.[18]

In contrast, the last main publishers of Hogg's fiction in this phase, the long-established London firm of Longman & Co., had reasons to welcome a competent 'imitator' of Scott, having lost the share that they had enjoyed in some of the earlier Waverley novels. All the evidence points to Longmans having acted firmly but fairly with Hogg in publishing *The Three Perils of Man* (1822) and *The Three Perils of Woman* (1823), each in the conventional three-volume form, in an impression of 1000. Hogg's request for anonymity in the first instance, and for an expansion into four volumes in the second, were both politely turned down; though an element of generosity was shown through advance payments in lieu of half profits, to the tune of £150 in each case. The firm also allowed the option of employing Edinburgh printers, facilitating the exchange of author's proofs. In the case of *The Private Memoirs and Confessions of a Justified Sinner* (1824) there are indications of Hogg's manipulating a situation whereby the little-known James Clarke, rather than James Ballantyne (Longmans' stated choice), carried out the job, allowing much fuller control of his text.[19]

With this title Hogg also managed to break the mould in producing an anonymous single-volume work, similar in physical appearance and strangely echoing in its contents the half-guinea upmarket titles then being produced by Blackwood from Scotland, with regular authors such as John Wilson and J. G. Lockhart. The work, as a result, sat strangely with Longmans' own fiction list, dominated by historical romances from regular female authors, and a new brand of didactic religious tales, such as Barbara Hofland's *Patience, A Tale* (1824). The record of sales suggests a near catastrophic situation from a publisher's point of view, with 515 of the print run of 1000 eventually being remaindered at a knockdown price of 9d. each. Identifying Longmans' Scottish agent Adam Black as a weak link, Hogg urged Blackwood to take a share in both this title and his new poem, *Queen Hynde*, due to be published by Longmans later in the year. Blackwood however showed little interest in the novel, and though eventually taking on a half share in the poem found little financial advantage there. Hogg for his part, in addition to receiving nothing for his novel, found himself saddled with a debt to Blackwood on account of the poem, for reasons which he claimed never fully to understand.

With the failure of a novel and a large poem in a single year, Hogg's prospects for finding outlets for long works must have seemed extremely limited. In Scotland especially the financial 'crash' of 1825–6 dissuaded surviving publishers from taking on imaginative literary works, Blackwood largely confining himself to works stemming from *Blackwood's Edinburgh Magazine*, in his eyes now a mainstay of his operations. It was Blackwood's insistence on delaying publication of the poetical miscellany *A Queer Book* (1832) even after its printing that precipitated Hogg's resolve to look for new channels for giving final form to his oeuvre. Shortly before leaving for his extensive trip to London in December 1831, Hogg made contact with the London publisher James Cochrane, with a view to publishing the full collection of his tales that Blackwood had repeatedly declined. If he had remaining doubts about the suitability of London as an alternative centre, these would have been allayed by his tumultuous reception during his visit there, promising liberation from the condescension attached to his various literary identities in Scotland. Though he had recently set up business on his own, Cochrane had previously worked for a leading marketer of novels in Henry Colburn, and was the publisher of *The Club-Book* (1831), edited by Andrew Picken, with contributions from a number of fellow Scots, including Hogg himself.

From Cochrane's smart premises in Pall Mall, plans were laid out for a twelve-volume set of *Altrive Tales* prefaced by an updated Author's 'Memoir' and to be issued by volume every two months. In a number of aspects, such as format, pricing, and the use of illustrations, the set was structured to match the Magnum Opus edition of Scott's Waverley Novels, which had commenced monthly publication in 1829, with sales rising from a projected 12,000 to some 30,000 a volume. In other respects, however, such as the plan to include new as well as old material by Hogg, the project bears comparison with a number other 'popular' sets being issued by the London trade, in an attempt to catch a new wave of emancipated readers. London then stood at the forefront of new technological developments in the trade, notably the use of stereotype plates for printing and advances in steel engraving, which enabled efficient production in much larger numbers. All must have looked set fair by the time Hogg returned to Scotland in March 1832, and early reports suggested a rapid sale of 1500 copies of the first volume, representing the first tranche of a printing of 3000. The sudden financial failure of Cochrane, however, brought an abrupt halt to the project, leading Hogg to liken events to the debacle with Goldie, and hoping for an another fortuitous outcome.[20]

While Hogg's first attempts to find a rescuer were directed at London, with approaches being made to both Smith, Elder & Co. and Richard Bentley, his efforts finally led back to his native Scotland, and with unexpected results. Having briefly sounded out Oliver & Boyd, Hogg turned to the Edinburgh and Glasgow publisher Archibald Fullarton, with whom he had recently contracted to provide an edition of Burns's work with a Memoir. In so doing, Hogg was entering a distinctly different sphere of book production, that of 'number' publication, a process involving the issue of titles in parts, allowing less wealthy readers to assemble larger works of literature as regular subscribers. Partly as a result of accident, the trail then led to the firm of Blackie & Son, Fullarton's old associates, themselves then out-and-out specialists in that mode of publication, with a highly centralised base in Glasgow, encompassing the functions of printer, illustrator, publisher and marketing in one enterprise.

Hogg was obviously attracted by the prospect of a radically enlarged sale, not only as a way of realising larger profits, but also as a means of making contact with a wider urban readership that he had long felt denied him. Blackies, however, proved extremely tight in their negotiations, evidently halving Hogg's demands for one-sixth of the retail proceeds, and by the nature of their operations left little or no space for authorial manoeuvring, especially once copy had been handed over. The posthumously published *Tales and Sketches of the Ettrick Shepherd* (1836–7), shortly followed by his *Poetical Works* in five volumes, placed a restrictive clamp on Hogg's output, governed partly by the mechanical nature of the operations involved and partly by ideological considerations. These distorted the nature of his original work and had the effect of holding back his literary standing for over a hundred years.[21]

CHAPTER THREE

Magazines, Annuals, and the Press

Gillian Hughes

Hogg's earliest attempts at writing were inevitably connected with eighteenth-century periodicals, which in the Scottish Borders gave ambitious young countrymen their chief access to a wider contemporary culture. The cost of newly published works was prohibitively high, so local book collections, such as the circulating library of Mr Elders in Peebles or the books owned by Hogg's Blackhouse employer James Laidlaw, would largely comprise older works of fiction, travel and theology, obtained either second-hand or in the form of cheaper reprints.[1] Information on current literature and affairs came largely from a weekly or thrice-weekly newspaper costing a few pence, or from a monthly magazine costing a couple of shillings, which also welcomed contributions from reader-correspondents. Hogg's old friend Alexander Laidlaw of Bowerhope, for instance, published the results of his investigation of 'a very destructive worm' that made its appearance on several farms in the vicinity of St Mary's Loch in the early summer of 1802 in the *Edinburgh Weekly Journal*.[2] Hogg's own first prose publications also appeared anonymously in periodicals:

> It was when engaged in *smearing* sheep at Blackhouse that the publication containing the first prose article of his which had the honour of appearing in print was handed to him by his master, and he was accustomed in after years to tell his confidential friends, in his own style of sly humour, how he felt affected on the occasion.[3]

These early published articles by Hogg are now almost impossible to identify, since they were amateur and unpaid contributions, customarily sent post-paid to the printing office and responded to only by publication, or by a brief rejection or promise of publication in the 'To Correspondents' paragraph of the relevant magazine. An issue typically mixed together largely anonymous articles, some produced by low-paid hack writers and others contributed gratuitously and anonymously by the magazine's readership. As James Grant recalled in 1836, 'It was a very rare circumstance for any author

31

of eminence to contribute, even anonymously, to the periodicals of the eighteenth century.'[4]

The official record of Hogg's early periodical publications is understandably misrepresentative. After the early poem 'The Mistakes of a Night' was printed in the Scots Magazine for October 1794, Hogg apparently contributed no more periodical articles until 'Sandy Tod, A Scottish Pastoral' appeared in the Edinburgh Magazine for May 1802. The first poem is only identifiable as Hogg's because it was alluded to as his in a subsequent magazine article, and the second because it was afterwards included in The Mountain Bard of 1807.[5] Anything Hogg published at this time that was neither alluded to nor reprinted elsewhere is unidentifiable, however unlikely it seems that an ambitious and proud author would not publish anything further for almost eight years after seeing his first poem in print. The above reminiscence of a prose article appearing during his years as a shepherd at Blackhouse farm suggests that he did indeed publish more periodical work.

Monthly miscellanies tended to treat poetry and prose articles rather differently, and poems are often easier to attribute. Anonymous prose articles were shared between sections featuring biography, history, geography, antiquities, criticism, agriculture, architecture, and so on. Poetry, however, was likely to be confined within a discrete section of each monthly issue under a title such as 'The British Muse', which flagged it as a forum for cultural pride and interchange.[6] Some poems were signed, but even within the prevailing periodical convention of anonymity regular contributors could build an identifiable authorial persona by the use of initials and pseudonyms, signalling regional or occupational identity and entering into debate with one another. Hogg's poem 'To Mr. T. M. C., London', for instance, was addressed to a regular contributor to the poetry section of The Scots Magazine in August 1805, and received a reply in the issue for March 1806.[7] When Hogg met Janet Stuart in 1808, he was pleased to discover her identity with the 'Adeline' of the poetry section of the Edinburgh Magazine. 'T. M. C.' himself proved in 1806 to be Thomas Mounsey Cunningham.[8] 'The Mistakes of a Night' was unsigned, and it was only after Hogg had learned to signal a magazine identity ('A Shepherd', a 'Scots Shepherd', or the more permanent 'Ettrick Shepherd') that he became more visible to contemporaries as well as to succeeding bibliographers. Recognition of a poetical corpus permitted the subsequent appearance of biographical information about Hogg in The Scots Magazine.[9]

These poems by Hogg formed a nucleus for The Mountain Bard (1807), while several of Hogg's contributors to The Forest Minstrel (1810) had also featured in Edinburgh periodicals.[10] This work would not, however, allow Hogg to move from unpaid amateur to professional periodical contributor: no editor or proprietor would pay for what, in the prevailing culture of writer–

readership, he could easily receive gratis. Although Archibald Constable had effected a revolution in periodical literature in 1802 by paying handsomely for well-informed critical articles in the *Edinburgh Review* he saw no need to extend this to the poetry and prose fiction of his other Edinburgh periodical, *The Scots Magazine*. When Hogg attempted to turn professional in Edinburgh after the failure of his Dumfriesshire farming schemes, his work was welcome only as that of an amateur:

> On going to Edinburgh, I found that my poetical talents were rated nearly as low there as my shepherd qualities were in Ettrick. It was in vain that I applied to newsmongers, booksellers, editors of magazines, &c. for employment. Any of these were willing enough to accept of my lucubrations, and give them public-ity, but then there was no money going – not a farthing; and this suited me very ill.[11]

Since the proprietor was the only person to make money from a miscel-lany periodical Hogg resolved to become a proprietor himself, and on 1 September 1810 the first issue was published of *The Spy: A Periodical Paper of Literary Amusement and Instruction*. Hogg's title signals that *The Spy* followed prestigious weekly essay-periodicals such as Addison's *Spectator* or Henry Mackenzie's *Mirror* and *Lounger*. The editor-author was a polite gentleman observing contemporary social life, supported by equally prestigious friends, and his work's appeal would lie partly in the ingenuity of the changes rung on familiar settings and themes. Hogg's subtitle, however, appealed to the more demotic and mixed modes of the miscellany market, promising poetry and popular prose fiction. Hogg's contributors accordingly included established Edinburgh professionals such as the Writer to the Signet Robert Sym of George Square, but also schoolteachers, printers and a number of women.[12] Radical ideas on matters such as education and slavery feature in *The Spy* as well as conventional literary forms. 'A Dialogue in the Reading-Room' echoes Johnsonian issues of authorship in a familiar urban setting, but Hogg's 'Story of the Berwickshire Farmer' (the prototype of the picaresque 'The Renowned Adventures of Basil Lee') includes scenes of rural life, foreign adventure, the supernatural, and illicit sex.[13] Such elements offended read-erly expectations of *The Spy* as an essay-periodical and led to the withdrawal of a significant number of subscribers: it was discontinued when the first year of weekly issues had been completed.

Since there was no lucrative periodical market for Hogg in Edinburgh, the benefits of participation were publicity and patronage. During his residence in Edinburgh he tried intermittently to record notable events through poems published in newspapers: he memorialised the deaths of the Tory politician Lord Melville and the Duchess of Buccleuch, a public dinner held in honour of Robert Burns, the entry of the allies into Paris at Easter 1814, and the institution of the Caledonian Asylum, a charity designed for the support of the families of fallen British soldiers.[14] As Peter Garside indicates in Chapter 2, Hogg's energies were largely devoted to the production of separate volume publications in the years following his success with *The Queen's Wake* in 1813. This situation, however, altered significantly in the autumn of 1817, when William Blackwood renamed his previously ineffective new monthly periodical *Blackwood's Edinburgh Magazine* and routinely paid ten guineas per sheet of sixteen pages for either poetry or prose fiction.[15]

While admitting the charm of a proprietor who affixed 'a price to the writers per sheet', Hogg was slow to recognise the revolution that Blackwood had effected in the status of the monthly miscellany, expecting well-known writers to 'disdain to continue writing for a two shilling Magazine' and offering 'any old thing worth publishing' among his own manuscripts rather than specially composed work.[16] He did, however, relish the social networking involved in production of the new magazine, securing its early success with the satirical 'Translation from an Ancient Chaldee Manuscript', involving himself in political rivalries occasioned by it, and replying to and continuing the work of other contributors. Hogg followed up articles by Walter Scott and William Laidlaw on the shepherd's dog, for instance, with another of his own.[17] As *Blackwood's* settled down from its early wildness into a respectable though lively organ of Toryism, Hogg settled down as a farmer in Yarrow valley, almost forty miles from Edinburgh. After Hogg's marriage in 1820, his relations with *Blackwood's* shifted. Living hand to mouth, Hogg could not sustain his household on the irregular though often substantial sums earned by his volume publications and became dependent for cash in hand on the regular monthly payments earned by work, which was now specially written for, and tailored to, the concerns of the magazine. Tom Richardson has estimated that by April 1835, a few months before his death, Hogg 'contributed more than one hundred works to *Blackwood's* and wrote perhaps another forty pieces for the magazine that were not published there'.[18] Such work was doubly lucrative, for Hogg could look forward to immediate payment and to receiving an additional lump sum when his songs, prose tales and poems were subsequently published in volume collections. *The Shepherd's Calendar* (1829), *Songs, by the Ettrick Shepherd* (1831), and *A Queer Book* (1832) all contain substantial amounts of material previously published in *Blackwood's*.

Hogg's participation in *Blackwood's* had a serious drawback, his magazine alter ego, the Shepherd of the *Noctes Ambrosianae*, a long-running series of popular dialogues about politics and culture between the magazine's supposed editor Christopher North and his cronies at a well-known Edinburgh tavern. In these the Shepherd varyingly stood as the acquiescent Tory peasantry of Scotland, a virtuoso of the Scots language, the power of imagination and natural taste uncorrupted by formal manners and education, and the butt of the condescending middle classes. The Noctean Shepherd became rather better known than Hogg the writer, a curious situation which Hogg alternately welcomed for publicity purposes and deplored as a misrepresentation.[19] Hogg's poetry was praised and his prose fiction disparaged, while his songs were embedded in the dialogues themselves: headnotes to many of the individual *Songs, by the Ettrick Shepherd* seek to restore the context of the *Noctes Ambrosianae* from which they had been abstracted for volume publication.

For good and ill Hogg remained, during most of the 1820s, tied to *Blackwood's Edinburgh Magazine*, since William Blackwood's pioneering professionalisation of the monthly miscellany magazine was followed only gradually by others. The bitter political divisions in Edinburgh between Whig and Tory meant that Hogg contributed to Archibald Constable's rival *Edinburgh Magazine* only intermittently and anonymously, except for periods when he had quarrelled with his Tory publisher. Hogg continued, however, to participate in old-fashioned amateur periodical networks. He became an enthusiastic contributor, for instance, to Henry Glasford Bell's *Edinburgh Literary Journal* (1828–31), which paid him with admiration rather than in cash, citing his opinions respectfully in editorials, reviewing his work handsomely, and printing items rejected by Blackwood as insufficiently decorous. It was flattering and refreshing to be consistently treated as an admired elder in the Scottish republic of letters.[20] Hogg also continued to contribute to Scottish newspapers, giving publicity to the St Ronan's Border Club by reporting on its meetings and social events, for instance. His newspaper work supported the interest of the Duke of Buccleuch, part of the implicit bargain by which he held the small farm of Altrive Lake rent-free. Hogg's authorship of some newspaper articles can be proved by letters or surviving manuscript fragments, for instance a report on a Carterhaugh cattle-show under the Duke's patronage or an account of a Border Games. His hand may be detected in other articles in which the poetry of James Hogg is cited, or local comment on the Buccleuch family is retailed in graphic Scots.[21]

The development of the literary annual, a hybrid between the one-off anthology and a magazine, brought London increasingly into focus for James Hogg as a market for his periodical work. With a year elapsing between issues, Hogg had plenty of time to send his work to editors, receive instructions, make corrections, and check that he had been properly paid for what had previously been used. Hogg could also tailor his work, as he preferred to do, to suit individual titles such as *The Amulet* (which favoured literature with a religious slant) or *Friendship's Offering* (which welcomed sentimental depictions of an author's own life experiences). Hogg was paid well for this work (as much as £1 for a small page by *The Anniversary*), and in the final year of his life estimated that by writing for annuals and magazines he made an income of 'from one to two hundred pounds annually'.[22] The advent of a regular and efficient steamship service from Leith during the 1820s also opened up the London monthly magazines for Hogg's work. *Fraser's Magazine*, begun in 1830, became a real rival to the Edinburgh-based *Blackwood's* in the final years of Hogg's life, paying him as well and being less censorious of Hogg's more extravagant subjects: more than thirty articles by Hogg appeared in its pages in six years, including his long poem 'Love's Legacy'. Hogg also favoured *The Metropolitan*, a magazine owned by his London publisher James Cochrane, and the *Royal Lady's Magazine* edited by George Glenny. William Blackwood no longer automatically had the pick of Hogg's best work, Hogg writing to him of his 'Ballad of Lord Maxwell', for example, that it had been written 'for a lady's Magazine in London and [. . .] sent off before your request for it arrived'.[23]

The advent of fast sailing ships across the Atlantic gave the largely illusory promise of an American market for Hogg's periodical writings in the 1830s. Hogg sent several articles to Simeon de Witt Bloodgood of Albany, for instance, but his experiment was unsuccessful as communications were plainly irregular. In September 1835 he wrote of his American admirers, 'I tried to prop several of their infant periodicals but I never yet could learn if any of my pieces reached their destination and I am convinced the half of them never did.'[24]

In the final years of his life Hogg, always willing to experiment with new markets for his work, made several contributions to *Chambers's Edinburgh Journal*, a weekly venture created in the wake of the 1832 Reform Act by his young Edinburgh friend Robert Chambers and priced at only three-halfpence to appeal to a lower-middle-class and aspirational working-class readership. *Chambers's*, however, did not normally include poetry and while Hogg was offered two guineas for a brief tale the paper's distaste for the supernatural and its relentlessly improving moral tone were hardly congenial. Hogg's 'The Watchmaker', for example, is only superficially consonant with the paper's warnings of the evils of the demon drink.[25] Rightly or wrongly, Hogg saw the spread of such cheap mass-circulation periodicals as threatening his livelihood, gloomily prophesying that 'we will soon all be beggars'.[26]

An unusually large proportion of Hogg's output was originally contributed to periodicals, reflecting a preference for the tale and the ballad over the three-volume novel and the long narrative poem. *The Three Perils of Woman* (1823) is subtitled 'A Series of Domestic Scottish Tales', while *The Queen's Wake* strings a succession of shorter narrative poems on the thread of a poetic contest at the court of Mary, Queen of Scots. Hogg was fortunate that his predilections coincided with a number of favourable changes in the periodical marketplace.

CHAPTER FOUR

Hogg's Reception and Reputation

Suzanne Gilbert

In 1944, French novelist André Gide encountered James Hogg's novel *The Private Memoirs and Confessions of a Justified Sinner*, into which he 'at once plunged with a stupefaction and admiration that increased at every page'.[1] Making inquiries, he found no one who knew of Hogg's work. In his introduction to the 1947 edition of the novel, Gide asks:

> How explain that a work so singular and so enlightening, so especially fitted to arouse passionate interest both in those who are attracted by religious and moral questions, and, for quite other reasons, in psychologists and artists, and above all in surrealists who are so particularly drawn by the demoniac in every shape – how explain that such a work should have failed to become famous?[2]

Several factors contributed to the obscurity of Hogg's masterpiece. On first publication in 1824 sales were sparse, and reviewers either ignored the novel, or were facetious or disapproving. 'Any degree of unqualified praise is hard to find', in Peter Garside's summary, with 'the general tendency being to see native talent marred by "extravagance", inelegance, and eccentricity'.[3] The novel's treatment of Calvinism disturbed readers who wanted their religion straightforward, and their God and demons readily distinguishable. Hogg's experimental impulse, evident in his 'postmodern' refusal to grant authority to a single narrative and his disruptive play with forms and conventions, was perhaps even less acceptable. Nor did publishers deem Hogg's book a marketable product. Austen, Edgeworth, Ferrier, Galt, Godwin, Peacock and other contemporaries remained in the public eye when, in the late 1820s, Richard Bentley bought the 'tail-ends' of copyrights of out-of-print novels for a series designed to exploit the expanding industrial-age literary market. As William St Clair explains, 'With a new title coming out every few weeks, *Bentley's Standard Novels* provided several years' worth of continuous serial reading, a delayed, carefully selected, series of most of the best fictional writing of recent times'; *The Private Memoirs and Confessions of a Justified Sinner*, along with Hogg's other novel-length fictions, failed to make the cut.[4]

The trajectory of Hogg's reputation has presented scholars with a range of difficulties and contradictions. This chapter traces key factors in that trajectory, including the early focus on Hogg's labouring-class roots, his complex involvement with the persona of the 'Ettrick Shepherd', and his contentious relations with the publishing world during his lifetime. It considers the distinctive North American reception of Hogg's work as well as its Victorian bowdlerisation, which contributed to its virtual disappearance from the modern literary canon. Finally, it traces the ongoing recovery of Hogg's reputation following Gide's reading of the *Confessions* in the mid-twentieth century.

Early reactions to Hogg's work turned on assumptions about his social status. Commenting on the (just published) *The Mountain Bard* (1807), the *Poetical Register* viewed Hogg as an example of the Romantic-era phenomenon of the peasant poet:

> The labouring class of society has, of late years, teemed with poets, and would-be poets. If it should much longer display the same fertility, there will not be a single trade or calling which will not have produced a bard. Mr. Hogg is the poet of the Shepherds; and is really an honour to them.[5]

The reviewer characterises shepherds as naturally fitted for poetry; they were 'always a poetical tribe', and Hogg's ballads 'are in the true style of that sort of writing': 'simple and natural, [containing] many spirited and picturesque ideas and descriptions, and, occasionally, strokes of genuine humour'.[6] *The Literary Panorama*, associating these qualities with an earlier, less civilised stage of society, voices another recurrent concern: Hogg's poetic success depends upon his knowing his place, and not neglecting 'his *proper* business'. He may dabble in writing, but he has also 'gained two prizes from the Highland Society, for Essays connected with the rearing and management of sheep'.[7]

Early reviews generally approve of Hogg's efforts, though the tone is inevitably patronising. Most assume that 'self-taught poets' lack originality: 'They are frequently the most servile imitators of the few, and often bad models, to which they may have gained access.' It was Hogg's best strategy to write about what he knew: 'to select a few of the traditional tales of his native district, about which the public curiosity had just then been excited, and attempt to relate them in a style resembling that of the ancient ballad'. The public's interest in ballads had indeed been raised by Scott's *Minstrelsy of the Scottish Border* (1802–3), and Hogg's efforts were deemed not 'altogether unsuccessful': his ballad imitations, 'though not sufficiently exact to deceive a connoisseur, have yet a very considerable likeness to their originals'.[8]

In general, reviewers devote far more space to appraising Hogg's life than to analysing his works. They dwell on the incongruity of a little-

educated shepherd managing to produce such writing, and express surprise
at his achievement 'considering the disadvantages of his situation'.[9] In the
advertisement to the second edition of *The Queen's Wake* (1813), Hogg's
publisher, George Goldie, assured readers that the poem was

> really and truly the production of *James Hogg*, a common Shepherd, bred among
> the mountains of Ettrick Forest, who went to service when only seven years of
> age; and since that period has never received any education whatever.[10]

Inflected with varying degrees of condescension or irony, this would remain
the dominant theme of critical responses to Hogg's work throughout his
career.

Hogg was heavily involved in his own construction as a self-educated
Ettrick poet who became 'king o' the mountain and fairy school', as distinct
from what he considered Scott's official but less authentic 'school o' chivalry'.[11] Hogg's arrival on the literary scene was modest and self-promoted;
coming from obscurity, he had to seek ways of putting himself before the
public. Recognising the value of the persona of the inspired rustic, he followed
the common practice of signing poems in magazines with epithets ranging
from 'A Shepherd', to 'Ettrick. A Shepherd', to 'the Ettrick Shepherd', to
'James Hogg, the Ettrick Shepherd'.[12] He reports that long before his literary
career took off he had enjoyed regional celebrity as 'Jamie the poeter', famous
for wooing the local lasses with his singing,[13] and he found a home for some
of those early songs in *The Scots Magazine*. His self-published first collection
of poems, *Scottish Pastorals* (1801), received almost no attention. Hogg's
involvement with collecting ballads for the third volume of *Minstrelsy of the
Scottish Border* marked a watershed. The enthusiastic reception of Scott's
work demonstrated a broad public appreciation for the traditional culture
that had produced the ballads, and Hogg was encouraged to put together his
own collection of original ballads and songs, *The Mountain Bard*.

Here the story of Hogg's reception takes an important turn. By far the
most influential way in which he shaped his public persona and reputation
was through the 'Memoir of the Life of James Hogg' that he wrote as an introduction to *The Mountain Bard*. In the 'Memoir' (conceived when his poetry
for *The Scots Magazine* began to attract queries about its unknown author),[14]
Hogg undertakes a strategic effort to authenticate his roots and narrate his
career in terms of an overcoming of early adversity. Hogg expanded the
'Memoir' for the revised *Mountain Bard* (1821) in order to frame and justify
his status as a professional writer, and he recast it again for *Altrive Tales*
(1832) to romanticise his origins from the standpoint of an established man
of letters. The connection between self-representation and reception was
irrevocably sealed. The 'Memoir' became a primary source for decades of

commentators, shaping Hogg's reputation in incalculable ways, defining –
and redefining – his literary legacy.

Other pressures shaped the subsequent reception of Hogg's work. He faced
censorship and misrepresentation, and consequently looked for ways to cir-
cumvent the various kinds of control that publishers imposed. As his career
developed, he sought to retain control of the 'Ettrick Shepherd' identity
while also distinguishing himself within wider circles, going 'professional'
with the 1810 move to Edinburgh, becoming '[n]o longer a Borders shepherd
and farmer who also wrote poetry but a would-be metropolitan writer'.[15] In
his weekly miscellany, The Spy, Hogg sought to consolidate his rural credentials while at the same time asserting his fitness to comment on Edinburgh's
cultural scene. As Ian Duncan puts it, however, 'the editors and reviewers
who monitored the literary marketplace would invoke [his rural] origins to
disqualify Hogg's attempts to write in metropolitan genres'.[16] Hogg acknowledged in the last number that as the identity of 'Mr. Spy' became known 'the
number of his subscribers diminished': 'The learned, the enlightened, and
polite circles of this flourishing metropolis disdained either to be amused or
instructed by the ebullitions of humble genius'.[17]

Hogg's next major work, The Queen's Wake (1813), met with unprecedented approbation. He was praised for 'genius, taste, and skill', and for
'versatility of talent' (Edinburgh Star). In the Monthly Magazine, Capel Lofft
effused:

> Greater ease and spirit, a sweeter, richer, more animated and easy flow of versi-
> fication, more clearness of language, more beauty of imagery, more grandeur,
> fervour, pathos, and occasionally more vivid and aweful sublimity, can hardly
> be found.[18]

The Theatrical Inquisitor commended Hogg for a 'natural and original' sense
of humour, 'decidedly superior' to Scott's.[19] Most reviewers continued to
emphasise his humble origins, as in the Scots Magazine's relegation of him to
'the first rank among men of self-taught genius'.[20] Publication of The Queen's
Wake was undoubtedly 'a life-changing event' for Hogg, making him a
'famous author', on friendly terms with Byron and Wordsworth; as Douglas S.
Mack notes, 'Now he could with justice feel that he was being taken seriously
as a poet'.[21] Six editions were published over the course of the decade, and his
name came to be coupled with the phrase 'the author of The Queen's Wake'.

Hogg's financial situation in the 1810s meant that he was constantly
scrambling to stay afloat, caught between the demands of a literary life in
Edinburgh and an agricultural one in Ettrick. Additionally, like other writers
of his class, he suffered repercussions from the social and political upheaval
of the period. Many of the most damaging representations of Hogg emerged

during the turbulent years of economic hardship and social unrest between the end of the Napoleonic Wars and the early 1820s. Hogg's writings drew criticism for the alternative viewpoints he offered on social issues and historical events, as in that 'challengingly egalitarian' narrative poem *Mador of the Moor* (1816),[22] and for his advocacy of traditional rural life, as in *The Brownie of Bodsbeck and Other Tales* (1818). Meanwhile, his increasingly audacious self-fashioning as a professional writer, driven in part by his precarious finances, led to strained relations with a succession of publishers.

When Hogg revised *The Mountain Bard* for publication in 1821, he expanded the introductory 'Memoir', including some controversial remarks about Scott and airing his disagreements with reviewers and publishers, in particular George Goldie. The targets of his attack, and the social circles that supported them, were deeply offended and responded accordingly. Reviews of the volume focus almost obsessively on the grievances detailed in the memoir, usually to the exclusion of talking about the poetry at all. Writing for the *Edinburgh Monthly Review*, David Laing accused Hogg of having 'acted unadvisedly' in making public 'what may have been said in ordinary conversation, or occurred in familiar and personal transactions'.[23] Hogg privately vented his exasperation with 'David Laing's canting and insolent review' and 'Goldie's notorious lies', adding: 'Wo is me if I am to be measured by the trade!'[24] During this period he also fell out with William Blackwood, mostly over the publication in *Blackwood's Edinburgh Magazine* of a vitriolic response to the 'Memoir' by John Wilson. A significant contrast may be seen in reviews from outside the volatile Edinburgh literary scene, which tended to reiterate the genteel condescension that greeted the 1807 *Mountain Bard*.

The trend of marginalising Hogg intensified throughout the 1820s, thanks largely to the appearance of the 'Ettrick Shepherd' in the popular series 'Noctes Ambrosianae', which ran from 1822 to 1835 in *Blackwood's Edinburgh Magazine*. As Garside observes, 'Publicity in the "Noctes" was as always a mixed blessing, on the one hand severely threatening Hogg's claim to be treated seriously as a literary figure, yet at the same time offering personal publicity on a scale that could not be found elsewhere' (p. lxvii).[25] Wilson's characterisation of the Shepherd as a naturally poetic buffoon certainly distorted Hogg's brand. In a burlesque of Romantic theories of inspired composition, Wilson represents Hogg as barely able to recall having written his own song:

When the book was sent out a' printed to Yarrowside, od! I just read the maist feck on't as if I had never seen't afore; and as for that sang in particular ['Come all ye jolly shepherds'], I'll gang before the Baillies the morn, and tak' my affi-davy that I had no more mind o' *when* I wrote it, or *how* I wrote it, or onything

whatever concerning it – no more than if it had been a screed of heathen
Greek. I behoved to have written't sometime, and someway, since it was there
– but that's a' I kent. – I maun surely hae flung't aff some night when I was a
thought dazed, and just sent it in to the printer without looking at it in the
morning.[26]

Features of the caricature resurfaced elsewhere, solidifying the connection
between the fictional Shepherd of the 'Noctes' and the writer James Hogg.
As Duncan has shown, Wilson depicts Hogg in terms of animal physicality
or 'hoggishness' in his unsigned review of *The Three Perils of Woman*: 'In one
page, we listen to the song of the nightingale, and in another, to the grunt of
the boar. Now the wood is vocal with the feathered choir; and then the sty
bubbles and squeaks with a farm-sow and a litter of nineteen pigwiggins.'[27] At
the heart of Wilson's representation, Duncan argues, is a 'satirical equation of
Hogg with his body'.[28] Reluctance to allow Hogg to overcome the perceived
limitations of his background, often expressed in terms of a physical appearance inassimilable to polite society, was not restricted to the 'Noctes'. John
Gibson Lockhart sketches a similar caricature in *Peter's Letters to his Kinfolk*
(1819):

> Although for some time past he has spent a considerable portion of every year
> in excellent, even in refined society, the external appearance of the man can
> have undergone but very little change since he was 'a herd on Yarrow'. His face
> and hands are still as brown as if he lived entirely *sub dio*. His very hair has a
> coarse stringiness about it, which proves beyond dispute its utter ignorance of
> all arts of the friseur; and hangs in playful whips and cords about his ears, in a
> style of the most perfect innocence imaginable.[29]

Critics ventriloquised Hogg as irrepressible, and therefore dangerous.
Wilson's Shepherd boasts, 'o' a' things whatsomever, be it in sacred matters
or profane, I detest moderation'.[30] The characterisation recurs in reviews
worrying that Hogg has gone too far, violating taste and decorum through
some combination of poor judgement, recklessness, and ignorance: the
symptoms of his low social origins. What reviewers of *Winter Evening Tales*
(1820) judged as 'indelicacies' Hogg saw as virtues: 'there was a blunt rusticity
about [the tales]; but I liked them the better for it'.[31] Nor was he conciliatory
towards his censors, taking them to task in the guise of the 'shepherd poet' of
Queen Hynde (1824):

> Bald, brangling, brutal, insincere;
> The bookman's venal gazetteer;
> Down with the trash, and every gull
> That gloats upon their garbage dull![32]

The *Westminster Review* remarked, 'It is very natural, that Hogg should fear and hate reviewers, and their readers.'[33] Given the rough – and excessively personal – treatment meted out to him, it is not surprising that Hogg complained that 'the whole of the aristocracy and literature of our country were set against me and determined to keep me down nay to crush me to a nonentity'.[34]

Social prejudice distorted assessments of Hogg's work throughout the nineteenth century and into the twentieth. This is obvious, for example, in the reception of *The Domestic Manners and Private Life of Sir Walter Scott* (1834; first published as *Familiar Anecdotes of Sir Walter Scott*). Hogg's handling of Scott's memory was met with outrage. William Maginn, writing in *Fraser's Magazine*, was notably scathing:

> If by domestic manners he had intended the manners of Sir Walter's domestics, there is no doubt that he is fully qualified, from taste, relationship, congeniality of sentiment, and considerable social intercourse with them, to do the subject justice; but as to the manners of Sir Walter himself, as well might we expect from a costermonger an adequate sketch of the clubs in St James's Street.[35]

Jill Rubenstein observes that 'the small-minded nastiness' of this review offers 'a vivid reminder of what Hogg endured as the accompaniment of any literary success he enjoyed in his lifetime'.[36]

When *Anecdotes of Scott* was published, Scott's official biographer and son-in-law Lockhart tried to get reviewers to ignore it. Lockhart's later characterisation in his *Memoirs of the Life of Sir Walter Scott* (1837–8) haunted Hogg's reception for well over a century. Lockhart evaluates Hogg's writing as 'exceedingly rugged and uncouth' but nonetheless showing 'abundant traces of [. . .] native shrewdness and genuine poetical feeling'. In his famous anecdote of the visit paid by the 'rustic genius' to Scott's town house in Edinburgh, Lockhart portrays Hogg, devastatingly, as a mannerless boor who presumes to emulate Lady Scott by stretching out on a sofa in his dirty clothing, his hands bearing 'legible marks of a recent sheep-smearing', dining 'heartily' and drinking 'freely':

> As the liquor operated, his familiarity increased and strengthened; from Mr Scott, he advanced to "Sherra," and thence to "Scott," "Walter," and "Wattie," – until, at supper, he fairly convulsed the whole party by addressing Mrs Scott, as "Charlotte".[37]

Hogg exposes himself as either ignorant of proper behaviour or blatantly disregarding it. Either way, the shepherd eclipses the author; Lockhart's monumental caricature of an uncouth upstart comes to stand for Hogg's entire career.

While reviewers often characterised Hogg as a provincial writer, his work found readers beyond Britain; *Winter Evening Tales* was translated into German, and *The Three Perils of Woman* into French. American publishers reprinted Hogg's poems, songs, stories, and all of his novels except for the *Confessions*. America also provided a home for original material, as Janette Currie has shown in her annotated list of his American publications from 1807 to 1911.[38] As Hogg wrote to a foreign correspondent for an American newspaper, 'I learned from many sources that my brethren beyond the Atlantic were sincere friends and admirers of mine and I tried to prop several of their infant periodicals.'[39] In 1834, *Familiar Anecdotes of Sir Walter Scott* first appeared in New York, and Hogg reports sending other material to its editor Simeon de Witt Bloodgood, which Bloodgood later published in the Albany *Zodiac*.[40]

There was, of course, a strong cultural base for the reception of Hogg's work in North America. The presence of a large population of well-educated Scottish emigrants and their descendants encouraged booksellers to publish material on Scottish subjects and by Scottish authors.[41] Describing Hogg's transatlantic readership as 'unquestionably large and enthusiastic',[42] Andrew Hook observes that he was 'probably the most popular [writer] in America as both poet and story-teller' on 'Scottish subjects and themes'; and that almost all his writings after *The Queen's Wake* 'received favourable attention'.[43] In 1834 the *American Monthly* reported a conversation between Hogg and an American visitor:

> 'They tell me', said he again, 'that my writings are kent in America.' I answered that they had all been reprinted there and were as well known and as much esteemed as in Scotland.[44]

The 'Shepherd' persona was also well known: 'In America the popularity of the *Noctes Ambrosianae* has been proved by the extent to which they have been republished and circulated in that country', wrote the work's American editor in 1864.[45] Outside literary Edinburgh Hogg's reputation seems to have suffered little from Wilson's caricature. Hogg was popular in nineteenth-century America because his personal narrative appealed to Enlightenment ideals of 'improvement' and self-help, and because the democratic and humanitarian impulses of his work paralleled those current in American political discourse.[46] An article in the *American Monthly Magazine*, 'The Ettrick Shepherd and Other Scotch Poets', rebuts the standard British assessments of Hogg and Burns:

> They were peasants indeed; but not in that sense in which the word would be understood almost anywhere out of their own country; for no peasantry in

Europe, we may venture to say, can be compared in equal terms with the peasantry of Scotland. There is not only none more generally furnished with the
rudiments of scholastic education, but none that values them more highly, or is
bettered prepared to profit by them, from a native characteristic intelligence,
which education gratifies but does not create.[47]

Hogg's innate 'knowledge of human and physical nature' supplements the
basic schooling of which he has made the best possible use.

After Hogg's death in 1835 his reception continued to be shaped by legends
and anecdotes – some of them self-constructed, others imposed. Some stories
of his colourful life and behaviour, such as Lockhart's regarding his visit to
Scott, achieved a kind of canonicity. Despite the distortions, however, he
inspired and influenced many nineteenth-century British writers, from the
Brontës to Robert Louis Stevenson.[48] Hogg's American popularity meant that
writers such as Irving, Cooper, Poe, Emerson, Hawthorne, Melville, Thoreau
and Longfellow were familiar with him, as they acknowledged in their own
published work and correspondence.

The posthumous editions of Hogg's *Tales & Sketches* (1837) and *Poetical
Works* (1838–40) published by the Glasgow firm of Blackie & Son omitted
many of his works and altered and bowdlerised those they did include; these
were the basis for subsequent editions, notably the Rev. Thomas Thomson's
two-volume *Works of the Ettrick Shepherd* (Blackie, 1865). In these watered-
down, relatively lifeless versions Hogg was read by the Victorians. *Confessions
of a Justified Sinner*, subject to especially grievous alteration in the Blackie
editions (under the title *Private Memoirs and Confessions of a Fanatic*), was
reprinted in its original version in 1894, evidence of a growing interest in
the work in the *fin de siècle*. However it was not until Gide's advocacy, half a
century later, that Hogg's masterpiece attained the status of a modern classic.
The appearance of Hogg's texts in their original versions in the Stirling/
South Carolina Research Edition, from the mid-1990s, has begun to bring
the entirety of his achievement to light and reshape his international reputation. Today many readers are able to echo Edwin Morgan's assessment that in
Hogg 'we have an author of unique interest, force, and originality'.[49]

CHAPTER FIVE

Hogg and the Highlands

H. B. de Groot

A modern reader tends to think of the Scottish Highlands mainly in geographical terms: the Highlands are in the north and are mountainous (unlike the Lowlands which are in the south and are hilly, and the Central Belt which is in the middle and is flat). In the time of James Hogg, the late eighteenth and early nineteenth century, the distinction would have been primarily cultural and linguistic: south of the Highland line the spoken language was Scots; above that line it was Gaelic.

An excursion to the Highlands was for much of the eighteenth century seen as a dangerous undertaking, because of the terrain, the lack of decent roads and accommodation, and the risk of being attacked by bandits. In the course of the century and in particular after the suppression of the 1745 rising, things improved for the traveller: a number of new military roads were constructed; the places of accommodation originally built for soldiers became regular inns ('change-houses'); crime was much reduced. The classic accounts of travels in the Highlands are those by the Welsh zoologist Thomas Pennant (1769, 1772), but he was preceded by Bishop Pocock (1747, 1750, 1760). Many others followed, including Samuel Johnson and James Boswell (1773), William Gilpin (1776), John Knox (1787), Sarah Murray (1796, 1801), Thomas Garnett (1798), and Thomas Stoddart (1799–1800).[1]

It would appear that Hogg visited the Highlands for the first time in 1791 when he went to the Trossachs, not as what would soon be called a 'Tourist' but as a drover of sheep. In the later eighteenth century wool was much in demand, principally to supply the Yorkshire woollen mills. The native Highland sheep were small and their wool was insufficient for the purpose. Consequently the eighteenth century saw the importation of sheep from the Lowlands: initially the short-haired blackface, later also the long-haired Cheviots. Hogg's 1791 Highland excursion should be seen as part of this process. Hogg went to the Highlands again in 1800, this time to the southeastern parts. It is clear from his letters that this journey had a practical purpose, as he was interested in renting a farm at the Spittal of Glenshee (in northern Perthshire).[2]

We know rather more about Hogg's subsequent visits, for he left detailed accounts of the 1802, 1803 and 1804 journeys.[3] It was probably Walter Scott who encouraged him to write up these accounts. The narrative was phrased as a series of letters to Scott and, when the first part of the 1802 *Journey* was published in the *Scots Magazine*, it was prefaced with a short Introduction by Scott (signed 'S. W.'). Hogg claimed in his narrative that his object in going to the Highlands was to find out more about the state of sheep-farming, but a rather whimsically expressed wish to find 'amongst the Grampian mountains a cheap and quiet retreat in the bosom of some sequestered glen' (p. 30) both suggests and half hides another practical purpose. The lease of Ettrick House, the farm where James and his parents lived, was to expire on Whit Sunday 1803, and James must have been on the lookout for alternative accommodation for himself and his parents.

The initial instalments of the 1802 *Journey* (see Figure 2) read like an old-fashioned eighteenth-century guidebook and it would seem that Hogg was still trying to find his way, but the narrative comes to life where he attended several horse races, saw two plays at the Theatre Royal in Edinburgh and, on crossing the Firth of Forth, was much amused by a boy on the ferry who had forgotten that it was Sunday and was whistling a popular tune. Much of the information provided in this first *Journey* was clearly written up later and cribbed from the *Statistical Account of Scotland* (something that is not true of the later *Journeys*). On the other hand, there are many fresh observations: when Hogg passed through Luncarty (a village just north of Perth), for instance, he was fascinated to find that people still remembered the battle between the Scots and the Danes that was supposed to have taken place in the tenth century.

The portions of the 1802 *Journey* published in *The Scots Magazine* stop after the sixth instalment, either because the conductors of the *Magazine* lost interest or because Hogg did not get the remaining material to the publishers before leaving on his 1803 excursion to the Highlands. The final two letters have been preserved in manuscript and are now at Stirling University. This is also the case with the outward journey of the summer of 1803 (first published by Hogg's daughter Mrs Garden in 1888), while most of the return journey has come down to us in a contemporary transcript now at Washington State University in Pullman.

In 1802 Hogg had travelled on horseback. In 1803 he was on foot and he travelled as far as the Outer Hebrides (see Figure 3). There is a sharp contrast between the night he spent in a shepherd's cottage at Loch Sloy in the Trossachs, accommodation shared with the cows and the hens, and the longer stay at Inveraray Castle, the residence of the Duke of Argyll, where Hogg was deferential and critical by turns. Further north he witnessed the preparations for the Sacrament Week (a week-long series of religious services which would

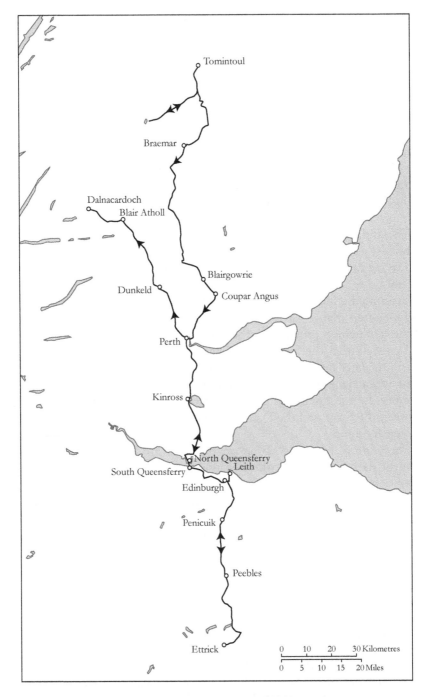

Figure 2 Hogg's journey of 1802

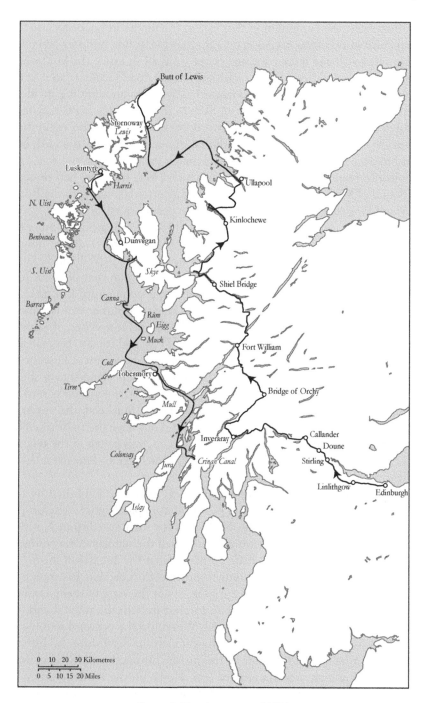

Figure 3 Hogg's journey of 1803

culminate with the Communion Service) at the manse in Lochalsh and left
us a picture of two sermons going on simultaneously: one minister preached
to the well-to-do and more educated people in English inside the kirk, while
another minister addressed those who only understood Gaelic from a 'tent'
(a portable pulpit) set up in the kirkyard. There was an alarming incident
when Hogg was on the way back from Skye to the mainland: Scots had been
in danger of being 'pressed' by the Royal Navy ever since the exemption
granted to them by the Lord High Admiral, the future James VII and II, had
been lifted in 1755. That danger became much greater during the war with
Napoleonic France. When the boat on which Hogg travelled had reached
the Sound of Mull, it was almost accosted by a cutter belonging to the Royal
Navy and Hogg came close to being forced to become a sailor.

The Scots Magazine did publish (belatedly in 1808–9) Hogg's account of his
1804 journey, which again took him to Harris (see Figure 4). Again he was
on foot, but this time he was accompanied by two friends: William Laidlaw
and John Grieve. The 1804 Journal is much shorter than that of 1803. It is
also much more sombre. Hogg tells us that in his community in Ettrick it
became known as 'the unfortunate journey'. Hogg was rather evasive about
what constituted the misfortune but, thanks to the researches of Janette
Currie, the situation has now become clearer.[4] Hogg had tried to become the
subtenant of Dr William MacLeod, who himself was the tenant at Luskentyre
on the Isle of Harris, with the intention of turning the land into a sheep
farm. In 1803 both signed a contract to that effect (the contract is now in
the National Library of Scotland). Alexander Hume MacLeod, the owner of
Harris, held the view that William MacLeod did not have the right to sublet
and took legal action. The case was resolved in 1809 in favour of the tenant,
but at that late date it was no longer possible for Hogg to become a sheep
farmer on Harris.

Hogg had hoped that the Highland Journeys would be published by the
Highland Society in book form and he wrote a supplementary essay on the
prospects of sheep farming in the Highlands for such an edition. Nothing
came of this plan and Hogg eventually published the supplementary essay in
1807 as part of The Shepherd's Guide – a book about the diseases of sheep.

Although Hogg reminded himself from time to time that his intent in
making these journeys was to find out more about the state of sheep farming
in the Highlands, he always showed an interest in both the natural and the
human worlds through which he passed. When, on the outward journey in
1802, he was staying at an inn at Dalnacardoch, in Perthshire, he hired a
guide, so that he could climb one of the nearby hills and get a good view of
the surrounding lochs and mountains (pp. 41–4); on the return journey he
left the drove road that took him south from Tomintoul in order to have a
look at Loch Avon (pp. 46–7). As for the human world: when travelling

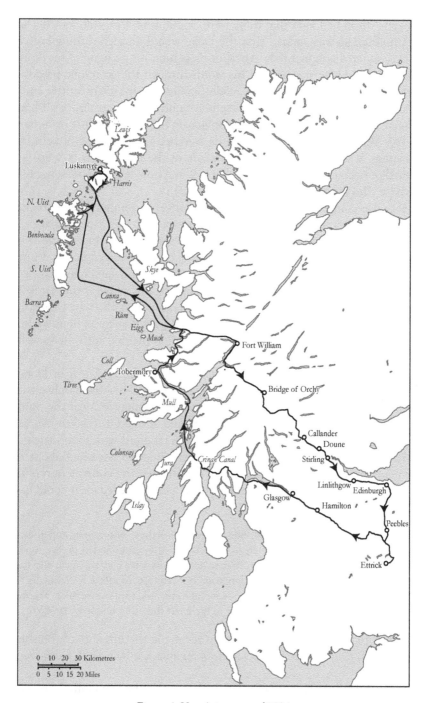

Figure 4 Hogg's journey of 1804

through Atholl he found that there were evictions on the estate of the Duke of Atholl. Hogg was amazed that the Duke would do such a thing but one of those evicted commented: 'Ah! Cot pless him, hit pe nane of his doing.' The fact that Hogg transmitted his words through the grotesque parody of Highland speech that had been made popular on the eighteenth-century London stage does not obscure his sense of outrage: the cottager still had a sense of loyalty towards a man who obviously felt none towards his tenants (p. 36). When Hogg was on Harris, he watched the gathering of kelp (the extraction of an alkali from seaweed made in the production of soap) and pointed out what a backbreaking task it was and how small the remuneration for those who did the actual work (pp. 131–2).

Hogg was committed to the expansion of sheep farming in the Highlands, both as an observer and as someone who aspired to be a participant. He was contemptuous of the primitive Highland sheep in contrast to the larger blackface and the Cheviot from the Scottish borders. He accepted that it was sometimes necessary to dispossess existing tenants and subtenants to make large sheep farms possible. On the other hand, he was aware of the hardships that resulted. When he travelled through Glen Shiel, in 1803, he wrote: 'I at length came to a place where there had been a great number of houses which were now mostly in ruins, the estate being all converted into sheep-walks' (p. 87).

Hogg put a lot of trust in aristocrats like the Duke of Argyll or Donald Cameron, the 22nd Chief Lochiel. On the other hand, he was sharply critical of a man like Robert Mackintosh, the owner of Dalmunzie (near the Spittal of Glenshee), who had neglected his estate and allowed it to go to rack and ruin (p. 48), or Hume MacLeod, an absentee landlord who took little care of the Isle of Harris (p. 133). Hogg was particularly concerned about the way many were driven to emigrate. He also felt that the construction of the Caledonian Canal was wasteful and that the money needed for it could have been better spent in other ways:

> if something is not done to provide assylum's for these brave men and their families, and to establish woolen manufactories; they [the landed proprietors] may live to see *their roads grow green, and a blue scum settle on their canal*; and to hear themselves addressed in the language of Scripture, *Matthew XVIII and 23* "Woe be to you ye blind guides! who strain at a gnat and swallow a camel! These things ought ye to have done and not to have left the other undone." (p. 85)

It seemed to Hogg that the best way to reconcile the interests of the sheep farmers with those of the tenants and subtenants was by way of 'feus', secure tenancies.

In his 'Memoir' Hogg wrote that, in later years, he 'generally went on a tour into the Highlands every summer'.[5] Clearly, these expeditions were of a different nature from the ones he had undertaken at the beginning of the century. The early tours are concerned with sheep farming and report the kind of thing which Hogg imagined would be of interest to the Highland Society. Later visits were more in the nature of holidays that provided opportunities for walking and fishing, eating and drinking. They also constituted experiences that Hogg would later work up in his fiction and in his poetry.

In 1814, while staying with Mrs Eliza Izett at Kinnaird House (in Perthshire on the river Tay between Dunkeld and Pitlochry), he fell ill and began writing *Mador of the Moor* there. According to his 'Memoir', his hostess told him to write a poem and she even prescribed his subject. Hogg accordingly 'determined immediately to write a poem descriptive of the river Tay' and decided that it was going to be in Spenserian stanzas.[6] That account should be treated with some suspicion, since Hogg had, on 14 November 1813, written to Alexander Bald that he had composed 1100 lines of a poem in Spenserian stanzas 'descriptive of Highland scenery and manners'.[7] Moreover, as James Barcus has pointed out, Eliza Izett's commands are uncannily reminiscent of the similar injunction which Lady Austen had imposed on William Cowper more than thirty years earlier.[8] Nor is *Mador of the Moor* a descriptive landscape poem, even though the Tay scenery remains important.

On 1 June 1816 Hogg wrote to Anne Bald that he had just returned from an excursion to Argyll and Perthshire and that these counties were going to be the setting of his poem *Queen Hynde*.[9] That poem takes us to the mythical west Highland world described in the poems of Ossian. A note links that world to what can now be seen by an enterprising tourist: 'It is altogether a singular and romantic scene; and being situated on the new road from Dalmallie to Fort-William, by Connel Ferry and Appin, is well worthy the attention of the curious, and, indeed, of every tourist interested in the phenomena of nature.'[10]

Hogg used his Highland experiences in a number of other works. His magazine *The Spy* includes an account of the landscape and the people from Uig in western Lewis, in the issue of 10 September 1810, while a two-part essay published on 1 and 29 June 1811 is set in the Trossachs and satirises the vogue of Scott's poem *The Lady of the Lake*.[11] Hogg recycled these essays in his 1820 collection *Winter Evening Tales* (the account of Uig is much extended and has become part of the story 'Basil Lee') and added another set in the Highlands: 'An Old Soldier's Tale', the fictional recollections of someone who had fought on the side of the government during the 1745–6 Jacobite rising. In this story the narrator tells us that at one point he found himself at Tomintoul, which he called 'a large and ugly looking village'.[12] This is anachronistic: since Tomintoul was a planned village and dates from 1779, the narrator could not have seen it in the 1740s, but his comments no doubt reflect what Hogg himself saw in 1802.

In 1826 Hogg had completed a story called 'The Adventures of Peter Aston', which again draws on his experiences in the return journey, from Tomintoul to Braemar, in 1802. It was published with several other historical tales as *Tales of the Wars of Montrose* in 1835.[13] Recently, another Highland tale, 'The Captain's Expedition', set in the Glen Shee area in Perthsire, has come to light.[14]

Whereas Hogg, in the *Highland Journeys*, had been confident that the interests of sheep farmers and the survival of Highland communities could be reconciled through guaranteed leases, his later comments on the Highlands are less optimistic. In 1810 he wrote in *The Forest Minstrel*:

> We stood by our Stuart, till one fatal blow
> Loos'd Ruin triumphant, and valour laid low.
> Our chief, whom we trusted, and liv'd but to please,
> Then turn'd us adrift to the storm and the seas.[15]

Both William Donaldson and Murray Pittock have convincingly argued that in such passages Hogg alludes not only to the devastation of the Highlands after the Battle of Culloden in 1746 but also to the later Clearances, where tenants and subtenants had to make way for sheep and either emigrated or were forced to relocate in crofts on the seashore.[16]

Already in the course of his 1803 *Journey* Hogg had remarked, on visiting the hiding places of Charles Edward Stuart after the defeat of his army in the 1745 rebellion: 'While traversing the scenes, where the patient sufferings of the one part, and the cruelties of the other were so affectingly displayed, I could not help being a bit of a Jacobite in my heart' (p. 81). In later years Hogg's interest in the Jacobite risings of 1715 and 1745 is most clearly seen in the collection, *The Jacobite Relics*, published in two parts in 1819 and 1821. The tone is set in the introductory poem:

> They stood to the last, and when standing was o'er,
> All sullen and silent they dropped the claymore,
> And yielded, indignant, their necks to the blow,
> Their homes to the flame, and their lands to the foe.[17]

The most eloquent statement by Hogg of what Highlanders had gone through in 1746 (and what, by implication, they were still going through) comes in the final part of his 1823 novel *The Three Perils of Woman*, in which a shepherd finds a 'mother and child [. . .] stretched together in the arms of death, pale as the snow that surrounded them, and rigid as the grave-turf on which they had made their dying bed. Is there human sorrow on record like this that winded up the devastation of the Highlands?'[18]

CHAPTER SIX

Hogg and Working-class Writing

Sharon Alker and Holly Faith Nelson

The robust working-class tradition in Scottish literature of this century and the last has been the subject of recent scholarly discussion. 'Following Alexander Trocchi', Robert Crawford observes, 'Gray, Kelman, Welsh and others [. . .] radically liberated Scottish fiction from the narrowly middle-class residually Presbyterian assumptions that still governed Scottish society in the 1950s and 1960s when these writers were growing up.'[1] Ian Brown spotlights the 'demotic vitality' of the theatre in modern Scotland, which David Hutchison notes has been dominated by plays 'about the life of the working class' 'from the 1970s' onwards.[2] And the verse of Scots currently writing in the working-class tradition, such as Liz Lochhead and Tom Leonard, has routinely been recognised as playing a critical role in the production of a vibrant populist Scottish aesthetic. However, the contemporary working-class voice in Scottish literature has only lately been situated in a comprehensive historical narrative. Douglas S. Mack has described 'a radical and deeply rooted tradition in Scottish writing' that 'seeks to give voice to the concerns and insights of people normally marginalized by mainstream society [. . . a] tradition grounded in the old oral ballads, and [. . .] in the writings of Alan Ramsay, Robert Fergusson, Robert Burns and James Hogg', which is 'carried on in our own day in different ways by writers such as James Kelman and Irvine Welsh'.[3] Both Welsh and Kelman have underscored the important place of James Hogg in this restored understanding of a working-class literary tradition.

The classification of Hogg as a working-class author, however, is far from simple, for several reasons: the 'working class', understood as a distinct 'class which must sell its labour-power in order to survive', was an emergent rather than fully developed category in Hogg's lifetime. Hogg had a strong association with the Tory periodical *Blackwood's Edinburgh Magazine*; and Hogg distanced himself from the politically radical, or at least actively reformist, working-class consciousness of his age.[4] In a letter of 14 May 1835 to Sir Robert Peel, twice Conservative Prime Minister, Hogg writes, 'I am ashamed of our Scottish radicals! Power is new to them and they are actually reform

55

mad; as little to be depended on as the Irish papists.'[5] In general, Hogg's writings pay little attention to the reforms proposed by working-class activists.

Nevertheless, Hogg is acutely aware of the social and economic significance of his humble station in life as a poor shepherd and its potentially harmful effect on his literary aspirations. He therefore reconfigures the category of plebian author from an ephemeral, provisional state of being to a stable, permanent position in life. This he accomplishes by engaging in an arduous struggle to control his own authorial persona, in which he learns to negotiate the complex Scottish, and later British, literary marketplace, characterised by an uneasy blend of residual patron–client relations and emergent capitalistic professionalism. Hogg also strove to subvert standard representations of labouring poets and their texts by renovating existing literary modes and genres and by inventing unconventional narrators, characters, and plots to convey the psychological and moral complexity, intellectual potential, and varied socio-economic relations of the lower orders. In the process, Hogg defies conceptions of literary taste and the ideal reader promoted by the literati. Thus, although Hogg was not committed to political reform, which he may have viewed as disruptive of social progress, he was deeply invested in the radical transformation of culture, a less blatant but perhaps more enduring way to influence and promote social change. This chapter charts the course taken by Hogg to solidify his place in the literary marketplace and to challenge conventional ideas of the place of labourers in literature.

Hogg's ability to rise 'to a higher nich[e] in the temple of Scottish literature than ever [. . . he] expected' is partly attributable to the historical moment in which he lived.[6] As Douglas Mack argues in this volume, as a shepherd-poet from the Scottish countryside, Hogg had a preordained place in the 'Scottish Enlightenment-Romantic century' as a primitive poet or natural rural genius.[7] However, such stereotypes restricted Hogg as a writer, since the form and content of his works were expected to coincide with particular notions of literary production associated with the labouring body. While Scottish ballads or rural songs would be deemed suitable genres for the rural labourer, for example, novels and epics were not.

Hogg was further constrained by those who governed the Edinburgh literary marketplace, men who sought to develop and reinforce middle-class values and taste. The literati positioned Hogg in a late-eighteenth-century category of 'peasant poet' that celebrated but also confined the work of working-class writers. At the same time, as critics extolled the author's connection to nature and antiquity, they emphasised the fragility of these properties in the urban world of print culture.[8] The vulnerability of working-class writers was stressed in 'narrative[s] of decline' in which poets from Stephen Duck to Robert Burns were considered as exceptional for their class and capable of exerting only a fleeting and modest influence on the field of letters.[9]

A cursory glance at Hogg's early career might suggest that he was destined to follow the path of many of his labouring-class predecessors. His early poetry collection, *The Mountain Bard*, did imitate, to a degree, the rural writing of earlier peasant poets and ancient balladry.[10] Yet even as he retains the persona of peasant poet and remains committed to his 'school' of 'traditional ballads', Hogg manages to complicate his creative output in radical ways during his literary career, resisting paradigms which sought to confine the lower orders to a bounded and sanitised cultural space.[11] One of Hogg's chief, if often underrated, contributions to the reconstruction of the category of plebian author is simply his ongoing literary output and lengthy publication record. Hogg unabashedly marketed his humble origins while maintaining his literary production in a wide variety of genres over more than thirty years, thereby successfully resisting the 'narrative of decline' and the rhetoric of pathos associated with the lives and texts of working-class poets. To sustain literary productivity while carrying out rural duties was no easy feat. Hogg had to assess on the go the changing conditions of the literary marketplace and to learn how to negotiate its nuances, courting and securing patrons, publishers and readers. He had to seek out new markets for his work, whether in Britain or North America. But by the end of his life he had created a new model of the working-class author as self-made man, capable of making his own way in the marketplace without renouncing his station in life.

Hogg also set the groundwork for later working-class writers by forging a new aesthetic that thematised plebian authorship and valued working-class voices. At times he openly mocks the gap between dominant cultural expectations of working-class authors and their actual achievements. In his periodical *The Spy*, produced shortly after he moved to Edinburgh to establish a literary career, Hogg introduces the figure of John Miller, the son of a poor rural schoolteacher, who wears a plaid, carries a staff 'like a Nithsdale Shepherd', and longs to become an author. His first meeting with 'Mr Spy' discloses the well-nigh impenetrable nature of the publishing industry to those without contacts or credentials. Although the Spy notes that Miller 'uses the broadest dialect of the district in common conversation', the works attributed to him, published in this and later issues, display his mastery of the literary arts and the English language. In the twenty-fourth and twenty-fifth issues, Miller tells a sentimental story in polite English about an impoverished woman caring for her child; the plot is tasteful and the characters virtuous. Miller's oral dialect is clearly only one of multiple registers in which he is fluent.

In reimagining the role of author as accessible to and viable for the impoverished and marginalised, Hogg continues a transformation of the idea of authorship that had begun in the mid-eighteenth century. In a study of

Tobias Smollett's *Roderick Random*, John Barrell argues that Smollett develops a new concept of the gentleman which becomes intertwined with the function of the author. Barrell contends that before Smollett, writers insisted that the intricacies of social relations could only be perceived by the impartial gentleman, whose status as an objective observer depends on 'his having no occupation'.[12] Distance from the degradation of the workplace encouraged linguistic purity. However, *Roderick Random* features an impoverished genteel protagonist whose ability to adapt to changing circumstances and experience in a range of occupations enable him to take on the role of author of his own life, for he can now 'grasp the relations of a multitude of social activities and practices'.[13]

Hogg foregrounds the benefits of labour and the ability to adapt that lie at the core of Smollett's conception of the gentleman and author, although Smollett's focus is primarily on professional rather than manual labour (despite Roderick's excursions into the world of domestic servitude). At times, like Roderick, Hogg's fictional authors have genteel connections or come from middling stock, as does the Spy. However, Hogg often challenges Smollett's connection between successful authorship and specific social origins. At the end of *The Queen's Wake*, for example, a poetic competition ultimately has two winners, one nobly born and the other a lowly Ettrick minstrel in an 'old gray plaid'.[14] Elsewhere, Hogg criticises middle- and upper-class authors for their misrepresentations of working-class life: praising John Wilson's *Trials of Margaret Lindsay* in a letter to William Blackwood (13 April 1823), Hogg, nevertheless, complains of 'misnomers regarding the character of Scottish Peasantry'.[15] Such defects undermine the author's claims on a representation of national life.

Clearly, however, Hogg does not advocate a specialist author who can only contribute sentimental rural poems informed by an accurate knowledge of farm labour. Luke Maynard notes that working-class writers who operate in a variety of social groups can access and deploy in their work an especially rich array of dialects, speech patterns and social customs.[16] Hogg often presents the working-class author as one who commands this comprehensive knowledge of the nation and even of broader universal truths. Labour is not merely something one does on the way to fuller knowledge, as the case of Smollett suggests. Rather, for Hogg, the labouring body is an essential component in the production of literary value, one which recognises the intricate rules and regulations of society at every level and adapts to them as the need arises.

Not content simply to promote the authority of working-class authors, Hogg also renovates the literary representation of working-class characters. He was capable of creating sympathetic impoverished or outcast figures in poetry and song, not unlike those in the works of Blake, Burns and Wordsworth. The suffering of the poor is highlighted both in his own early poetry and in works by others included in his collections. However, Hogg, unlike many of his contemporaries, offers more than tender well-worn images of those who must labour or beg to survive. Barrell observes: 'If we can be sure of anything about the eighteenth century, it is that English society at the time was minutely stratified and subdivided'; yet artistic representations of the rural poor consistently set them within 'a stable, unified, almost egalitarian society'.[17] Hogg, in contrast, sets out to capture the minute stratifications of working-class social relations, the local diversity of language, manners and attitudes, and the full range of 'the practical aspects of rural life'.[18]

Hogg's was not a wholly new endeavour. It had been anticipated, for example, by several middle-class novelists, such as Samuel Richardson (*Pamela*), William Godwin (*Caleb Williams*), and, in Scotland, Elizabeth Hamilton (*The Cottagers of Glenburnie*). In a more extensive and sustained manner than these precursors, Hogg invests many of his lower-class characters with the pliability and complexity of his authorial persona. In his works we discover well-rounded, intelligent labourers who struggle with moral issues and, at times, move across class boundaries. 'The Poachers', published in *Ackermann's Juvenile Forget Me Not*, features the son of a 'poor man of all work' who is treated abominably by his employer, a baronet, and resorts to poaching to support his family after his father's death.[19] The story represents the boy, Benjamin Little, as admirable not only for his ability to survive but also for his virtue and desire to better himself through education. In the end he becomes a 'respectable Presbyterian clergyman' while remaining the 'deadliest shot on the moors'.[20] Hogg plays up Benjamin's retention of the skills he has inherited from his father – and even his ill-gotten gains – in his new social station.

Hogg also disturbs class boundaries by deploying the trope of the nobleman or prince concealed (unwittingly or not) as a peasant. The trope was traditionally invoked to support a conservative vision of the nobility as inherently superior to the peasantry. However, Hogg uses it with such frequency, always emphasising the skill of the ordinary man, as to interrogate rather than reinforce the social hierarchy. In 'Duncan Campbell', first published in two issues of *The Spy* and reprinted in *Winter Evening Tales*, a young vagabond boy and his dog are taken in by the family of the narrator, who fondly recalls their childhood together: when 'Duncan herded my family's cows all the summer – so did I – we could not live asunder'.[21] Their shared physical labour turns to shared intellectual endeavour: 'Duncan and I were sent to the parish school, and began at the same instant to the study of that most important and fundamental branch of literature, the A, B, C.'[22] Duncan ultimately discovers that he is the heir to the Laird of Glenegle and claims his inheritance. Yet the story dwells on the virtues not of the upper ranks (Duncan's birth family is rather dysfunctional) but of the working classes, their sympathy towards the homeless boy, and the benefits Duncan acquires from hard labour on the farm and solid schooling in the local parish. The labouring body can be intellectual whether it is that of a laird or farmer.

This strategic reimagining of the peasant/prince trope recurs in A *Queer Book*, published late in Hogg's career. In 'Jock Johnstone the Tinkler', Lord Douglas is goaded into fighting the eponymous tinker and is mortified to lose, until he discovers that his opponent is really the Lord of Annandale. This discovery comes at the very end of the tale, after the tinker rebuffs Lord Douglas's offer of patronage:

> 'Wo worth thy wit, good Lord Douglas,
>   To think I'd change my trade for thine;
> Far better and wiser would you be,
>   To live as journeyman of mine.'

> 'To mend a kettle or a casque,
>   Or clout a goodwife's yettlin pan;
> Upon my life good Lord Douglas,
>   You'd make a noble tinkler man.'[23]

Hogg revels less in the tinker's final unmasking than in his prior acts of self-assertion, and in the lord's lamentation for his defeat at the hands of an apparent peasant.

A *Queer Book* also features poetry centred on intrepid and intelligent working-class men. In 'Robyn Reidde', the young peasant-protagonist is dismissed by the Scots as a fool. When serving Lord Douglas in a contest against the English Lord Scrope, Robyn's physical strength and talent with a bow impress Scrope so much that he claims him as his own. Robyn follows Scrope and, after a series of adventures, wins a fencing tournament against a French champion. The intellectual capacity of working-class men is evident in 'Will and Sandy', in which two shepherds debate recent political events while tending their sheep, and appeal to history to support their respective positions. This is not to say that Hogg's working-class characters are unfailingly courageous, clever, or even virtuous. His concern, rather, is with their complexity. 'The Goode Manne of Allowa' (also in A *Queer Book*) features a poor old man who lacks the means to realise his desire to be charitable. When magically transported to a shipwreck in which he finds the drowned corpse of a bejewelled maiden, the 'goode man' has no qualms about mutilating the body to get the treasure, which he then keeps for himself. In fashioning his working-class characters as diverse, ambiguous and complicated beings capable of an assortment of thoughts and acts, Hogg does for them what eighteenth-century writers had done for the 'middling sort'.

Hogg does not always trouble categories of social class as overtly as these examples suggest, particularly when the literary conventions he adopts prove restrictive. The developing genres of prose fiction were especially well equipped for representing the complexity of individual consciousness and a wide range of social voices and settings. By around 1800, several novels had represented characters from the lower ranks to appreciative readers. Hogg continues this practice, following the fate of a servant, Sally Niven, in *The Three Perils of Woman* and the rise of a yeoman farmer, Charlie Scott, in *The Three Perils of Man*, and tracing the various patterns of working-class lives in contributions to annuals and gift books. Hogg's disruption of social norms is also evident in *The Brownie of Bodsbeck*, his novel on the persecution of seventeenth-century Scottish Covenanters. Walter Laidlaw, the protagonist, is a prosperous tenant farmer, one of the middling sort, but he lives humbly and simply, evident in the opening scene in which he sits in front of his 'little parlour fire' watching his wife 'airing a pair of clean hosen'.[24] Though 'a substantial, and even a wealthy man', Walter is no stranger to manual labour, on which his income depends.[25] He 'drive[s] a neighbour's flock from his pasture' and supervises his shepherds, and his family are involved in a variety of physical work on the farm.[26] Here Hogg blurs the usual distinction made between the labouring body and middle-class existence. In a rural context, farmers, shepherds and servants all perform much the same sort of work, both domestic and agricultural. Worth is determined not by rank but by ethical action.

In *The Brownie of Bodsbeck*, Hogg also tackles social distinctions in a less obvious way. As Mack argues in Chapter 7, Hogg's treatment of the Covenanters should be read as a form of class commentary. The novel shows royalist aristocrat forces harassing and brutalising the common borderers, as in the scene in which Viscount Graham of Dundee, known as Claverhouse or 'Clavers', orders one of Walter's shepherds to burn an old shepherd 'on the cheek, cut off his ears', and stay with him until 'he pay[s] [. . .] down a fine of two hundred merks' for admitting he attended a conventicle.[27] This is but one of many similar acts of cruelty, in which the viscount seems less concerned with correcting religious dissent than with oppressing the lower and middling sort, who have little or no redress from the depredations of his 'savage troopers'.[28]

In contrast, the Covenanters are responsive to the daily needs of ordinary people.[29] They constitute an alternative community, hiding out in the borderlands, defiantly courageous in the face of tyranny, loyal both to its members and to the local folk who befriend them. The Covenanters rescue Walter's daughter from being raped by a clergyman, although doing so risks alerting the authorities to their presence, and none of those who are captured turn informant on Walter, even to barter for their lives. Hogg's Covenanters outwit enemies who command far greater resources, they value music and learning, and they work adeptly with their hands. When Walter is arrested on suspicion of sympathising with them, the Covenanters labour in secret on his farm to ensure that the harvest will be saved and his flocks cared for: '[U]pwards of an hundred ewes had been smeared during the night, by the officious and unwearied Brownie of Bodsbeck'.[30] This strange disembodied labour (carried out at night) is viewed by the Borderers as magical and fearful. Happening outside the proper order of things, it threatens orthodox society. Indeed, the Covenanters devise and operate their own society in a way that defies traditional boundaries, as is evidenced by the social make-up of this sympathetic and forlorn group of outcasts, 'auld gray-bearded ministers, lairds, weavers, and poor hinds, a' sharing the same hard fate'.[31] Hogg sanctions a community held together not by the vagaries of birth or social or economic standing but by shared belief, need and individual skill. Representing a cohesive yet fluid and mobile group with their own distinct cultural practices who live outside the official social order allows Hogg to question and destabilise the notions of rank and hierarchy in which that order is rooted.

The strategies with which Hogg constitutes his authorial persona and writes working-class characters and experience into his texts also shape the third element of the 'rhetorical triangle': the reader. Hogg resists the category of reader that the Edinburgh literati were developing by producing imaginative literature that was accessible and appealing to readers who, like the author, must earn their keep. Hogg's works thereby reveal the ideological and artificial construction of the canons of 'taste' promoted by the literati who excluded from the literary field whole classes of readers skilled in critical inquiry and debate.

It is not surprising that Hogg should conceive of his readership as varied and diverse, and believe in his work's appeal to a broad mix of readers across class lines. In the introduction to his song collection *The Forest Minstrel* he declares that songs are favoured by all ranks 'but especially the genteel in town and the plebians in the country', and adds that 'among the peasantry in particular, there is an insatiable desire for new productions of this kind', together with qualities of 'taste and discernment that are, in their circumstances, and with their opportunities, perfectly unaccountable'.[32] In his later works Hogg reminds readers that current notions of 'taste and discernment' are policed by a literary party that seeks to elevate itself to genteel status. Instead, Hogg wishes to constitute a reading audience with what we might call a secular Presbyterian hermeneutic: one that encourages individual readers from every rank to rely on their own discriminating conscience in engaging with his writings and determining their worth.

In brief, while Hogg's role in the development of a working-class aesthetic is not radical in a political sense, it can certainly claim the label of literary radicalism. At the moment in which *Blackwood's* and its circle were formulating a very particular sort of middle-class Scottish Romanticism, Hogg was, through his diverse literary output, noisily and doggedly insistent that the concept be expanded to accommodate the labouring intellectual and the professional and working-class reader far more comprehensively than had previously been the case. His works suggest that the rich complexity of a national public cannot be located in artificial concepts of taste, which fail to reflect the lived experience of most of its members. Instead, that public is more fully engaged through a broad range of styles and genres which may speak to social and cultural communities hitherto marginalised in or excluded from the field of British letters. It is this legacy of a productive resistance to class stereotypes and a literary reframing of the working-class author, character and reader that makes Hogg's contributions to Scottish Romanticism so fruitful for later working-class writers, Scottish and British alike.

CHAPTER SEVEN

Hogg's Politics and the Presbyterian Tradition

Douglas S. Mack

During Hogg's lifetime there were three major political groupings in Scotland: Tories, who were supporters of the status quo; Whigs, who advocated measured and moderate reform; and Radicals, who sought fundamental changes that would create a society based on the French Revolution's principles of liberty, equality and fraternity. As he often said, Hogg was a Tory. Nevertheless, some of his closest friends (for example, James Gray) were people of Whig or even Radical sympathies,[1] and his own attitudes were consistently and assertively egalitarian. This chapter explores the paradoxes and complexities of Hogg's political position, and in doing so traces connections between his political views and his roots (which he shared with the politically radical Robert Burns) in the working-class Presbyterian religious tradition of Lowland Scotland.

Hogg's Tory sympathies seem to have derived in part from his reservations about aspects of the Whig master-narrative that had shaped the view of history widely accepted among the intellectual elite of the Scotland of his era. This master-narrative was deeply influenced by Adam Smith's famous theory that there are four stages in the development of human society: nomadic hunting, shepherding, agriculture and commerce. Adam Smith had first set out his theory in a series of lectures on jurisprudence at Glasgow University, as part of an examination of the development of the rights of property. His four stages are thus best understood as a conceptual scheme rather than as an empirical description of actual historical developments. Nevertheless, the four-stage scheme encouraged the writers of the Scottish Enlightenment and their heirs to understand history in terms of the progress of society from one stage of development to another, more advanced stage. Additionally, Adam Smith's scheme tended to encourage assumptions that the law-abiding and commerce-based modern Lowland Scotland of the Enlightenment era was well on its way to becoming a fully evolved society – one in which civilised values and high culture could be expected to thrive.

Enlightenment-influenced assumptions of this kind underlie the series of major novels in which Hogg's friend Walter Scott explores the histori-cal processes and events through which the Scotland of the Enlightenment era had arrived at its happy state of advanced modernity. For example, the Jacobite rising of 1745 sought to restore the exiled Stuart dynasty to absolute power, and Scott's *Waverley* (1814) presents this project as a doomed attempt to put back the clock by returning to an earlier stage of social development. Scott's emotional commitment to aristocracy and the Tory cause meant that, for him, the traditional loyalties and the heroic violence of the world of the royal Stuarts had a strong romantic appeal. Nevertheless, at an intel-lectual level he accepted the Enlightenment-influenced Whig assumption that the future lay with the law-abiding commercial society established under the limited constitutional monarchy of Britain's eighteenth-century Hanoverian kings. In Scott's novel, Edward Waverley is initially carried away by the romantic appeal of Prince Charles's insurrection, but by the end of the novel reason has reasserted itself, and Edward begins a new life of prosperous and uneventful domestic tranquillity in the British modernity evolving in the second half of the eighteenth century.

However, Adam Smith's four-stage theory of social development pre-sented certain difficulties for someone like Hogg, who had grown up within the traditional oral culture of the peasantry of Ettrick Forest. Smith's theory pigeonholed such a person as the product of a society at a comparatively primitive and backward stage of social development: a society so backward, indeed, that in the late eighteenth century it was still under the spell of absurd ancient superstitions about witchcraft, and still in awe of supernatu-ral creatures such as ghosts and brownies. Under the influence of Smith's theory, the Edinburgh intellectual elite of Hogg's era had a tendency to make a simple binary distinction between the world of the Enlightenment (seen as straightforwardly true and valid), and pre-Enlightenment culture (seen as backward and deluded). In this context, there was a tendency for Hogg himself to be viewed as someone not to be taken entirely seriously: an inter-esting and exotic specimen, no doubt, but decidedly a backwoodsman, the product of a primitive stage of social evolution.

In setting out to challenge this set of assumptions, Hogg did not adopt a strategy of establishing a simple binary distinction of his own, in which pre-Enlightenment culture would be presented entirely positively, and the Enlightenment would be presented entirely negatively. Nevertheless, he did try to assert that the traditional society in which he grew up could have its own kind of worth and validity. For example, in his poem 'Superstition', first published in 1815 in *Pilgrims of the Sun*, he writes with regret that the 'cold Saturnine morn' of the Enlightenment has banished traditional beliefs which (Hogg claims) had encouraged a kind of Wordsworthian awareness of the transcendental glory of the divine:

Those were the times for holiness of frame;
   Those were the days when fancy wandered free;
That kindled in the soul the mystic flame,
   And the rapt breathings of high poesy.
   Sole empress of the twilight – Woe is me!
That thou and all thy spectres are outworn;
   For true devotion wanes away with thee.
All thy delirious dreams are laughed to scorn,
While o'er our hills has dawned a cold saturnine morn.[2]

As an adult, Hogg was fully aware that he was living in a post-Enlightenment world, and he recognised that 'Superstition' was no longer empress of his native Ettrick. Nevertheless, he had a Tory dislike of the tendency of self-confident modernisers to despise and dismiss out of hand the traditional customs, values and beliefs of the old oral peasant culture in which he had grown up. His attitude about such matters emerges in a playful late short story entitled 'On the Separate Existence of the Soul', in which Robin Robson, a very old-fashioned shepherd who (with the help of an angel, no less) decidedly gets the better of his master, the laird of Gillian Brae. The laird is a smart-alec young man driven by the assumptions of post-Enlightenment modernity. Robin, on the other hand,

> steadily upheld the propriety of keeping by old-established customs, and of improving these leisurely and prudently; but deprecated all rash theories of throwing the experience of ages aside as useless and unprofitable lumber, as if the world were void of common sense and discernment, till it brought forth the present generation, the most enlightened of whom, in his own estimation, was the young laird of Gillian Brae.[3]

Hogg was by no means entirely out of sympathy with the Enlightenment. In *The Private Memoirs and Confessions of a Justified Sinner*, the 'Editor' (very much a man of the Enlightenment) describes how young George Colwan, climbing a hill early in the morning, sees 'a bright halo in the cloud of haze'. The Editor eloquently provides a rational and scientific explanation of 'the lovely vision':

> [George] soon perceived the cause of the phenomenon, and that it proceeded from the rays of the sun from a pure unclouded morning sky striking upon this dense vapour which refracted them. But the better the works of nature are understood, the more they will be ever admired. This was a scene that would have entranced the man of science with delight, but which the uninitiated and sordid man would have regarded less than the mole rearing up his hill in silence and in darkness.[4]

Even as the Editor conveys the excitement and value of the scientific methods and insights of the Enlightenment, there is a jarring note in his dismissal of 'the uninitiated and sordid man'. Hogg's enlightened and urbane Editor has his blind spots: he is all too ready to assume that men of science – enlightened and highly educated men like himself and the laird of Gillian Brae – have a monopoly of wisdom. As many critics have remarked, Hogg's novel has undermined many of the Editor's confident certainties by its final pages. It achieves this in part through the interpolation of a folk tale about the Devil, an oral narrative current among 'the auld wives of the clachan', which is retold to Robert Wringhim by his servant, the 'peasant' Samuel Scrape.[5] Although he can empathise with the Editor's delight in a scientific understanding of the ways in which the rays of the sun can be refracted by a 'cloud of haze', Hogg nevertheless rejects the Enlightenment's tendency to discard the experience of ages as useless and unprofitable lumber: he is consistently willing to see potential value in old wives' tales and the local knowledge of countryfolk. *Confessions of a Justified Sinner* ensures that the voices and insights of non-elite people are heard and valued, for example when the powerful oral testimony of the prostitute Bell Calvert plays a crucial role in undermining the certainties of the Editor's world view. This egalitarian aspect of Hogg's political thinking meant that he and his friend Walter Scott were very different kinds of Tory, and the nuances of Hogg's views will become clearer if we examine the nature of his political disagreements with Scott.

Shortly after Scott's death in 1832, Hogg produced some manuscript anecdotes about his friend, in the second paragraph of which he writes:

> The only blemish or perhaps I should say foible that I ever discerned in my illustrious friend's character was a too high devotion for titled rank. This in him was mixed with an enthusiasm which I cannot describe amounting in some cases almost to adoration if not servility. This was to me the strangest disposition imaginable! For me who never could learn to discern any distinction in ranks save what was constituted by talents or moral worth. I might indeed except the ministers of the gospel for whom I had always a superior veneration? But this was the class that Sir Walter cared least about of any.[6]

We get a glimpse of Scott's assumptions about 'titled rank' in the discussion of the origins of the French Revolution early in his *Life of Napoleon Buonaparte* (1827):

> In La Vendée alone, the nobles had united their interest and their fortune with those of the peasants who cultivated their estates, and there alone were they found in their proper and honourable character of proprietors residing on their own domains, and discharging the duties which are inalienably attached to the

owner of landed property. And – mark-worthy circumstance! – in La Vendée alone was any stand made in behalf of the ancient proprietors, constitution, or religion of France; for there alone the nobles and the cultivators of the soil held towards each other their natural and proper relations of patron and client, faithful dependents, and generous and affectionate superiors.[7]

For Scott, as for the Editor of *Confessions of a Justified Sinner*, it seems natural and appropriate for political power to lie in the hands of an enlightened gentry and aristocracy. Hogg, on the other hand, 'never could learn to discern any distinction in ranks save what was constituted by talents or moral worth' – a view very much in line with the egalitarian assumptions of the demotic Presbyterian tradition of Lowland Scotland. This tradition asserted, in Liam McIlvanney's summary, that 'authority ascends from below; that government is a contract, and political power a trust; and that even the humblest members of society are competent to censure their governors'.[8]

In the seventeenth century, the Covenanters, a militant Presbyterian movement originating in the south-west of Scotland, had risen in armed rebellion in defence of the rights of the people against what they regarded as arbitrary abuse of royal power by the Stuart monarchs. The memory of the Covenanters was revered during the era of Scott and Hogg by the people of Lowland Scotland, not least by political radicals, and debate about the Covenanters provided the context for a memorable dispute between Scott and Hogg about two recent works of fiction: Scott's anonymously published *Old Mortality* (December 1816) and *The Brownie of Bodsbeck and Other Tales* (March 1818). *Old Mortality* represents extreme Covenanters as dangerous and deranged fanatics, prototypes of the revolutionaries who had driven the excesses of the Terror in France during the 1790s. In short, Scott used *Old Mortality* to advance the Tory cause by depicting the era of the Covenanters in a way that would serve as a warning against the subversive radicals who were working for revolutionary change in Britain in the 1810s. In his anecdotes about Scott, Hogg records a dispute between them that took place on the day following the publication of *The Brownie of Bodsbeck*:

> His shaggy eyebrows were hanging very sore down, a bad prelude, which I knew too well.
> "I have read through your new work Mr Hogg" said he "and must tell you downright and plainly as I always do that I like it very ill very ill indeed."
> "What for Mr Scott?"
> "Because it is a false and unfair picture of the times and the existing characters altogether An exhaggerated and unfair picture!"
> "I dinna ken Mr Scott. It is the picture I hae been bred up in the belief o' sin' ever I was born and I had it frae them whom I was most bound to honour and believe. An' mair nor that there is not one single incident in the tale not one

which I cannot prove from history to be literally and positively true. I was obliged sometimes to change the situations to make one part coalesce with another but in no one instance have I related a story of a cruelty or a murder which is not literally true. An' that's a great deal mair than you can say for your tale o' Auld Mortality."

"You are overshooting the mark now Mr Hogg. I wish it were my tale. But it is *not* with regard to that, that I find fault with your tale at all but merely because it is an unfair and partial picture of the age in which it is laid. [. . .] I only tell you that with the exception of Old Nanny the crop-eared Covenanter who is by far the best character you ever drew in your life I dislike the tale exceedingly and assure you it is a distorted a prejudiced and untrue picture of the Royal party."

"It is a devilish deal truer than your's though; and on that ground I make my appeal to my country."[9]

Clearly, the vehemence of Scott's response to Hogg's *Brownie* derived from their very different views about 'the Royal party' in the era of the Covenanters. *Old Mortality* represents the royalist officer John Graham of Claverhouse as cultivated and gentlemanly: a complex man whose capacity for ruthlessness is balanced by an admirable loyalty to his cause. *The Brownie of Bodsbeck*, on the other hand, depicts Claverhouse as a ferocious persecutor of the Covenanters, in effect a war criminal. Hogg draws on the oral tradition of his native region as he tells how various bands of Covenanters took refuge among the hills of Ettrick Forest after their defeat at the Battle of Bothwell Bridge in 1679, only to be pursued by Claverhouse and his troops. *The Brownie of Bodsbeck* focuses on the ways in which some of the people of Ettrick Forest risk their own lives by giving help and support to the fugitive Covenanters.

Hogg's short novel was published as part of a collection entitled *The Brownie of Bodsbeck and Other Tales*. Each of the three tales in the collection paints a portrait of the society of Hogg's native district at a different stage of its historical development: 'The Hunt of Eildon' is set in the Middle Ages, when Ettrick was a royal hunting forest; *The Brownie of Bodsbeck* deals with the era of the seventeenth-century Covenanters; and 'The Wool-gatherer', a modern love story, explores class divisions in the Ettrick of Hogg's own period. The origins of the collection can be traced back to the early 1810s, and we get our first glimpse of it in a letter Hogg wrote to Scott on 3 April 1813:

I would fain publish 2 vol^s 8vo. close print of *Scottish Rural tales* anonymous in prose I have one will make about 200 pages alone some of the others you have seen in the Spy &c. Some people say they are original and interesting. I mention all these for your advice when I come.[10]

The long story referred to here was probably 'The Bridal of Polmood', which was not published until it appeared in Hogg's *Winter Evening Tales* in 1820.[11] At all events, Scott's 'advice' about the new project seems to have been favourable. In a letter to Bernard Barton of 5 July 1813, Hogg reports:

> Mr Wal[r.] Scott says in a letter 'If I may judge from my own feelings and the interest I took in them the tales are superior at least in the management to any I have read: the stile of them is likewise quite new.'[12]

No doubt encouraged by Scott's reaction, Hogg offered his projected collection to the publisher Archibald Constable in a letter of 20 May 1813:

> I have for many years been collecting the rural and traditionary tales of Scotland and I have of late been writing them over again and new-modelling them, and have the vanity to suppose they will form a most interesting work. They will fill two large vols 8vo price £1 or 4 vols 12mo price the same.[13]

This offer was declined and, as a result, Hogg's rural and traditionary tales seem to have gone on the back burner for a time. About a year and a half later – in December 1814 – Hogg had business dealings for the first time with the rising Edinburgh publisher William Blackwood, and in due course this gave him the opportunity to offer his tales to Blackwood. Blackwood accepted another long tale, 'The Brownie of Bodsbeck' but refused 'The Bridal of Polmood'. Hogg replaced the latter with 'The Wool-gatherer', revised from *The Spy* (where it had appeared as 'The Country Laird', February 1811), and a new tale, 'The Hunt of Eildon', to make up a two-volume set.[14] If the set sold well, another two volumes would follow. In January 1818 Hogg sent Blackwood the text of an advertisement:

> In the press and speedily will be published Vols 1 and 2 of Mr Hogg's *Cottage Tales* containing *The Brownie of Bodsbeck* and *The Wool-Gatherer*. These tales have been selected by him among the Shepherds and peasantry of Scotland and are arranged so as to delineate the manners and superstitions of that class in ancient and modern times &c &c.[15]

In May 1818 Blackwood duly published *The Brownie of Bodsbeck and Other Tales* as a two-volume set, and *Winter Evening Tales* (published in two well-filled volumes by Oliver & Boyd in 1820) finally carried Hogg's sequence of 'rural and traditionary tales' to its projected length of four volumes.

The Brownie of Bodsbeck has often been read as a pro-Covenanter response to Scott's *Old Mortality*, but Hogg's short novel is not really about the Covenanters. Rather, it is about the response of the people of Ettrick Forest to Claverhouse's persecution of the fugitive Covenanters in the period remembered in Ettrick tradition as 'the killing time'. Walter Laidlaw, farmer of Chapelhope, is the central character of the tale. Walter is no Covenanter: indeed, his instincts prompt him to support the authority of king and land-lords. Nevertheless, out of common humanity, he secretly gives succour and protection to a group of Covenanters who have taken refuge among the wild hills of his remote sheep farm, in spite of the fact that in doing so he is putting his own life and property at serious risk as an abettor of rebels.

At the end of the novel, when the killing time is over, Walter discov-ers that his daughter Kate has been secretly assisting another group of Covenanters. Kate is apologetic:

> "O my dear father," said she, "you know not what I have suffered for fear of having offended you; for I could not forget that their principles, both civil and religious, were the opposite of yours – that they were on the adverse side to you and my mother, as well as the government of the country."
>
> "Deil care what side they war on, Kate!" cried Walter, in the same vehement voice; "ye hae taen the side o' human nature; the suffering and the humble side, an' the side o' feeling, my woman, that bodes best in a young unexperienced thing to tak."[16]

Like Walter and Kate, Hogg instinctively sympathised with 'the suffering and the humble side'.

It will be remembered that, in his anecdotes about Scott, Hogg contrasted Scott's 'too high devotion for titled rank' with his own inability 'to discern any distinction in ranks save what was constituted by talents or moral worth'. Hogg was not a party-political animal, nor was he a class warrior. Instead, and in line with the egalitarian assumptions of the Presbyterian tradition, he was willing to recognise, like, and admire 'talents and moral worth' in any kind of person: Whig or Tory, duke or shepherd. His political position seems to have been similar to that of Dickens, as described by George Orwell:

> Dickens is not *in the accepted sense* a revolutionary writer. But it is not at all certain that a merely moral criticism of society may not be just as 'revolutionary' – and revolution, after all, means turning things upside down – as the politico-economic criticism which is fashionable at this moment. Blake was not a politi-cian, but there is more understanding of the nature of capitalist society in a poem like 'I wander through each charter'd street' than in three-quarters of Socialist literature. [. . .] Two viewpoints are always tenable. The one, how can you improve human nature until you have changed the system? The other, what is the use of changing the system before you have improved human nature? They appeal to different individuals, and they probably show a tendency to alternate in point of time. [. . .] 'If men would behave decently the world would be decent' is not such a platitude as it sounds.[17]

Hogg was a Tory who believed that it is foolish to throw 'the experience of ages aside as useless and unprofitable lumber'. Nevertheless, he
shared Dickens's 'revolutionary' tendencies. Like Dickens, Hogg sympathised
instinctively with 'the suffering and the humble side'; and, like Dickens, he
believed that 'if men would behave decently the world would be decent'. As
George Orwell remarks, this is not such a platitude as it sounds.

CHAPTER EIGHT

Hogg and Nationality

Caroline McCracken-Flesher

In 1832, James Hogg visited London, where *The Morning Chronicle* termed him 'the great object of attraction at all literary dinners, *conversaziones*, and *soirees*'.[1] Hogg communicates his delight through a rollicking list of invitations:

> the public parties are the most agreeable. I have dined in many of these The literary fund society gave me a dinner The Canada Company A private Club of M.P.'s &c The society of true Highlanders and I dine with The Highland society of London to morrow.[2]

What did all this celebration mean? Two London Scots give the author in this moment a context both national and problematic. Allan Cunningham declared: 'James Hogg [. . .] is acknowledged on all hands to be the living and visible head of this national school of song; his genius seems the natural offspring of the pastoral hills and dales of the Border.'[3] Thomas Carlyle was dubious: 'Is the charm of this poor man chiefly [. . .] that he *is* a real product of nature, and able to speak naturally [. . .]? An "unconscious talent", though of the smallest, emphatically *naïve*.' Carlyle found Hogg 'a very curious *specimen*', but presumed most Londoners would see him as 'a mere wooden *Punch or Judy*'.[4] Even to Hogg's friends and compatriots, and at the moment of his British success, a battle was being waged over whether the poet was a natural genius or a laughable naïf. If the first, was his work a *lusus naturae*, so unlikely as almost to merit scientific investigation: or did it have national status and pedagogical force?

Although Hogg was on display in London, the nation was of course Scotland, and Londoners understood that his gift was Scottish. In 1831, the *Athenaeum* (positively) found the poetry directed to 'every Scotchman who desires to have his own green hills [. . .] brought back to his fancy'.[5] Then in 1835 it (negatively) remarked 'a national tone and feeling [. . .] with which we southerns do not wholly sympathize'.[6] Hogg's writings, however much they were applauded in the metropolis, marked a literary and psychological border with the south. How far, then, did they characterise the north? Cunningham and Carlyle suggest that this might be problematic: to parse Walter Scott's designation of the Ettrick Shepherd as 'the great Caledonian Boar', was Hogg indeed 'Caledonian', or just a 'boar', with all that term's implications of crudity, excess and tedious disruptiveness?[7] This chapter argues that Hogg enacts the nation as both Caledonian *and* a boar. He manifests a literary and national space which is distinct but by no means unified. In so doing he implies a different understanding of what constitutes Scotland.

Moreover, his work challenged contemporary ideas of the nation in ways that can contribute to theories of the nation today. Traditions derived from Scotland's own Enlightenment, and those in formation during the Romantic period, imagined the nation as a product of sequence and a manifestation of coherence. The Scottish Enlightenment privileged a universal stadial progression which advanced logically from inferred origins; Romanticism emphasised the uniqueness of places and people as indicators of significant identity; both found a compelling example in Scotland. By contrast, Hogg's texts, with their hiccupping structures and disparate and overlaid voices, and Hogg himself, with his unsteady authorial persona, pointed to the nation as a practice not just of difference but of discomfort. That discomfort troubled the coherence of Scotland, and jostled the bounds that conventionally cir-cumscribe one nation as opposed to another. Given Scotland's dual role as central player in discourses about nationhood and as representative nation, Hogg stood to shift the very idea of national 'identity'. Today, his contribu-tion can be recognised and applied in a complex understanding of the nation as variable and barely containable.

At first glance, Hogg fits nicely into theories of national coherence that inherit Scottish thinking about the nation. Benedict Anderson's idea of the 'imagined community' stresses that nations are not old, but new: we look back and choose the origin that produces the nation according to the needs of our day.[8] Although sceptical, Anderson's theory allows us to imagine a coherent progress from origins. To contemporary and even modern critics, Hogg fits this pattern; he seems 'natural' and perhaps simple to the sophisti-cated Thomas Carlyle, and rustic and labouring classes, thus somehow more authentic, to post-Marxian scholars.[9]

Hogg also fits theories of the nation informed by postcolonialism. Scotland, subject to the Union with England (1707) and also, as Tom Nairn terms it, a 'highly successful partner in the general business enterprise of Anglo-Scots imperialism', had a particular use for this manifestation of uncouth origins.[10] Frantz Fanon notes that colonial dominance 'distorts, disfigures, and destroys' the past of the colonised: it requires the past not to be 'natural' but gro-tesque. A local who wants to get ahead under this imported narrative must 'leave certain of his intellectual possessions in pawn'.[11] Other rising talents like John Gibson Lockhart were only too eager to pawn off the shepherd. Lockhart expressed Scottish 'inferiorism' in relation to England, implying his own sophistication by depicting his countryman as a boor:[12]

> [Hogg] has spent a considerable portion of every year in excellent, even in refined society, [but] the external appearance of the man can have undergone but very little change since he was a 'herd on Yarrow.' [. . .] His very hair has a coarse stringiness about it [. . .] and hangs in playful whips and cords about his ears, in a style of the most perfect innocence imaginable.[13]

Hogg is at once compared to Wordsworth's naturally noble Pedlar and fenced off from polite society. This is Hogg as Carlyle's Punch and Judy.

But as the 'other', Hogg participates in Homi Bhabha's theories of 'the otherness of the people as one'.[14] Although ideologues may stress the nation's shared ethos, the people, through their variety, will always perform the nation differently. And Hogg shows many non-standard ways of being a Scot: he is a fiddler; a shepherd; part of the folk; a friend of Walter Scott; a traveller; and so on.[15] This is what Ian Duncan remarks as Hogg's 'synchronicity', and Murray Pittock suggests functions as 'altermentality'.[16] Hogg betokens an alternate reality, perhaps a more 'natural' one, but one in any case at odds with respectable traditions and terms.

Hogg certainly expresses the 'otherness' of the people, but perhaps not 'as one'. From his many differences, we might pose a more rambunctious definition of otherness – a definition that challenges even the idea of a 'oneness' that somehow comprises 'otherness'. Hogg implies no alignment between varieties of Scottishness. Rather, Hogg's cluttered texts with their clashing dynamics and their author's multiple and contesting personae evoke a lumpiness, an excess, an unpredictable otherness in one person and his works, never mind in the people at large, which challenges any idea of a cohesive, bounded nation. Hogg suggests complications too many and variable to be contained 'as one'.

Such complications may be strategic. This becomes clear when we consider Hogg in the context of that 'heaven-taught ploughman' and 'national' incarnation, Robert Burns. The shepherd posited Burns as a model for himself as poet of the people, claiming that when he heard 'Tam o' Shanter' and was told Burns's story,

> I wept, and always thought with myself – what is to hinder me from succeeding Burns? I too was born on the 25th of January [. . .]
> I remember in the year 1812 [. . .] I told my friend [. . .] that I should yet live to be compared with Burns; and though I might never equal him in some things, I thought I might excel him in others.[17]

Did Hogg believe he was born on Burns's birthday? Did he seriously mean he could contend with Burns in 1812?

The supposed parallelism with Burns provoked hostile reactions. In 1832 a pamphlet by 'An Old Dissector' quoted Hogg's claim that, 'I TOO WAS BORN ON THE 25TH OF JANUARY', and fulminated: 'the devil you was!'[18] The 'Dissector' poured scorn: 'What a pity that the whole of this magnificent fabric of apparent castle-building should rest on no more solid foundation than an *ex post facto* fiction' (11). But Hogg himself knew as much, and presented his assertion as always questionable, taking care to include a resistant audience. Thus, one friend defends Hogg, but another 'reprobated the idea, and [. . .] told it as a bitter jest against me in a party' (*Memoir*, 12). Hogg may be 'mortified', but he recounts his mortification. Moreover, Hogg himself often ridicules his alignment with Burns. In 1834, he recalled that

> I expected to die at the same age and on the very same day of the month. So when the 21st of August began to approach I grew very ill – terribly ill and told the people who were waiting on me that I feared I was going to die. They said 'they hopet no' But before midnight I was so ill and so frightened, that I was skirling and haudding by the blankets. (*Letters*, vol. 3, pp. 214–15)

Hogg's self-positioning with regard to Burns was 'tongue-in-cheek' (Bold, p. 65). But what did it achieve? Not the unproblematic sequencing between ploughman- and shepherd-poets that a cohesive national narrative might prefer. Hogg's energetic assertion instead raises questions of his inadequacy. He is admitted to the Burnsian tradition, but often resentfully and mockingly, as a misfit – an add-on that does not add up. Through a comparison with Burns made impossible by time (they do not occupy the same moment) and place (two bodies cannot occupy the same physical or, it seems, poetic space), Hogg turns our attention away from sequence and towards the difference, the excess, that will always undermine coherence. Hogg's nation is at once composed and decomposed by jostling times, persons, modes of writing and being, and stories told.

This becomes obvious in the comparison Hogg strenuously invites between himself and Walter Scott. Hogg and Scott became friends, so far as the divisions of class and Scott's stature as the pre-eminent author of his day allowed. This makes doubly interesting Hogg's long-term positioning of himself as both less and more than his fellow author. Hogg typically posited himself as 'not Scott'. Scott's *Lay of the Last Minstrel* (1805) is echoed and critiqued through Hogg's *The Queen's Wake* (1813); *The Lady of the Lake* (1810) is similarly recast through *Mador of the Moor* (1816). Once more, the issue is not to assign places to poets in some tidy pattern. When Hogg produced *The Forest Minstrel* (1810) after Scott's *Minstrelsy of the Scottish Border* (1802), he stood less as supplement than as rival – a role he sharpened in subsequent works, which assertively occupy space already mapped out by Scott. Here we see Hogg beginning to claim not just difference but priority for his belated texts. The most notorious case involves Scott's *The Tale of Old Mortality* (1816) and Hogg's *The Brownie of Bodsbeck* (1818). When his book came out in 1818, Hogg wrote to the editor of *The Scotsman*, 'The Brownie was written long before Old Mortality [. . .] Scott knows this well enough' (*Letters*, vol. 1, p. 351). Given that both books focus on the Covenanters in the 'killing times', but in very different ways, what was at stake in Hogg's hint that Scott stole his idea? If Hogg belatedly occupied Scott's space on other occasions, here he suggests that he was the one already in place.

Hogg's relationship to Scott, like his relationship with Burns, produces the Ettrick Shepherd as an unassimilable excess – and produces Scott as an unlikely excess, also. When Hogg stages the relationship as a rivalry – as when Scott finds the insolvent Hogg a job as shepherd under condition that 'I was to put my poetical talent under lock and key for ever!' – he becomes visible as an invader of Scott's space.[19] And Hogg shows Scott's national and literary eminence as far from secure or self-evident – even in the moment he represents as their first meeting. In what Gillian Hughes calls 'one of the great moments of Romantic myth-making', Scott is rebuked by Hogg's mother, the source for some of his poems in the *Minstrelsy*: 'there war never ane o' my sangs prentit till ye prentit them yoursel', an' ye ha spoilt them awthegither' (Hughes, p. 42; *Familiar Anecdotes*, p. 38). Scott is the cuckoo in the nest. Together, in Hogg's shifting and strategic rearrangements, the Heaven-taught Ploughman, the Wizard of the North, and the Ettrick Shepherd expose the literary space of the nation as jumbled, contested, disrupted, unboundable.

Hogg reveals excess as a characteristic of the nation in his stories, too. Though he sometimes centres his fictions on queens and kings, the cohesive narrative that monarchy should enforce always fails. *The Queen's Wake* echoes one such tale, that of return.[20] Queen Mary returns to Holyrood, and Scotland seeks to coalesce around this figure of beauty and wholeness:

> Scotland, involved in factious broils,
> Groaned deep beneath her woes and toils,
> And looked o'er meadow, dale, and lea,
> For many a day her Queen to see;
> Hoping that then her woes would cease,
> And all her vallies smile in peace.
> (*Queen's Wake*, 'Introduction', ll. 91–6)

The Queen, too, desires a reconciliation that will unify the nation. The herald inviting minstrels to court proclaims, 'Peace, peace to Scotland's wasted vales'. Yet if Scotland is to be peaceful, something must be left out:

'No ribaldry the Queen must hear, [. . .] / No jest, nor adulation bland, / But legends of our native land' (ll. 309–12). Predictably, Mary does not get the stories that will peacefully restore past to present. The minstrels come 'Forcing [their] way' to Holyrood; their tales clash; the Queen's candidate, Rizzio, does not win (l. 387). National order and resolution seem as far away at the end of the poem as they were at the beginning.

Mador of the Moor likewise undoes a royal tale aimed at national cohesion.[21] Here, the monarch goes among his people in disguise. Conventionally, this folk tale motif foregrounds the worth of people and king through a mutual recognition which binds them as one.[22] But Hogg's king is an irresponsible young man, winked at by a corrupt court. This monarch is not quietly doing good among his people; rather, masquerading as a minstrel, he is seducing their daughters. Although ultimately he weds his commoner (who tracks him back to court), the poem ends with the King setting off again: 'Haply to distant land I now may roam' (Canto V, l. 280). Monarchs themselves, it seems, resist integration into a singular national narrative.

Moreover, Hogg shows that Mary does not represent her people. When Rizzio loses the minstrelsy contest, the Queen orders her squire to 'call the votes again' ('Conclusion', l. 65). This exercise of sovereign power reveals only its weakness: 'Her favourite's voters counted o'er, / Were found much fewer than before' (ll. 68–9). In a Scotland made up of excessive otherness, whatever you grasp, you shall lose. The Scots make sure of it: 'She found out with whom she had to do', the poet sardonically remarks (l. 71). Indeed, this is a theme running through Hogg's interrogation of nation as in/coherent state. In 1822, celebrating George IV's visit to Scotland and perhaps hoping for a pension, Hogg greets his sovereign through similarly wayward locals.[23] Even the First Sea-Nymph, who has guided the portly king across the turbulent main, avers: 'I judged there were greater crimes / Than giving my Prince a touch of the times; / So I whispered to him, in haughty tone, / What element he journeyed on.'[24] Any would-be coherent narrative of the nation stands subject to its subjects.

It is subject to them individually and severally – which for Hogg comes disturbingly to the same thing. Repeatedly in his novels, characters and roles double and contend in the same space. In *The Three Perils of Man* (1822), two ladies dress as squires and one of them makes a squire dress as her; they argue over two knights; meantime, border lords wrestle for power.[25] An embassy designed to clarify when and how to fight is full of doubled characters: the beautiful captive turns out to be the child of the friar's lost love; Tam Craik is the murderous Jock of folklore; the poet is the child once lost and now found by Charlie Yardbire; Muckle Charlie will become Sir Charles Scott; the friar is Roger Bacon and thus a Hoggean surrogate. Such conflations flip and confound narrative times, too – for instance, in *The Three Perils of*

Woman (1823), earlier stories are told late.[26] These doublings and multiplica-
tions even produce the temporal impossibility of death and life in one body,
when Gatty Bell falls into and out of a years-long trance. And of course, they
undermine any possibility of a singular time, place, or person in *The Private
Memoirs and Confessions of a Justified Sinner* (1824). Here, brothers, doctrines,
stories, editors, even sections of the book struggle against one another – to no
resolution.[27] In themselves and as a nation Scots are multiple, excessive and
irreconcilable.

What stands forth from all this jostling is James Hogg – a carefully constructed site and source of contention. In *The Queen's Wake*, a shepherd from
Ettrick appears several times. Once he stands in shreds and tatters, subject
to barbs and jests, to play and lose (but he gains a 'wild' Scottish harp). His
double, another Ettrick Shepherd, speaks at the beginning and end of the
poem. This poet implies that though minstrels fade, stories live:

> 'Tis said that thirty bards appeared,
> That thirty names were registered, [. . .]
> But some are lost, and some declined.
> Woe's me, that all my mountain lore
> Has been unfit to rescue more!
> (*Queen's Wake*, 'Conclusion', ll. 19–26)

Specifically, stories live in this inheritor who is not Walter Scott, not a relic
of the past, not a winner, but who rather, in himself and as a representative
of previous minstrels, manifests a clash of desires, resentments and potentials.

This is the Hogg of whom *The Athenaeum* cautiously remarked on his
death: 'he kept a somewhat voluminous journal: [. . .] we [. . .] hope [. . .] that
it will not be sent "unhousel'd unanointed" before the public'.[28] Why was the
cultural establishment so bothered by James Hogg? Why did even his friend
Allan Cunningham reductively insist, 'Hogg is what he represents himself,
a shepherd'?[29] Persistently, Hogg exposed the fractures within a supposedly
coherent nation. *The Athenaeum* senses the problem. So much the more
did Scots like Cunningham, with their peculiarly colonial and postcolonial
anxieties of influence and order.

Hogg's various autobiographies make the case clear. Hogg was notori-
ously tactless when it came to including others within his own story. George
Goldie, his early publisher, is outed as a bankrupt who undermined Hogg's
sales; Walter Scott poaches on his literary territory; Scott's wife Charlotte
may be illegitimate and a drug addict. Not surprisingly, this sort of thing
provoked a firestorm of criticism. In 1821 Goldie published a twenty-four
page pamphlet in his own defence, and in 1832 the 'Old Dissector' complained for twice that length.[30] Mocking 'the notoriety which [. . .] Mr Hogg

has acquired', Goldie decried his 'distempered imagination', his 'miserable object of creating an interest with the public', and his 'really fabulous' narrative (Goldie, pp. 6–7). Hogg had implied a scandalous complexity and inconsistency – perhaps even multiplicity – in an upstanding citizen, catching him on the raw.

Hogg did not recant. The Dissector's anger was magnified in 1832 because the author was now repeating libels for which he had been taken to task in previous years (Dissector, p. 17). So the only strategy left was to reduce the Shepherd into that singularity: a liar. 'Any thing will be believed of him, except what he says of himself' (Dissector, 11). Ironically, this move exacerbates the problem, as *Blackwood's Edinburgh Magazine* discovered. *Blackwood's* had transformed the self-avowed shepherd from Ettrick into the literary character 'the Ettrick Shepherd'. It displayed Hogg as other enough to define social and Scottish margins for Blackwoodians like Lockhart, but not so excessively other as to undermine them. It consequently mocked Hogg's 1821 Memoirs:

> I take the liberty of sending back Hogg, which has disgusted me more severely than any thing I have attempted to swallow since Macvey's Bacon. He is liker a swineherd in the Canongate, than a shepherd in Ettrick Forest. I shall never again think of him without the image of an unclean thing; and for his sake, I henceforth forswear the whole swinish generation. Roast pig shall never more please my palate – pickled pork may go to the devil – brawn, adieu! – avaunt all manner of hams – sow's cheek.[31]

Having invoked Hogg, the magazine wrestles to force him into the limiting grotesquery of swinish metaphor. But metaphor only multiples the possibilities: Hogg generates a cascade of porcine comparisons. The writer struggles on:

> I undertake, in six weeks, to produce six as good poets as he is, from each county in Scotland [. . .]
>   Besides, how many lives of himself does the swine-herd intend to put forth?
> ('Familiar Epistles', 43)

The ramped-up attempt to stop Hogg's torrent of lives promises only to beget six more of his ilk – potentially with the same problems. The Hogg who spins disruptive stories becomes the more conspicuous and uncontainable the more that critics try to shut him down. Worse, he makes the Blackwoodians themselves appear all the more obsessive, anxious, fractured and out of control.

That Hogg had no interest in playing a coherent part – and some enjoyment in upsetting his anxious fellows – is obvious in his fraught relationship with *Blackwood's*. At times, Hogg resisted Blackwoodian caricatures of himself as the Ettrick Shepherd. When the *Blackwood's* review followed close behind Goldie's attack, he wrote angrily to William Blackwood, impugning 'the ribaldry and mockery that has been so liberally vomited forth on me from your shop' (*Letters*, vol. 2, p. 109). But typically, a reconciliation followed. In 1820, the *London Magazine* attacked *Blackwood's* – and Lockhart and Scott in particular – for their abusive treatment of 'poor Hogg, the delightful Shepherd Poet'.[32] Yet Hogg remained a *Blackwood's* man. That is, the 'delightful Shepherd Poet' determinedly aligned himself with men who in education, class and interests were his opposites. He seemed to prefer a context in which he visibly did not fit, would always appear excessive, and would provoke excess in others.

David McCrone notes that a 'national "story" usually contains a foundation myth [. . .] which provides an alternative history or counter-narrative predating ruptures or dispossessions'.[33] Hogg, however, suggests that what supposedly belongs to the 'past', whether 'delightful Shepherd' or swinish grotesque, might productively unsettle the present through its lack of coherence. His tales enact fraction, not resolution, and as shepherd, Spy, *Blackwood's* persona, Burnsian inheritor, and Scott competitor, he enacted it himself. Hogg stood to Scotland as that gristly, indigestible chunk of 'Macvey's Bacon', the excess that undoes the reductive coherences of state nationalism, and reveals the nation as a hearty soup of roiling differences.

CHAPTER NINE

Hogg, Gender, and Sexuality

Silvia Mergenthal

The eponymous hero and first-person narrator of James Hogg's 'The Renowned Adventures of Basil Lee'[1] is a ne'er-do-well Lowland Scot who, after having run through most of his patrimony, eventually purchases an ensign's commission, joins the British army and promptly finds himself on his way to America. There he becomes involved, on the British side, in the War of Independence.[2]

Basil's commanding officer is a Highlander named Colin Fraser, whose mistress, Clifford Mackay, Basil seduces, whereupon Fraser challenges him to a duel. Basil does not quite see the point of fighting duels, although Fraser's Irish second, Macrae, tries to explain that, as an officer in the British army, Basil will have to rise to the challenge, or else be disgraced for ever. He is still not convinced, arguing that he is quite prepared to publicly admit that he has wronged Fraser, and to apologise to him – and besides, 'I do not approve of fighting duels. My religious principles do not admit of it.'[3] Given his career up to this period of his life, even well-disposed readers will suspect that it is less Basil's piety than his habitual cowardice which is at the root of his refusal to fight.[4] But his own intended second, an English 'gentleman', informs Basil that he will at least have the right of choosing his weapon; after some deliberation, Basil settles on the broadsword, and the duel does take place.

The challenge to a duel, issued by a Highlander to a Lowlander and fought over the possession of a Highland woman, as well as the responses to this challenge are couched explicitly in national terms and reflect conflicting constructions of masculinity, one of which – Basil's – can be termed residual, whereas the other, by the late eighteenth century, has become dominant, namely, the behavioural code of imperial masculinity. It takes a Highlander, an Irishman, and an Englishman to initiate Basil into it, and although he adopts it somewhat reluctantly here, later episodes in his military career will show that he only ever masters it incompletely; by contrast, the proverbial martial spirit of the Highlander has already been incorporated into it. Of course, Hogg's tale satirises this behavioural code of imperial masculinity as well – while Basil's cowardice turns out to be an effective survival strategy.

The period around 1800 is generally regarded as a time in which conflicting notions of gender as well as divergent attitudes towards sexuality coexist. In the case of gender, these notions ranged from Mary Wollstonecraft's neo-Cartesian insistence on the non-gendered nature of the human mind to early articulations of a 'separate spheres' ideology by Hannah More. The latter position would come to dominate nineteenth-century literature and culture, but even in the period under consideration, it had already rendered literature, for instance with regard to the distribution of literary genres, a gendered field. As for sexuality, Evangelical – or, in Scotland, Calvinist – strictures on unlicensed physical expressions of love clashed with more liberal (occasionally libertine) sexual mores, as authors from Burns to Byron would learn to their detriment.

This chapter investigates how James Hogg negotiates the gender/sexuality discourses of his time, focusing on two of his major novels, *The Three Perils of Man: War, Women, and Witchcraft* (1822) and *The Three Perils of Woman: Love, Leasing, and Jealousy* (1823). Underlying this investigation, and the analysis of 'The Renowned Adventures of Basil Lee' so far, are two assumptions regarding gender which have, by now, become widely accepted among scholars who employ gender as a category of literary analysis: first, that gender is discursively constructed, intersecting with discourses of nationality, as in the case of Basil Lee's duel, or religion; second, that gender is (inter)actively performed, by both the individual whose gender is to be established and by those who are expected to recognise and acknowledge it. Both participants in this interaction need to have certain abilities, but they also have rights and duties: the ability to act 'like a man' or 'like a woman' on one side, and the ability to recognise the signs of masculinity or femininity on the other; the right to be treated appropriately, as a woman or a man, and the right not to be deceived; the duty to behave so as to not confuse one's partner in the interactive process, and that partner's duty to neither question nor ignore one's gender (self-) identification.

However, this chapter also shows that gender issues are intimately linked to three other characteristics of Hogg's work: to what might be called the generic instabilities of his texts; to his key preoccupation with the question whether, and how, one can remain identical to oneself under pressure; and, finally, to his championship of residual – and hence, potentially alternative and oppositional – cultural practices. For examples of all these concerns, and for the connections between them, one can turn, once again, to 'The Renowned Adventures of Basil Lee'. With regard to the generic instabilities of the story, it combines, or rather juxtaposes, the formal and stylistic conventions of the autobiography, the sermon, the picaresque novel, the imperial adventure story, the ethnographical essay, the tale of terror, the comedy of manners, and the domestic tale. As these genres also differ considerably in how explicitly sexual practices can be represented in them, their juxtaposition, and the tonal tensions which it creates, account for the comic incongruity of the moral message which Basil delivers in the final (prose) paragraph[5] of the tale:

> It may be deemed by some, that I have treated female imprudence with too great a degree of levity, and represented it as producible of consequences that it does not deserve; but in this, I am only blameable in having adhered to the simple truth. Besides, I would gladly combat the ungenerous and cruel belief, that when a female once steps aside from the paths of rectitude, she is lost for ever. Nothing can be more ungracious than this; yet to act conformably with such a sentiment, is common in the manners of this volatile age, as notorious for its laxity of morals as for its false delicacy.[6]

This message is comprehensible in the discursive context of either a sermon or a domestic tale, and it is applicable to the constructions of gender roles inscribed in and by these discourses. It is, however, incommensurate with the picaresque arena of sexual exploits in non-metropolitan (rural or colonial) environments, in which femininities and masculinities may be performed quite differently, as in the story in fact they are. As a consequence, in 'Basil Lee' as in other Hogg texts, characters appear to be written by the generic conventions they find themselves caught up in and, as a result, often cease to be intelligible to themselves, and to one another: Basil, on his translation from the picaresque novel to the imperial adventure tale, 'from being a good natured, careless, roving, absurd fellow [becomes] all at once proud, positive, and obstreperous'.[7] He later fails to recognise Clifford, once she has metamorphosed from a *fille du regiment* into a gentlewoman.

Finally, as to Hogg's championship of residual cultural practices, one only has to recall the number of 'fallen women' who populate nineteenth-century fiction to appreciate the very different trajectory which Clifford's life will take, bearing in mind, however, that Clifford's good fortune is shadowed not only by what might have become of her but also by what happens to other Highland women in Hogg's tale. Clifford first marries a wealthy American, and after his death, seeks out Basil, who has, in the meantime, returned to Scotland. There the two live happily ever after, Clifford's husband having left his son – probably fathered by Basil – heir to his fortune, but with its interest at Clifford's disposal.

In the opening sentences of both *Three Perils of Man* and *Three Perils of Woman*, the gendered space of late eighteenth- and early nineteenth-century fictional genres is invaded by Hogg – or rather, by one of his narrators and one of his characters, respectively – with startling abruptness: 'The days of the Stuarts, kings of Scotland, were the days of chivalry and romance.'[8] And: '"I fear I am in love," said Gatty Bell, as she first awakened in her solitary bed in the garret room of her father's farm-house.'[9]

With regard to *Three Perils of Man*, critics have paid attention to the sinister aspect of chivalry:

> The role of the chivalric knight is to protect the weak, especially women, but the knight can only genuinely take on this role of defender if the threat to women is real. Rape, as the ultimate physical attack on a woman, is thus a necessary other side of the chivalric system.[10]

In *Three Perils of Man*, there are three episodes in which male and female characters are brought together for the ultimate purpose of sexual congress. In Aikwood, the yeomen who have come to the rescue of Charlie and his companions are introduced by Michael Scott to thirty lovely maidens, who, the morning after, are transformed into horrible hags.[11] But, as Gibbie Jordan recounts in Chapter XXXII of the novel, hags can be deceived in their choice of partners as well: in some of the most terrifying scenes which he becomes privy to during his captivity at Aikwood, witches are married, night after night, to the devil in disguise. However, while, in the novel as a whole, the Aikwood scenes are embedded in the siege of Roxburgh frame narrative, the two mass couplings involving witches frame a Roxburgh event that is endowed with all the cultural capital which the chivalric system has accumulated, namely, a mass wedding, sponsored by the King and Queen, between successful champions and their mistresses. It is surely no coincidence that the devil employs the same feudal rhetoric as the King and Queen; hence the unions between yeomen and witches, and between witches and the devil, shed a sinister light on the marriages enforced (with equally diabolical cunning) by the royal couple. At the very least, the witches' weddings are, respectively, an uncanny foreshadowing of, and an unkind commentary on, the disillusionment experienced by the knights and the ladies in their marriages.

Through concentration on the fantastic and extreme elements of chivalry, *Three Perils of Man* offers a critique not only of chivalry itself, but, by implication, of the modern literary forms in which it is encoded, namely, the historical romance and the Gothic novel. *Three Perils of Woman* serves a similar purpose vis-à-vis the domestic or conduct novel and the national tale.[12] One of the key structural topoi of the national tale, the cross-cultural marriage, has already been introduced into *Three Perils of Man*, when Charlie Scott – perhaps not under entirely favourable auspices, as we have just seen – marries Lady Jane Howard, who is English. *Three Perils of Woman* is constructed around a whole sequence of cross-cultural marriages between three generations of Highland men and Lowland women: in the first, the Culloden generation, these marriages spell unmitigated disaster, while their consequences can still be traumatic even among the generation to which Hogg himself belongs. The third generation does appear to finally get it right when a Lowland lass is transformed into a 'blessing to the human race'.[13] However, this chronological sequence of 'real history' is, of course, reversed in the actual novel so that the story of Gatty's and the second M'Ion's courtship and marriage is framed by the cautionary tales of Mrs Johnson and the first M'Ion, and of Sally Niven and Alaster Mackenzie. In addition, even Gatty's elevation to the status of a Highland chieftain's wife – and to near sainthood – is bought, quite literally, at the expense of Cherry; and it is haunted, as Antony J. Hasler has shown,[14] by the spectre of the Highland Clearances. Meanwhile, the advice on questions of conduct which the narrator proffers (when he remembers to do so, which is rarely) is as comically inadequate throughout the novel as it is in 'Basil Lee', and for the same reasons.

The question of identity, and its link to gender discourses in the two novels, can be approached by analysing their techniques of characterisation and by describing some of their character constellations. Both *Three Perils of Man* and *Three Perils of Woman* highlight forms of male bonding through, and over, the bodies of women. The storytelling competition in *Three Perils of Man* is driven by the storytellers' sexual and/or carnivorous desire for Delany, and while Delany will be neither raped nor eaten, she will be gifted by Michael to Charlie Scott, thus cementing a relationship between them, the ultimate purpose of which is the aggrandisement of their mutual kinsman, the Warden. In *Three Perils of Woman*, the two rivals in Sally Niven's affection, her husband Alaster and her one-time lover, Peter Gow, having just exchanged what will turn out to be mortal blows, now find themselves on 'two soft beds of flowery heather, strewed [. . .] over with mosses', and with 'their feet to each other, and their heads to the sod-wall'. When Sally eventually encounters them there, their responses to her presence mirror one another: 'both of them uncovered their pallid faces at the same instant, and both of them uttered a groan of tender compassion, as in concert'. Over the next few days, Sally slowly loses her mind – as well she might – and 'symptoms of derangement began to manifest themselves in the demeanour of both the patients'.[15]

Another character constellation, on which *Three Perils of Woman*, in particular, can be said to be predicated, is that of love triangles, either with two female and one male or with one female and two male 'corners'. For the first type, there are Cherry, Gatty and M'Ion, and Sally, Peter Gow's wife, and Peter Gow; for the second type, there are Richard Rickleton, the married lawyer and Katie, followed by Sally, the Minister of Balmillo and Peter Gow, and finally, once again Sally and Peter Gow, now with Alaster Mackenzie. As this list indicates, triangular love relationships are presented in both comic and tragic versions. It is the comic versions that expose the imbalances of power inherent in these relationships most clearly. If, as Katie succinctly explains to her husband, he refuses to acknowledge her son, whose biological father is the married lawyer, as his own, her whole fortune – or at least those parts of it which she has not lent to her lover – will be at his (that is, Richard Rickleton's) disposal.

On the level of individual characters, most readers and critics of *Three Perils of Man* or *Three Perils of Woman* – and of other Hogg texts – are gripped, on their first encounter with them, by a profound sense of unease, amounting, in some instances, to positive dislike: compared to his contemporaries, from Jane Austen to Walter Scott, Hogg does not seem capable of, or interested in, creating what in old-fashioned critical terms can be regarded as 'round characters'. It is simply not possible to conceive of Yardbire and Sir Charles Scott in *Three Perils of Man*, or of Cherry and Cherubina, Gatty and Agatha, Sally and Sarah in *Three Perils of Woman*, as actually one and the same person(s), as they seem to change their personalities according to how they think of themselves, how they are addressed by others, and how they are referred to by their narrators. The most extreme cases of these 'identity crises' are the numerous grotesque – dead, semi-dead, or living – female and male bodies with which both novels are haunted: the most grotesque of these is surely Gatty's (in *Three Perils of Woman*), whose trance-like state seems to have been precipitated by sexual intercourse,[16] closely followed by Gibbie Jordan's (in *Three Perils of Man*), who is made to witness his own physical dissolution over and over again. While, on the surface, Gatty's and Gibbie's plights could not be more dissimilar, the near death of the one and the triumphant survival of the other are both indebted to a concept of human identity according to which (male or female) bodies are inhabited by non-gendered souls. This is a concept which is, of course, fairly orthodox in religious terms, but it also resonates with contemporary feminist ideas, specifically, with Wollstonecraft's neo-Cartesian insistence on the non-genderedness of the human mind.[17] In addition, as has already been indicated, the boundaries between two bodies or two souls, or perhaps even one person's body and another person's soul, are anything but impermeable. Thus, in *Three Perils of Woman*, there is 'sympathy between [M'Ion's] frame and the body of the deceased', that is, Gatty's, and Sarah's madness spreads to Alaster Mackenzie and Peter Gow, 'whether [. . .] from feelings of sympathy, from inflammation of the wounds, or a deep consciousness of their deplorable condition'.[18]

Finally, a plot element which features prominently in both *Three Perils of Man* and *Three Perils of Woman* is that of cross-dressing, with all the cross-dressers women disguised as men: Princess Margaret, Lady Jane Howard, and Bessy and May Chisholm in *Three Perils of Woman*, Lady Sybil, the daughter of the old Chief of the Clan-More and Sally Niven in *Three Perils of Man*. None of these women can 'pass' as men for any length of time, that is, they cannot, in Harold Garfinkel's definition of 'passing', 'achieve and make secure their rights to live in the elected sex status while providing for the possibility of detection and ruin'.[19] Hence, in both novels, the respective narrators and the two sets of characters, that is, the cross-dressing women and those they come into contact with – which, in the case of Princess Margaret and Lady Jane Howard, may well be other cross-dressing women – catalogue signs of, respectively, masculinity or femininity: height, complexion, posture, pierced ears, the tendency to blush, voice, clothes, hair-styles, and sexual attractiveness in accordance with the heterosexual matrix. Some of these signs turn out to be unreliable: while Margaret eventually realises that Jane is female, mainly because she has inadvertently come into contact with her rival's breasts, Jane is fooled by Margaret's greater height and darker complexion. And with regard to the heterosexual matrix, the following description of the first physical contact between Margaret and Jane, coming at a point when each of them knows herself to be female, but believes the other to be male, is perhaps somewhat ambiguous:

> they joined hands on the bargain; but they had no sooner laid their hands into one another's than they hastily withdrew them, with a sort of trepidation, that none of the lookers on, save the two pages, who kept close by their masters, appeared to comprehend. They, too, were both mistaken in the real cause; but of that it does not behove to speak at present.[20]

The 'trepidation' is, of course, neither caused by a male–male handshake, as the 'lookers on' believe, nor by a male–female one, as the participants and their respective pages assume, but by one between two women. It seems to be the function of these cross-dressers, in their respective novels, to alert the reader to the performativity of gender, as well as to the fact that the way in which masculinity and femininity can be performed varies diachronically, that is, across different historical periods, and synchronically, between different social classes or ethnic communities. These variations are, once again, inscribed in different discourses: among these are, as we have seen, the domestic or conduct novel, the historical romance, the Gothic novel and the national tale, but also, crucially, oral forms of narration such as the folk tale or the Border ballad. One of the reasons, then, why Hogg's men and women do not become 'round characters' is that they are situated at the interfaces of conflicting constructions of, respectively, masculinity and femininity. Unlike some, or perhaps most, of his contemporaries, Hogg resists the temptation to homogenise, and thus to naturalise, these constructions.

What, then, of Hogg's championship of residual cultural practices? This can best be documented by referring, once again, to the character constellations of the more unsettling of the two novels, *Three Perils of Woman*. While, in two of the love triangles, women are sacrificed to dynastic and economic aspirations (Cherry, and arguably Gatty), or else to political manoeuvring (Sally and Peter Gow's wife), the female 'corner' of the third, the 'fallen woman' Katie, is singularly lucky in that her husband, Richard Rickleton, is prepared to act as father to a child he has not fathered, even though this will mean that this son, once acknowledged, will inherit the Rickleton lands. This comes as a surprise to both her and the reader: Rickleton has a history of fighting duels with whoever questions his manliness. Rickleton, then – in this respect, though perhaps not in others, quite unlike Basil Lee – learns to resist the allures of the behavioural code of imperial masculinity. He is rewarded with 'social happiness' and, more importantly, with the brotherly affection of the man who has always been his greatest rival.

CHAPTER TEN

Hogg and Music

Kirsteen McCue

In his first 'Memoir' of 1807 James Hogg describes an important moment in his early life when he attended a dance at the home of Mr Scott of Singlee. '[Being] admitted into the room', Hogg writes, he was 'all attention to the music'. He proceeds to give an entertaining account of returning alone to his barn, picking up his fiddle and roughly 'essaying some of the tunes' which he had just heard, frightening the evening's musician into believing that these invisible sounds are emanating from the Devil himself.[1] As is often the case with Hogg's personal accounts, the realities are used for wider creative ends. In fact, several contemporary reports attest to Hogg's prowess as a performer. His fiddle playing resulted in his creating several tunes and he was frequently invited to sing at social gatherings, including some of the earliest 'Burns suppers'.[2] H. B. de Groot has suggested, with reference to the musical descriptions in 'Highland Journeys', that Hogg was in possession of an especially sensitive musical ear, and enjoyed good relative pitch.[3] Hogg's songs were his first and some of his last creations, and his collections, often with musical accompaniments, show his passion for the genre as well as his wider interest in music. The decisions he makes as a song collector and editor often reveal an innate knowledge of things musical, and his enthusiasm and attention to detail in these roles clearly illustrate a vested interest in the developing fashion for the publication and performance of national song.[4]

Information about Hogg's musical education is scant. He prefaces the above story of his devilish fiddling with information about the acquisition of his first fiddle – which he had saved for – at the age of fourteen, and which he would play for up to two hours per day.[5] His musical ear had developed from an early age and appears to have been much encouraged at home. Hogg's mother, Margaret Laidlaw, was widely known for her considerable abilities as a singer: famously, it was she who had sung ballads to Walter Scott for his *Minstrelsy of the Scottish Border*, the project which brought Scott and Hogg together in 1802.[6] Elaine Petrie has already commented that much of Hogg's early musical education was an oral one and was heavily influenced by his agricultural environment and from listening to psalms and traditional ballads sung by members of the Ettrick community.[7] Like Robert Burns, of whom he had no knowledge in his early years, Hogg's first poetic or 'rhyming' attempts were songs and they were thus some of his first works to appear in print, as part of *Scottish Pastorals* (1801) and *The Mountain Bard* (1807).[8] Alongside a range of pastoral and sometimes bawdy love lyrics (such as 'O Shepherd, the weather is misty and changing' in *Scottish Pastorals*) Hogg displayed his considerable flair for national song in 'Scotia's Glens' and 'Donald Macdonald' (both in *The Mountain Bard*). The latter was to be something of a calling-card for Hogg: he referred to it as 'my first song', and it was indeed the first of his songs to appear in a popular song-sheet issued in Edinburgh by John Hamilton in 1803.[9]

Hogg's *Highland Journeys* at this time also reveal his interest in songs and singing. He notes, in his first *Journey* of 1802, that his fellow Borderers have a 'generally musical ear' and discusses the shared provenance of many tunes or melodies from the Borders, the South West and up to Perthshire.[10] His 1803 *Journey* refers to a 'Dutch concert' (akin to a *ceilidh*) performed by the birds at Loch Katrine, 'from the small whistle of the wren, to the solemn notes of the cuckoo, sounded on E. and C. a double octave lower'.[11] Another description of his friend John Grieve's 'musical ear' is found in his 1804 *Journey* where he refers to keys ('sharp key'), cadences, musical intervals ('a fifth') and note lengths ('a minim').[12] Such references show that Hogg's musical knowledge was not purely oral, and support the theory that he may have had relative pitch. While we have no clear evidence of a formal musical education, this confident use of musical terminology must have resulted from either spending considerable time with knowledgeable musicians or reading musical textbooks. And Hogg must have done either or both, as these comments and his descriptions of musical performances elsewhere in his work (for example in the 'Holy symphony' which is Part II of his poem *Pilgrims of the Sun*, 1815) illustrate.[13]

Hogg's private letters to Walter Scott make reference to his plans for a proper volume of songs as early as 1803, but it was not until 1810 that such a collection appeared.[14] *The Forest Minstrel* was pulled together shortly after Hogg's arrival in Edinburgh and, as noted by Peter Garside and Richard Jackson, it was influenced by major collections of Scottish songs already in circulation. Like David Herd's 1776 edition of *Ancient and Modern Scottish Songs, Heroic Ballads etc.* and Joseph Ritson's *Scotish Songs* of 1794, this collection classified its content, in this case into four areas: 'Pathetic', 'Love', 'Humorous' and 'National' songs.[15] Of the 83 songs included, Hogg contributed 56, across all four categories, and the remainder came from a group of his friends. Hogg commented later in his 1821 'Memoir' that the songs included were 'in general not good, but the worst of them are all mine, for I inserted every ranting rhyme that I had made in my youth'.[16] This volume did not

create the public stir for which Hogg had wished, but displayed a wide range
of songs from tender youthful lyrics such as 'Blythe an' Cheery', to a spirited
sense of comedy in 'Love is like a dizziness' or 'Dr Munro'. The process of
transforming early, often oral, informal song lyrics into a formal collection
for a literate audience was a new departure. And, as the new Garside/Jackson
edition illustrates, it also exemplifies something of Hogg's knowledge of and
interest in music and melodies, and thus reveals his wider interaction with
similar contemporary publications.[17]

Leaving behind the poor sales figures and lack of public interest, *The Forest
Minstrel* allowed Hogg to begin to seriously build his profile as a songwriter.
He had declared himself the font of knowledge of Scottish Border ballad
tradition in *The Mountain Bard* in 1807.[18] *The Forest Minstrel* project revealed
his abilities as a songwriter and editor. But in 1813 he proceeded to promote
and secure his position by his presentation of the 'Master Singers' in his long
narrative poem *The Queen's Wake*, which did meet with public success.[19] The
narrative structure of a bardic competition was not just an ingenious solution
to incorporating a diverse range of ready-made songs and ballads; it was a
major statement about Hogg's position as a national songwriter.[20] Across the
three nights described in the poem, songsters and balladeers from all corners
of the Scottish nation make their unique regional contributions. The first
prize is given to Gardyn, the experienced Ossianic bard 'of ancient Caledon';
although Mary, Queen of Scots has a penchant for the Italianate lyrics of her
courtier David Rizzio. But the young Bard of Ettrick – clearly Hogg himself
– makes a forceful presence, persuading the Queen to award him the popular
'Caledonian Harp'. Showing himself adept at writing songs in all styles, as
well as projecting his own position as the Bard of the moment, it was *The
Queen's Wake* that first truly celebrated Hogg's role as both a national and
'natural songster'.[21] Commissions from musicians and music publishers followed quickly. Between 1813 and 1819 Hogg launched his songs to a wider
English audience through his involvement with John Clarke Whitfeld's
Twelve Vocal Pieces (c.1817), where 'There's naething to fear ye' and 'The
Lark' (later known as 'The Skylark'), posthumously Hogg's most widely
circulated song, appeared.

At around the same time he also provided lyrics for a set of Byron-
inspired *German Hebrew Melodies* with London publisher Charles Christmas
(c.1818).[22] Closer to home he contributed to Alexander Campbell's *Albyn's
Anthology* (1816 and 1818) and forged important connections with the
Edinburgh civil servant and music editor George Thomson. His *Select
Collection of Original Scottish Airs* (Volume 5 of 1818) brought Hogg's lyrics
together with Beethoven's musical arrangements – 'Bonnie Laddie, Highland
Laddie' (beginning 'Where got ye that siller moon') is a notable example.[23]
Moreover, Hogg's developing friendship with Edinburgh musicians and music

publishers Nathaniel Gow & Sons resulted in Hogg's first personal music volume. A *Border Garland* of 1819 comprised nine Hogg songs with music by William Heather, the composer with whom Hogg had just been working on Hebrew melodies, and his new friend Niel Gow junior, grandson of the most famous Scottish fiddler of the eighteenth century. Hogg's own fiddle tunes appeared with four of the nine songs (including 'The Women Fo'k' and 'The Laird o' Lamington'). And 'The Lament of Flora MacDonald' with music by Gow was issued simultaneously as a single song-sheet with piano or harp accompaniment.[24]

By the mid-1810s Hogg's reputation as a noted Border and Scottish songster was secured. Alexander Campbell sought him out for Border songs for *Albyn's Anthology*, but Campbell's collection was the first to feature Highland and Hebridean songs with both Gaelic text and music. The singing of Gaelic song had impressed Hogg during his Highland journeys and two of his songs for *Albyn's Anthology* were given Gaelic tunes ('Why should I sit and sigh' and 'My Mary is my only joy').[25] Discussions between the Highland Society of London and George Thomson resulted in Hogg being chosen as editor of a new collection of Jacobite songs, and consequently the two 'series' of *The Jacobite Relics of Scotland* appeared in 1819 and 1821. As Murray Pittock's work has demonstrated, this project brought Hogg into contact with the transmission and adaptation of much older songs, but also with an active living tradition of political and national Scots song.[26] Hogg's editorial decisions (for example, the inclusion of many Whig songs but omission of others with Episcopalian roots) did not always meet with approval and there was much criticism that the material included was not suitably refined. Colonel Stewart of Garth, writing in connection with the society's initial involvement, believed that the overall aim of the project – to show Scottish song as 'equal to if not superior to any other Country'– had not been met.[27] But time has proved otherwise and *Jacobite Relics* is now regarded as a 'canon-making collection'.[28] The editing of its melodic content again reveals elements of Hogg's innate musicality. Hogg was inspired by both Thomson's work and James Johnson's *Scots Musical Museum* (1787–1803), and the *Relics* featured melodies and texts. In addition to seeking out more local and specialised musical sources, Hogg's correspondence with the publisher Oliver & Boyd referred to the importance of placing page turns helpfully for the musician.[29] Musical antiquary William Stenhouse acted as a consultant, but Hogg disagreed with his alteration of many of the tunes included. Hogg's note for 'Farewell to Glen-Shalloch' comments that while Stenhouse's choice of Gaelic air might be easier to sing, the 'true air' for the song is another found in Simon Fraser's *Airs and Melodies Peculiar to the Highlands of Scotland and the Isles* of 1816.[30] Here and elsewhere Hogg's personal preference for the wild and irregular Highland and Gaelic melodies comes to the fore.

Throughout the 1820s Hogg's songs appeared in several Scottish and London-based song publications (e.g. those of R. A. Smith and James Dewar in Edinburgh and Goulding, D'Almaine & Co. in London) and as single popular song-sheets for the growing domestic music-making market.[31] They were found in literary annuals and gift books and in periodicals, including, most importantly, *Blackwood's Edinburgh Magazine*, which featured Hogg as the often drunken shepherd songster of the *Noctes Ambrosianae* and published several of his key social and bacchanalian songs (for example 'The Noctes Sang' and 'The Village of Balmaquhapple').[32] Hogg described this wide range of outlets in several letters to William Blackwood throughout 1830 in which he tried to persuade the publisher that a volume of 'my best songs out of all the periodicals in the Kingdom &c' would be a good idea.[33] Hogg's plan was to produce a volume of less than 'one third of my songs', which the public had deemed 'popular in the first place', as the first volume of a 'cabinet edition' of his popular work.[34]

Hogg's persistence triumphed and early in 1831 *Songs by the Ettrick Shepherd* appeared. This compact volume of 113 songs included those published in earlier collections; Hogg also reclaimed songs which had appeared elsewhere across his career, including those in several of his literary works. A fine example is his love song 'When the kye comes hame', which had first appeared in his novel *The Three Perils of Man* (1822) and was then sung by the Shepherd in the *Noctes* (1823). While *Songs by the Ettrick Shepherd* did not include music, Hogg provided headnotes to each song, giving a history of its creation, often an entertaining anecdote about its performance and frequently a reference to an existing musical setting. These headnotes add the 'personal touch', and, by giving the broader context for each song, they do a wonderful public relations job for Hogg. Without these notes the reader, while appreciating the wide-ranging patriotism, humour, tenderness and feistiness of the lyrics alone, would have little idea of just how important the genre of song was to Hogg's developing career, or of his wider musical celebrity.

After *Songs by the Ettrick Shepherd* there were no other major publications of Hogg's songs during his lifetime, but in the decades following his death several of his songs established their place in the canon of national and, indeed, popular song.[35] His 'Lament of Flora Macdonald', 'Bonnie Prince Charlie' (or 'Cam ye by Athole'), 'Donald MacDonald', 'The Skylark' (or 'Bird of the Wilderness') and the timeless 'When the kye comes hame', in particular, found favour with editors and music publishers throughout the nineteenth century, and his position as the key 'Scottish Songster' after Burns was secured. This is a fact that would have pleased Hogg, for in his final, substantially expanded 'Memoir' of 1832 – written just after he had compiled *Songs* – he retrospectively declared his intentions to 'follow in the steps of Burns'.[36] Hogg's self-deprecating anecdote of scraping tunes on his fiddle after the dance at Mr Scott's gave way to the confident affirmation that his soul had been invested with a 'heavenly gift' for 'immortal song'.[37]

CHAPTER ELEVEN

Hogg as Poet

Fiona Wilson

James Hogg's poetry can be described as 'Romantic' in ways as various as that much contested term itself. Most immediately, it emerges from the historical era still described as the Romantic period, an age shaped by revolution, war and, in Britain, by the growth of an increasingly democratised reading – and writing – public. Hogg wrote poetry in response to the first two circumstances and, as an author, saw himself as inevitably engaged with the third. Repeatedly, his poetry invokes the scenario of an ideal circle of readers and writers, a notional public before which he performs. In his earliest works, that public is grounded in Lowland culture, in balladry and in the example of Burns; later poems show the effects of the poet's move to Edinburgh and his abrupt immersion in metropolitan print culture.

Like other Romantic poets, Hogg explored such popular conventions as minstrelsy, romance, verse narrative, natural description, and flights of Promethean vision. Similarly, he pushed metrical experiments that, for example, put pawky ballad rhythms cheek by jowl with the consciously urbane patterns of the Spenserian stanza. Where Byron mugs the tragic aristocrat, Hogg performs the natural poet; where Coleridge frets about the Satanic imagination, Hogg considers the benefits of space travel. Yet, even as Hogg seeks to create a community, his poetry is often marked by a sense of struggle. This struggle shows up in his competitive relations with other writers and in his simultaneous embrace and distrust of Romanticism as an ideology (a Romantic gesture in itself). For Hogg, the contradictions of Romantic poetry are far from abstract; they represent the direct consequence of his all-too-real fight to survive in the bruising creative economy of the nineteenth-century poetry market.

Perhaps all poets begin with the experience of language as problematic pleasure, pleasurable problem. Certainly, Hogg's first exposure to the possible languages of poetry was complex, derived as it was from both oral and written traditions. The first poetry he ever heard surely came from the mouth of his mother, the ballad singer Margaret Laidlaw; other rhythms arrived via writers like Alexander Pope, Oliver Goldsmith, and James Beattie, 'old canon' precursors that Hogg at once absorbed and kicked against. From the sentimental writer Allan Ramsay, Hogg learned how to perform the pastoral poet, a persona he draws upon in his first publication, *Scottish Pastorals* (1801); still, Hogg's performance as Arcadian naïf is already complicated by the far-from-naive presence of Robert Burns. Hogg's account of the shocked delight he felt on hearing 'Tam o' Shanter' recited in 1797 reveals much about his excitement at encountering the Scots language used by a brilliant, experimental labouring-class poet. Burns offered Hogg a powerfully enabling example of what could done at the interface of oral and written poetry – as well as a warning, of course, of the risks of being typecast as a 'natural' or 'peasant poet'. With *The Mountain Bard* (1807), his first 'official' published book, the new author invoked a broader circle of writers and readers and further developed his self-presentation: the pastoral poet was beginning to be replaced by the more culturally prestigious figure of the bard.

In taking up the mantle of Scottish bard, Hogg was, of course, provoking a print exchange with yet another writer: Walter Scott, best known to the reading nation of 1807 as the ballad-collector of *The Minstrelsy of the Scottish Border* (1802–3) and as the author of *The Lay of the Last Minstrel* (1805), both of which deeply affected Hogg's poetry, opening up creative possibilities but also provoking instinctive objections – a sense of difference that was to be critical to his notion of himself as a poet. One of Hogg's major objections to the *Minstrelsy* was Scott's refusal to include a stash of Hogg's own recent ballad imitations; and in important ways *The Mountain Bard* is the consequence of that objection, 'an answer', as Suzanne Gilbert writes, to Scott's project in the form of ten ballad 'imitations' and eleven 'Songs Adapted to the Times'.[1] The parallels are overt: some ballads expand upon themes introduced in *The Minstrelsy*, others commemorate the Scott family in Border tales that, Hogg deliberately reminds us, include *his* ancestors too; the whole is buttressed, antiquarian-style, with lengthy notes. Yet, even as *The Mountain Bard* nods towards a shared history, Hogg carefully stakes out his own, often critical, perspective. For the son of Margaret Laidlaw, the ballad is not a fly in the amber of polite culture, but something living and creative, part of a tradition still undergoing transformation as it moves from speaker to speaker, to writer and reader – especially where the reader is a poet too. Moreover, if Hogg is in dialogue with Scott, he is also in the business of tracing another ideal circle of writers and readers (living and dead). The second part of *The Mountain Bard*, 'Songs Adapted to the Times', exhibits Hogg's skills as a lyricist along with his links to other labouring class writers, including Burns, as well as the brothers Thomas and Allan Cunningham. Hogg's relationship with Scott was part of a larger network of different possibilities for Hogg as a writer.

The Mountain Bard is a more crafted book than it has sometimes been given credit for. However, it was Hogg's forced decision to move to Edinburgh in 1810 and 'push my fortunes as a literary man' that truly transformed the practice of his art, as well as his conception of himself as a poet.[2] Within months, the former shepherd was at home in a cultural metropolis at once intellectual, convivial, competitive – and deeply responsive to the work of writers such as William Wordsworth, Walter Scott, Robert Southey, Thomas Campbell and, soon, George Gordon, Lord Byron. It took effort, at first, for Hogg to find his feet as a professional writer, but he quickly became an enthusiastic theatregoer and public debater, and his talent for friendship propelled his involvement in a series of overlapping literary circles, from booksellers and publishers to polite female readers. These aspects of Hogg's Edinburgh life – his interest in theatricality and in different registers of speech; his shocking, if exciting, immersion in the cut-and-thrust of early nineteenth century print culture; his painful awareness of the power of audiences and readers to decide success; and his ambition to outperform other poets – very much shaped his future productions, most markedly *The Queen's Wake* (1813), Hogg's best known poetic work and the major success of his career.

At first glance, *The Queen's Wake* is pure costume drama spectacle, all starched ruffs and jingling reins, a verse romance set in a safely picturesque sixteenth-century Scotland. The volume's frame tale concerns the fictional establishment by Mary, Queen of Scots of a 'wake', or nightly bardic competition, to entertain and pacify her unruly new subjects. Closer consideration, however, suggests that the spectacle on hand is really that of early nineteenth-century Edinburgh. Mary as listener is conflated with Princess Charlotte, the dedicatee of the book and, further, with the female readers who increasingly composed a significant part of the British reading public and whose 'courtesy' and 'friendship' are repeatedly appealed to by the poet. Gillian Hughes rightly connects the bardic contest to the kinds of competitive spectacle Hogg loved to watch and participate in (for example, the public debates at the Edinburgh Forum), but the contest can also be seen as a version of the poetry market writ large.[3] Hogg actually insets into the book portraits of writers he knew, the circle of his most immediate peers and readers: the Fourteenth Bard is John Grieve, the Ettrick-born businessman who supported Hogg in his early days in Edinburgh; the Fifteenth Bard is the Reverend James Gray, Hogg's future brother-in-law; the Sixteenth Bard is Allan Cunningham. Hogg appears as 'himself' twice, as the Tenth Bard and as the narrator of the frame tale, a self-duplication that permits him to manipulate the risky role of the natural poet – just as Hogg's countryman Byron had so recently manipulated the role of the decadent aristocrat in the first two Cantos of *Childe Harold* (1812). Though the Tenth Bard is initially the object of snobbish scorn, his skill ultimately wins him the second place prize of the Caledonian Harp – and, one intuits, the symbolic first prize.

Still, the form of the *Wake* has other purposes too – not least, the fact that it allows Hogg to further stage his versatility as a poet. The First Night, for example, pits three distinctly different performers and rhetorical styles against each other: Mary's Italian favourite, David Rizzio, presents 'Malcolm of Lorn', the overwrought tale of a sensitive mama's boy; the Second Bard, Gardyn, follows with 'Young Kennedy', a piece of Highland *Sturm und Drang*; the unidentified Eighth Bard sings 'The Witch of Fife', a vigorous ballad about a witch's night-time shenanigans – and the unfortunate fate of her nosy husband. This group of alleged period pieces represents key aspects of Romantic taste. Where Rizzio's polysyllabic rhymes suggest a dig at the popular 'tirly-whirly' Italian music Hogg so disliked (and just possibly at the developing taste for all things Italian among metropolitan readers), Gardyn's stark melodrama draws on the powerful cultural capital of the northern sublime. Together they propose a Burkean binary, Rizzio's feminised 'beautiful' versus Gardyn's manly 'sublime' – a malign pairing satisfyingly interrupted by the battle of the sexes in 'The Witch of Fife'.

With its moonstruck pleasures and driving ballad rhythm, 'The Witch of Fife' looks forward to the best-loved poem of *The Queen's Wake*, 'Kilmeny'. A young maiden lies down in the greenwood, falls asleep, and disappears for seven years. Waking in 'ane farr cuntrye', she is instructed by spirits and shown a surreal tapestry of Scotland's future: an enthroned lady (Mary) is bitten by a snake, a coffin appears on a plain, a lion (Scotland) is crowned with the rose and clover leaf, a fierce people (the French) burst forth with revolutionary fervour; the British lion fights with and defeats the French eagle ('Night Second', l.1408).[4] 'Kilmeny' represents a fascinating intervention into British Romantic poetry because of the way it marries traditional tales of dream-travel, such as the story of Tam Lin, with the apocalyptic futurity of Romantic idealism. Like Coleridge's *The Rime of the Ancient Mariner* (1798) (a poem which Hogg certainly knew), 'Kilmeny' deploys a funky, faux-medieval language to tell the story of a character who crosses the boundary between the real and spirit worlds. Like Shelley's 'Queen Mab' (1813) (a poem which Hogg almost certainly did *not* know), 'Kilmeny' features a heroine gifted with a vision of things as they are and may yet be. But 'Kilmeny' also displays qualities quite specific to Hogg's own sensibility. Though Kilmeny is celebrated for her bold imaginative quest, her position is ironised by her inability, on her return, to communicate where she has been or what she has seen. Worse, in a further rap to Romantic idealism, the recital of Kilmeny's tale by the Thirteen Bard (Drummond) produces little more than a yawn from the weary courtiers, who fail to recognise in the ballad a prophecy of Mary's future destruction. It is a wonderful touch, and it brings the entirely modern and historical implications of the *Wake* sharply back into focus. In 'The Conclusion', although the Tenth Bard does win recognition from the court, his victory emerges from a background of fractious struggle and it is the image of the mob of competing bards that persists. As Hogg would later complain of the increasingly politicised environment of Edinburgh publishing, '['t]was party all, not minstrel worth . . .' ('Conclusion', l. 83).

That Hogg, by 1813, saw himself as moving onto a larger creative stage is clearly indicated by the projects that followed *The Queen's Wake*: *Mador of the Moor* (1816), *Pilgrims of the Sun* (1815), and the planned compilation of a 'Poetical Repository', a collection of poems from leading British writers to be published half-yearly. Hogg was active in seeking contributors for the Repository and, within months, had introduced himself to the superstar poet of the moment, Lord Byron. In September 1814, he travelled with future *Blackwood's* editor John Wilson to Grasmere to visit William and Dorothy Wordsworth, where he also met Robert Southey and Thomas de Quincey. The visit was a mixed success. Wordsworth's demand in the famous 'Preface' to *Lyrical Ballads* for a poetry rooted in rural life and written in a 'language really spoken by men' could be seen as a virtual programme for a writer like Hogg; Wordsworth's and Coleridge's avant-garde ballads, furthermore, are, in themselves, a form of modern imitation.[5] Yet, the visit of 1814 produced evidence of rivalry too, including the notorious incident in which Wordsworth allegedly snubbed Hogg's enthusiastic praise of the 'meeting of the poets' with the rejoinder, 'Poets? Poets? – What does the fellow mean? – Where are they?'[6]

For his part, Hogg was greatly amused by the Lakers' self-congratulatory coterie; later, when the anticipated contributions to the Poetical Repository failed to materialise, he simply substituted his own parodic imitations. *The Poetic Mirror* (1816) shamelessly, hilariously mocks Wordsworth, Coleridge, Byron, and Scott, among others (including the author himself). 'The Stranger' sends up Wordsworth's 'The Recluse'; 'Isabelle' – sleepless maiden, upset dog, lots of unanswered questions – skewers Coleridge's 'Christabel'; Byron gets a ribbing in 'The Guerrilla', and Scott in 'Wat o' the Cleuch'. The satire, however, is more contact sport than evisceration; Hogg parodies these writers because they matter to him. As Hogg moved forward in his career, the importance of Scott – and increasingly of Byron – continued to fuel his poetry.

Of all the works considered so far, *Pilgrims of the Sun* (1815) most fully reveals Hogg's desire to be recognised among the first rank of British poets, a goal flagged upfront by the volume's dedication 'To the Right Hon. Lord Byron'. Typically, the Dedication offers homage – and also a challenge – as Hogg announces his wish to 'fondly try / With thee a wild aerial strain'; at the same time, the Dedication sketches another ideal circle, invoking community between himself and Byron as fellow *Scottish* poets ('Dedication', l. 8).[7] The poem itself falls into four parts. The ballad narrative of the first section introduces another visionary medieval heroine, one Mary Lee of Carelha', a figure comparable to Kilmeny but more sophisticated and complex. While Mary's origins in Border tradition are signalled by her name ('Carelha' is Carterhaugh, the home of Tam Lin, the famous traveller to faeryland), her vision is less a matter of being 'away with the fairies' than a process of lucid, open-eyed exploration. Considerable emphasis is placed, for example, on her self-taught, sceptical intelligence, having learned 'to read, when she was young, / The books of deep divinity':

> And the more she thought, and the more she read
>   Of the ways of Heaven and Nature's plan,
> She feared the half that the bedesmen said
>   Was neither true nor plain to man. (Part First, ll. 33–4, ll. 37–40)

While this habit of questioning seems meant to cast Mary as a proleptic Protestant, it also evokes Hogg himself, a poet whose intellectual and creative curiosity pushed him, like other writers of the period, to 'dream' far beyond his given social status.

Mary's dream-journey begins with a 'shivering throb' as her soul is separated from her body. Accompanied by a spirit-guide ('Cela'), she travels into the sky '[t]o see what maid hath never seen, / And do what maid hath never done' (Part First, ll. 287–8). In Part Second, Cela and Mary fly ever closer to the sun, eventually recognised as the seat of God; Mary witnesses an inhabited universe, '[w]orlds beyond worlds', in which her beloved earth is no more than a 'cloudy spot' (Part Second, ll. 55, 137) and observes the terrible fall of a dying planet. Eventually, it becomes clear that all of the worlds Mary sees are simply possible versions of earth; two such versions are described in Part Third: Venus, 'the land where faithful lovers dwell' (Part Third, l. 39) and Mars, a place of eternal war, where 'hamlets smoked in ashes on the plain', much as Europe must have appeared after its recent battles (Part Third, l. 243). In the final section we read of Mary's difficult return to her body. Brought, like Blake's Thel, to the very pit of the grave, Mary chooses – as Thel does not – to embrace the terrestrial knowledge of eros and of death and, in the poem's final lines, she marries a mysterious wandering minstrel, Hugo of Norroway, in whom she recognises the earthly form of Cela.

As even this (drastically) truncated summary indicates, *Pilgrims of the Sun* is an audacious book: what more literal image of Romantic Prometheanism could there be than Mary Lee's out-of-body flight towards the sun? *Pilgrims* aims high formally too, each of its four sections displaying Hogg's skill with a different metrical style: the ballad rhythms of the first section are succeeded in the second by the blank verse of the Miltonic 'Harp of Jerusalem', and in the third by the rhyming couplets of Dryden and Pope and of the gleefully appropriated harp of 'Imperial England'; Part Fourth, in which Mary returns home, circles back to the same – but different – territory of iambic tetrameter (Part Second, l. 1). Meiko O'Halloran has deftly shown how these strategic literary moves can be understood, in part, as representative of a Romantic response to Dante and Milton, and usefully compared, for example, with Coleridge's *Ancient Mariner* and Byron's later *Cain* (1821).[8] Hogg's intellectual goal, O'Halloran argues, is an ecstatic marriage of Christian and pagan traditions of worship. Nevertheless, as so often with Hogg – and with Byron too – sublime yearnings must tough it out with material realities; Mary's return to her body describes a painful, but necessary, return to human history.

While *Pilgrims of the Sun* initiates a conversation with Byron, arguably the most provocative and speculative writer of the age, *Mador of the Moor* (1816) revisits Hogg's earlier creative exchanges with Scott. Contemporary readers immediately discerned the presence of Scott's *The Lady of the Lake* (1810) in Hogg's new metrical romance, and the charge of imitation was widespread: both poems begin with a royal hunt; both feature James V and draw on the 'prince-in-disguise' stories associated with that king; and both deploy the Spenserian stanza. Yet as James Barcus argues, perhaps we should be thinking less about the closed system of mimicry than the open-endedness of dialogic engagement (p. xxiii).[9] Hogg was sceptical about *The Lady of the Lake*, complaining in *The Spy* that the fancifulness of Scott's poem glossed over actual history, leading the mind to pursue 'an illusion, and [interest] itself in a professed fiction' – a statement that, coming from the future author of *Pilgrims of the Sun*, may seem a little rich, but is perhaps best understood as a comment on class and narrative, a way of saying that there is more to history than lords and ladies.[10] Certainly, *Mador* takes a pronounced interest in the illegitimate and dispossessed in telling the story of Ila Moore, who falls in love with a wandering minstrel – James V in disguise – and is left holding the baby when her lover abruptly absconds back to court.

From its opening pages, Hogg positions *Mador* in an ambivalent relationship to Scott and to the politics of literary Edinburgh; the volume's epigraph (from a poem by John Wilson: editor, Tory, frenemy) is placed in productive tension with its dedication (to John Grieve: fellow Borderer and participant in what Susan Manning describes as the 'alternative' literary Edinburgh of booksellers, female readers, and self-taught provincials).[11] Interestingly, Hogg seems to view himself as uneasily placed between both circles, with Scott – Hogg's patron? mentor? fellow author? student? – representative of everything Hogg must negotiate. In this light, Barcus's view of *Mador* as a revisionary, or 'made o'er', *Lady of the Lake* gets strong support from the poem itself. In place of Scott's courtly hunters, Hogg's readers encounter a pack of violent, privileged men whose assault on nature is implicitly compared to war and sexual predation; in place of Scott's chivalrous monarch, we meet a canny, deceptive king, full of the tricky Stuart charm, but singularly lacking in the right stuff, or at least, the stuff readers expect from heroic rulers. Though the lovers are eventually reunited and James brought to acknowledge his bastard child and his royal duties, *Mador*'s repeated allusions to ballad treatments of illegitimacy, child murder and faithless lovers set in play social tensions hardly resolved by the 'happy' ending.

Hogg's last major poetic work, *Queen Hynde* (1824), long in the making and large in scope, is an epic poem 'about the origins and roots of the Scottish nation'.[12] In imagining an ancient, pre-Christian Scotland, Hogg draws on the big-screen drama of the *Iliad*, James Macpherson's Ossianic poem *Fingal* (1762), and Scott's novels and verse romances, specifically *The Lord of the Isles* (1815). Still, with regard to the latter at least, Hogg was as ever insistent on the differences between himself and his old friend and rival: 'Dear Mr Scott', he archly insisted, 'ye could never think that I was in the chivalry school like you. I'm the king o' the mountain an fairy school a far higher ane nor your's [sic]'.[13] And, if the Clash of the Titans quality of *Fingal* is definitely present, Hogg is often busy defusing Macpherson's high solemnity with bursts of absurd, even grotesque, humour, a quality that has produced the memorable description of *Queen Hynde* as '*Fingal* with jokes'.[14] If there is a joker in this epic pack, though, it may well be Byron's *Don Juan* (1818–24), with which Hogg's poem may share a common ancestor in Ludovico Ariosto's *Orlando Furioso* (1516). Like *Don Juan*, *Queen Hynde* is a mock-epic with a serious, displaced commentary on national identity. Most interestingly, both poems provoke an aggressive dialogue with their reading audiences.

Broadly put, *Queen Hynde* describes a Scottish Arcadia threatened with foreign invasion and ultimately saved by a prince disguised as a peasant. 'There was a time – but it was gone', the poem begins (coyly invoking Scott's *Waverley* novels), when Scotland was ruled by the young and innocent Queen Hynde (Book First, l. 1). Paradise is lost, however, when a Viking army, led by Eric of Norway, invades the capital city of Beregon, a metropolis paralleled with Macpherson's Selma and (elliptically) Edinburgh as ideal capital of Scottish culture. An unexpectedly chivalrous lot, the Norwegians agree to a trial by combat, with Hynde and the crown of Scotland as reward for the victor. Things look bad for Caledonia, but at the last minute, M'Houston, a prince disguised as a peasant – in the archaic Scots word, 'hind' – bursts from the crowd to thrash Eric and take the queen's hand: in short, the hind wins Hynde and becomes king.

The story is complicated, full of subplots and minor characters with important roles. (One subplot, for example, concerns Saint Columba of Iona and the establishment of Christianity in Scotland; another focuses on the flirtatious hi-jinks of Hynde's lady-in-waiting, Wene.) The traditional 'high' matters of epic – love and war – get a full airing, but are frequently punctured by 'low' material, such as the moment in which Hynde's prophetic dream of invasion issues in the image of herself attacked by the black bull of Norway and, in absurd slow motion, '[t]ossed up the air a heideous height / On point of blood-stained horn to light!' (Book First, ll. 474–5). Much comedy is extracted from the hypocritical misogyny of St Oran, Columba's deputy on Iona; scenes of extreme violence, as in *Don Juan*, also provoke dark laughter. The poem is always conscious of its own outrageousness: 'Eternal God! What is it now?' the narrator pleads at the end of Book Fourth (l. 1144).

However, it is Hogg's repeated poking and prodding at his reader that is one of the most fascinating aspects of *Queen Hynde* (as well as the most suggestive of *Don Juan*). Once again, Hogg envisions a circle of readers that is significantly female: 'the virgin daughters of Caledonia', subsequently figured as the symbolic 'Maids of Dunedin' (i.e., Edinburgh) ("Dedication," Book First, l. 454). These addresses appeal to a female reading public that Hogg seems to feel he must woo, although he resents and resists its power – even as he also recognises the parallels between himself and his female readers as outsiders to official literary culture. 'Maid of Dunedin, thou may'st see', he warns at the close of Book First,

> That now I've changed my timid tone,
> And sing to please myself alone;
> And thou wilt read, when, well I wot,
> I care not whether you do or not.
>
> Yes I'll be querulous, or boon,
> Flow with the tide, change with the moon,
> For what am I, or what are thou . . . ? (Book First, ll. 1060–8)

That last line, of course, is distinctly Byronic, reminiscent not just of the metaphysical speculation Byron indulges in *Childe Harold* and mocks in *Don Juan*, but also of the increasingly needy, aggressive, quasi-erotic relationship of poet to reader in a market where reputation is everything, determined so often by 'party', including the politics of nationality, class and gender. Towards the end of *Queen Hynde* the bard addresses his female readers again, boldly indicting all those he refuses to include within his ideal literary circle: those who skip to the end; those who put their faith in critics; those who read at night; those who read by day; those who read without feeling or understanding; those who are in love; those who weep; those who are immodest; those who prefer foreign tunes to '[t]heir native measures'; those who sing before breakfast; those who have no sense of poetic rhythm; and, most despised of all, those who censor, rashly wielding the word 'INDELICATE' (Book Fifth, ll. 2258, 2263). It is a brash, rambunctious, obviously somewhat tongue-in-cheek assault, but at the same time a poignant appeal to the public on whose favour the poem, after all, depends.

CHAPTER TWELVE

Hogg and the Theatre

Meiko O'Halloran

This chapter examines Hogg's attempts between 1810 and 1817 to use the theatre as a vehicle for his aspirations to become a major British Romantic writer. Amid the expanding Georgian theatre and Walter Scott's project to launch a new Scottish dramatic tradition through the work of Joanna Baillie, Hogg began attending the Edinburgh Theatre Royal and trying his voice as a theatre critic in his weekly paper, *The Spy* (1810–11). After making his name as a poet with *The Queen's Wake* (1813), he attempted to launch himself as a playwright. Sharing the Romantic veneration for Shakespeare and aspiring to participate in an increasingly competitive national theatre, Hogg tried to create a new kind of historical play, *The Hunting of Badlewe* (1814), for the London stage. Using Shakespearean sources and interweaving five plots, he explored the destructive behaviour of an early Stuart court, perhaps hoping to make his fortune by mythologising the Stuarts as Shakespeare had immortalised the Tudors. The play was never performed and received no critical attention when it was published. The disappointing reception of Hogg's subsequent collection of plays, *Dramatic Tales* (1817), ended his efforts as a playwright. This chapter suggests that, though unsuccessful, Hogg's experimental theatre criticism and playwriting were crucial to the innovative narrative techniques that emerged in his fiction in the 1820s. Hogg would use competing narratives and shifting perspectives far more successfully in his prose tales and novels. However, the formative process of repositioning himself in relation to his audience and rethinking the role of readers began in the theatre in the 1810s.

By his own account, Hogg composed his first play, a comedy called 'The Scotch Gentleman', as early as 1795, while he was a shepherd in the Scottish Borders.[1] Over the following years, he developed an admiration for the work of Shakespeare. Stopping at Edinburgh en route to the Highlands in the summer of 1802, he saw a production of *Hamlet* ('one of the best plays of my favourite author'); the following year his feelings were 'wrought to the highest pitch of horror' on reading the 'monstrous tragedy of *Titus Andronicus*' as he travelled to Lewis in the Outer Hebrides.[2] Following his failure as a tenant-farmer, Hogg moved from the countryside to Edinburgh in February 1810 to become a professional writer. He attended the theatre regularly, observing the reactions of urban audiences and the potential rewards (accolades and profit) of a successful production. His knowledge of Dr Johnson's work may have prompted him to recall that Shakespeare himself had entered the literary kingdom with no advantages: 'The genius of Shakespeare was not to be depressed by the weight of poverty [. . .]; the incumbrances of his fortune were shaken from his mind, "as dewdrops from a lion's mane".'[3] With his innate talent and resilience in the face of adversity, Shakespeare epitomised the kind of active and vigorous natural genius which Hogg, as a peasant poet facing material hardship, found profoundly inspiring. The density of Shakespearean allusions in Hogg's first serious play, *The Hunting of Badlewe*, suggests that he had read most of Shakespeare's plays by the time he began composing it in the spring of 1813.

Shakespeare was also a source of national inspiration, attracting widespread veneration in the eighteenth century and the Romantic period as a literary forefather who strengthened Britain's changing identity. By the time Johnson wrote his 'Preface to Shakespeare' (1765), he had been canonised as a national poet whose cultural authority was felt to reflect Britain's transformation from a Stuart autocracy to a modern commercial society under the Hanoverians.[4] Throughout the embattled era of the French Revolution and the Napoleonic wars, Shakespeare seemed to fulfil the role of an ancestral bard, bringing the past to life and celebrating Britain's heritage. As the popularity of his English history plays continued to shape the national consciousness, Scottish playwrights naturally sought to bring Scottish stories to the stage as part of a new era in British history.

In December 1756, the first performance of John Home's tragedy *Douglas* in the Canongate Theatre appeared to offer a new dawn for Scottish theatre. 'Whaur's yer Wully Shakspere noo!' an excited patriot was said to have shouted.[5] But a substantial indigenous dramatic tradition failed to take immediate root.[6] However, by the time Hogg moved to the city, the Edinburgh Theatre Royal was beginning a new lease of life and he was impressed by the opportune moment for new Scottish drama. Under Scott's direction, the Edinburgh Theatre Royal reopened on 29 January 1810 with a spectacular production of Baillie's *The Family Legend* (1810), which played to crowded houses for three weeks. Writing in *The Spy* about the audience's enthusiastic applause for the Highland music, Hogg wondered why Scottish theatregoers did not 'assert their rights' to hear more Scottish music in their theatres, especially after London theatregoers had 'made good their right of chusing [sic] their own prices of admission' in the newly rebuilt Covent Garden Theatre in the Old Price riots of 1809.[7] 'Performers are paid for the purpose of pleasing people,' he argued, 'not for shewing [sic] them their superiority in the art.'[8] In this passage, as elsewhere, Hogg is interested in breaking down the authority of a 'high' artistic performance and making the theatre an inclusive experience in which members of the audience have a 'right' to expect their own tastes and views to be represented.

As an ambitious writer who was eagerly 'spying' out new literary roles for himself, Hogg was fascinated by the power of theatre audiences to reject or endorse performances. In the early 1810s, as Hogg joined the Edinburgh theatrical milieu, a wealth of criticism on the drama reflected the increasing power of the Georgian theatre to shape the national character. Leading critics included Coleridge, Charles Lamb, Leigh Hunt, Elizabeth Inchbald and, most prolifically, William Hazlitt, whose essays on the drama began to appear regularly in *The Morning Chronicle* in 1813. Critical discussions of the theatre stimulated Hogg's aspirations as both a critic and a dramatist. His editorial persona, 'Mr Spy', aptly suggests the power of viewing to gain a purchase on society. Although the name implies a surreptitious onlooker, Hogg was a familiar and welcome figure at the Edinburgh Theatre, the manager, Henry Siddons, even allowing him to attend plays without charge.[9] The theatre became a panorama in which Hogg observed a social spectrum of actors, writers, directors, and audience members. His enjoyment of theatre-going is captured in his role-playing as a critic. Turning his observations of the Edinburgh Theatre into semi-fictional pieces of theatre criticism, which appeared alongside his poems and stories in *The Spy*, Hogg explored ways of shifting his perspective from the actors' performances to the audience's reactions.

By multiplying his critical personae in *The Spy* and dramatising the reactions of a group of spectators, Hogg was able to present a range of perspectives on theatre performances. At the start of the theatre season in November 1810, Mr Spy attends a performance of *The Clandestine Marriage* with his country-bumpkin friend, John Miller (another avatar of Hogg), and 'a charming young lady from the country' (Hogg's future wife, Margaret Phillips).[10] With no previous experience of the theatre, Miller gently criticises the appearance and abilities of the actors in his homely Scots register ('he speaks no that ill, puir chiel, but he has unco glazed, empty-like een'), making naive references to characters such as '*the dawtie*' (the darling or pet).[11] By displacing an unpretentious and instinctive enjoyment of the theatre on to Miller and showing Mr Spy's interest in his friend's opinions, Hogg is able to value Miller's clear-sightedness while developing a more refined critical voice for Mr Spy, whose critique of the management of the theatre and the strengths and weaknesses of the principal actors exhibits his extensive knowledge of the company. Collectively, John Miller's candid remarks, Margaret's laughter, and Mr Spy's opinions serve to break down the boundaries between the audience and the actors.

The combination of the functions of theatre critic, director, and actor anticipates the Ettrick Shepherd's directions to his imagined audience of modern female readers in *Queen Hynde* (1824). In this mock epic, which Hogg began composing after *Dramatic Tales*, the narrator repeatedly upbraids and teases the 'Maids of Dunedin' for their feeble acting abilities and slow responses to the protagonists' performances. The theatricality of Hogg's multiple responses in *The Spy* begins to suggest that what happens on stage is not so much 'high art' as an extension of the social role-playing that goes on in the audience. For the rest of his career, Hogg sought to expand the role of readers through his role-playing and his frequent shifting of narrative perspectives. In poems such as *The Queen's Wake* and *Queen Hynde*, readers are guided by the reactions of a fictional audience. In his novels and stories, however, Hogg often challenges readers by removing a stable sense of narrative authority. In *The Private Memoirs and Confessions of a Justified Sinner* (1824), the Editor is both a reader of the sinner's memoir and the biased narrator of a rival version of events; the open-endedness of the novel invites readers to interpret the competing narratives for themselves. In his playwriting too, Hogg tested his audience's expectations of a work of art and their relationship to it.

Following his success with *The Queen's Wake* in January 1813, Hogg sought to participate in the making of British theatre by composing a new kind of historical drama which he hoped to offer for performance in London. Hogg was among many Romantic poets who hoped to gain fame and fortune as a playwright. By the 1810s theatres could hold several thousand spectators, and the profits for commercially successful plays were huge. Coleridge, for example, made £400 from the successful run of his tragedy, *Remorse*, for twenty nights at Drury Lane, beginning on 23 January 1813.[12] Actors such as Sarah Siddons and John Philip Kemble were hailed as celebrities of the Romantic age. The enormous popularity of the theatre made this an especially exciting moment for an ambitious Scottish dramatist to enter the London scene. However, Hogg was acutely aware that the elevated genre of the drama was not the traditional territory of peasant poets; shepherds might compose ballads or appear in pastoral dramas such as Allan Ramsay's *The Gentle Shepherd* (1725), but writing a history play or a tragedy for an educated urban audience was a bold enterprise for a labouring-class autodidact.

Hogg worked on his play for a year, confiding his efforts only to a handful of supporters, from whom he requested the strictest secrecy.[13] After reading the play, his friends advised him against offering it to a theatre. Instead, *The Hunting of Badlewe; A Dramatic Tale* was published in April 1814, under the gentrified pseudonym 'J. H. Craig of Douglas Esq.', with a preface in which the author explained his 'experiment in dramatic composition'.[14] If the play was well received, Hogg could triumphantly reveal his authorship, but to his disappointment, his attempts to get admirers of *The Queen's Wake*, such as Robert Southey and Lord Byron, to read the play proved futile.[15]

The Hunting of Badlewe (retitled 'The Profligate Princes' in *Dramatic Tales*) presents a sinister culture of profligacy, in which a group of Scottish princes and courtiers disguise themselves as lesser nobles in order to pursue and ruin the wives and daughters of Scottish barons. Hogg dramatises a power struggle between the nobility and the crown which overshadowed the reigns of Robert III of Scotland (1390–1406) and his forefathers, Robert II (1371–90) and David II (1329–71). Since the five King Jameses were direct descendants of Robert III and Annabel Drummond, the hero and heroine of Hogg's play, it seems likely that Hogg was aiming to cultivate a Stuart mythology much as Shakespeare had done for the Tudors. Adapting historical events from Raphael Holinshed's *Chronicles of England, Scotland, and Ireland* (1577), Hogg invented a romantic betrothal between Robert and Annabel which rescues the nation.[16] In fact, they had been married for over a decade before Robert succeeded to the throne at the age of fifty-three and they even had a twelve-year-old heir. Hogg carefully promotes Robert and Annabel as guardians of the nation, whose love will save the precarious Scottish court from Robert's illegitimate brother, the Earl of Buchan – the notorious 'Wolf of Badenoch' who terrorised his countrymen in the lawless interim in 1390 between his father's death and his brother's succession. Lord Badenoch is the most treacherous of the hunters in Hogg's play. In reinventing historical figures for the stage, Hogg freely drew on different phases of their careers, explicitly aligning his approach with that of Shakespeare: 'we should never have seen a RICHARD or a MACBETH, had the Author confined himself to any single period of their lives' (pp. vi–vii).

For his chief innovation in *The Hunting of Badlewe*, Hogg interweaves five concurrent plots. Although the multiple plots are confusing, Hogg gives compelling reasons for his 'dissent' from the dramatic unities. The conventional structure of one main plot with 'one great leading action' was too restrictive, he argued in his preface, in that it reduced characters to 'the influence of that one passion, which predominates [. . .] in the particular circumstances, in which that individual may be placed' (pp. v–vi). Here, Hogg implicitly takes issue with Baillie's 'Introductory Discourse' to her *Plays on the Passions* (1798). Whereas Baillie had focused each of her plays on a single ruling passion such as love or hatred, Hogg wanted to find a way of depicting the 'many various passions and feelings [which] sway the human heart, at the different periods of life' (p. v). Instead of representing a single major incident, he approached his play as 'a tale or history' in which he drew on a range of the individual's experiences (p. vi). By presenting an array of interrelated plots, he hoped to display the characters more fully, thereby engaging the feelings of the audience. Unfortunately, these ideas are not borne out

in the play. Hogg's use of multiple plots restricts the psychological development of the characters, leaving little room for the audience to enter into
their feelings. He would use an extensive temporal scope more effectively in
Queen Hynde and his novels; indeed, the runaway success of Scott's *Waverley*
(1814) a few months later demonstrated the exciting possibilities for the
novel's accommodation of an epic approach to history. While Hogg did not
succeed in his aims in the drama, he experimented with several provocative
storytelling techniques in *The Hunting of Badlewe* which he carried forward
and developed in his fiction.

Hogg sought to involve his audience in his play by breaking down familiar
dramatic forms and conventions. His sprawling use of plots seems intended
to draw readers into the disintegration of social order faced by the protagonists. Hogg spells out the wider implications of the breeding of moral
corruption from the royal court in a speech by one of the wronged barons,
who articulates the devastating social and national consequences of the
hunters' lawless pursuits. After discovering that the chief villain, Badenoch,
is Prince Alexander Stewart, heir to the Scottish throne (historically, he was
a younger son of Robert II), Lord Crawford finds his faith in God's authority
shaken. He laments:

> that those in stations dignified,
> Who stand as patterns to be copied forth
> By rank to rank succeeding, thus should stain
> The annals of our land, by open violence
> Of every precept that enlinks mankind,
> And marks the bounds of honour and of shame!
> Misrule, so palpable and so unvarnished,
> Make's [sic] one to doubt of heaven's supremacy,
> And wrangle with his Maker.[17]

As Crawford's soliloquy suggests, the abuse of authority by those who are
appointed to rule society has a pervasive effect. The careful preservation
of 'stations dignified' from 'rank to rank succeeding' is disturbed by a moral
darkness which 'stain[s] / The annals of our land' – seeping into the writing
of national history and inciting rebelliousness against the God-given social
hierarchy. In a similar way, the mysterious structure of Hogg's third novel,
The Three Perils of Woman (1823), sweeps readers into the relentless turns
of individual and national fortune experienced by the protagonists. Moving
through a bewildering series of 'circles' (rather than chapters), readers find
themselves entangled in plots which repeatedly shift between comedy and
tragedy, beginning in Edinburgh in the 1820s and moving backwards to
the harrowing aftermath of Culloden. Just as readers of the novel are left to
interpret the implications of Hogg's enigmatic rewriting of Scottish history,

so readers of *The Hunting of Badlewe* have their faith in a guiding literary authority shaken.

Hogg further alerts readers to the moral disorder of his protagonists' world through his unconventional use of Shakespearean motifs. Far from being derivative, Hogg's allusions to Shakespearean drama highlight his originality. He introduces motifs which invite the reader's sense of familiarity, only to depart from well-known dramatic situations in surprising ways. For example, in keeping with Shakespearean comedy, we might expect Badenoch to be unaware that his page is actually a noblewoman, Elenor March, in disguise. However, Hogg unexpectedly employs disguise and cross-dressing for tragic effect. Unlike Viola in *Twelfth Night* or Rosalind in *As You Like It*, Elen is kept in thrall by Badenoch as an object of sexual convenience. Badenoch's violation of the conventions of comic romance makes his villainy all the more shocking.

Hogg also challenges his readers' expectations by introducing characters who repeatedly borrow and discard Shakespearean roles. Their continuous role-playing has the effect of forcing readers to attend closely to possible literary allusions in order to keep up with the changing inflections of the narrative. The most striking example of this occurs when Badenoch abandons Elen with their unborn child and kills her father for challenging him. At this crisis point, Elen moves through a succession of Shakespearean likenesses, none of which fully fits her. Lord Crawford's description of Elen's madness as she stands at the edge of a stream 'in strange fantastic mood', gazing at 'something by wild imagination framed', strongly recalls Gertrude's account of the death of Ophelia, drowned in a brook while wearing 'fantastic garlands' of flowers.[18] After drowning a single flower in place of herself, however, Elen begins to resemble Lady Macbeth, obsessively 'washing her fair hands' and attempting to extinguish an imaginary lamp. Elen's successive transformations in the perceptions of those around her heighten our impression of her solitariness, suggesting that no literary archetype can capture her individual experience.

Elen's frantic attempts to wash her hands may remind readers that although she has none of Lady Macbeth's culpability, there is nevertheless a stain on her purity. Her subsequent appearance as a 'country maiden' in 'fantastic russet dress', and the way in which she communicates her experience of rape through the image of a 'little virgin flower' ravished by a poppy, makes a disturbing contrast to the scene in *The Winter's Tale* in which Perdita discourses on the significance of gillyvors ('which some call nature's bastards') and the merits of assisting nature by 'marry[ing] / A gentler scion to the wildest stock'.[19] Elen's passing resemblance to Perdita is filled with tragic irony, since she has lost her innocence to the wildest of princes and is carrying their illegitimate child. Hogg's use of shape-shifting characters builds on his earlier interest in the interaction of audience and performers in *The Spy* and *The*

Queen's Wake. His protagonists' role-playing now, in effect, invites readers to participate in the drama by occupying a series of different roles in relation to the characters. To miss an allusion in *The Hunting of Badlewe* is to miss one's cue as a proactive reader on an ever shifting narrative stage.

Hogg repeatedly attempted to launch himself as a dramatist between the composition of *The Hunting of Badlewe* in 1813 and the publication of *Dramatic Tales* in 1817. As Karl Miller remarks, his other plays are full of Shakespearean allusions: to *Romeo and Juliet* and *Othello* in 'Sir Antony Moore', to *A Midsummer Night's Dream* in 'The Haunted Glen', and to *Macbeth* in 'All Hallow Eve'. And although Hogg's plays look back to an ancient world, his exploration of moral darkness in 'All Hallow Eve' also looks forward to *Confessions of a Justified Sinner*, as Miller goes on to suggest.[20] Hogg later reflected that during the mid-1810s he had adopted 'the resolution of writing a drama every year as long as I lived, hoping to make myself perfect by degrees, as a man does in his calling, by serving an apprenticeship'.[21] As his 'resolution' implies, Hogg found playwriting a labour-intensive and restrictive exercise. Nevertheless, his experiences as a theatregoer, a theatre critic, and a playwright crucially informed his innovative narrative techniques. In the competing narratives of *Confessions of a Justified Sinner*, his characters appear in various roles: Robert Wringhim is a hypocrite, a victim, a fanatic, a murderer, a possible schizophrenic, the Devil, a bewitched body, and a disintegrating corpse. Through a series of distorting narrative lenses, readers are invited to view the breeding of Robert's moral corruption and the mysterious manifestations of a satanic antagonist who has the 'cameleon art' of changing his appearance.[22] The novel's competing narratives demand a correspondingly protean performance from his readers. Just when readers are convinced that Robert is mad, one reviewer complained, the novel produces witnesses to substantiate his delusions, forcing readers to readjust their interpretations – 'as great an annoyance as if the audience were compelled to change their dresses three or four times during a performance, instead of the actors'.[23] In the fluid medium of fiction, Hogg created his most exciting and original work, forcing readers to react to the characters' performances – an impulse that arose directly from his experience of the theatre.

CHAPTER THIRTEEN

Hogg and the Short Story

John Plotz

In the story of the short story, James Hogg has perpetually found himself out of place, out of time, and surprisingly out of luck. Hogg belongs after all to the first generation of authors who in Scotland, England, America, and even Russia began to produce substantial numbers of works that bore many of the features associated with the modern short story. The peak of Hogg's reputation, in the 1820s, coincides with the appearances of masterworks – by Walter Scott, Washington Irving, Edgar Allan Poe, Alexander Pushkin – that for nearly two centuries have struck a surprising range of critics as embodying the genre's essential features.

Far from being hailed as a forefather, though, Hogg barely rates a mention in most histories of the modern genre. It was compression, psychological penetration, and above all singleness of effect that Poe picked out as the essence of Nathaniel Hawthorne's short fiction in 1842 – and scholars have generally shaped their generic taxonomies around some variant of the same list ever since.[1] Even more than the novel, Brander Matthews proclaimed a generation later, the short story 'is one of the few sharply defined literary forms. It is a *genre* [. . .] a species as a Naturalist might call it, as individual as the Lyric itself'.[2] A remarkably durable consensus, critical and creative alike, coalesced around the insistence that, in Poe's terms, 'a certain unique or single *effect*' would be the acme of the author's ambition, and that 'the immense force derivable from *totality*' would henceforth be understood as an unmistakable impression produced on the reader by a single event.[3]

This formal constraint, if rigorously applied, makes unavailable to the short story a range of other options, many of them essential components of the realist novel. Oscillation between detachment and absorption appears to be out of the question, for instance, as does the temporal unfolding, the delay, and experiential accumulation that Ian Watt identifies as crucial to eighteenth-century notions of fictive realism. If post-1830 novels can succeed by varying or combining different temporal schemes, so that effects are spread out through flashback, concentrated to a sensation, or understood only retrospectively, short stories have no such luxury: every detail must 'tell'. Goethe influentially described the short story as presenting an eruption of the fantastical into the everyday – 'a singular or unprecedented event which occurs as part of everyday reality'[4] – but even here the 'singular' has its place. It is the moment of fantastical disruption around which all explanations, and all of the story's actions, must coalesce.

Poe's categories have, however, been rethought in a number of productive ways recently.[5] Recent attention to the role that *The Thousand and One Nights* played in shaping emerging conceptions of fiction in early modern Europe provides a welcome alternative to a straightforward history that walks dutifully through *Spectator* sketches (of the 'Inkle and Yarico' variety) and the performative arabesques that structure Eliza Haywood's *Fantomina* to arrive, by a kind of motiveless teleology, at Maria Edgeworth's moral and national tales.[6] The various pre-genres to the modern short story – among them the fabliaux, dirty jokes and shaggy dog stories that crop up in Aesop, and migrate in various ways from *The Thousand and One Nights* to *The Decameron* and Chaucer – offer a much more varied set of contributing antecedents to nineteenth-century short fiction.

That development bodes well for the case of Romanticism. Both Dean Baldwin's influential 'delay' hypothesis – that Britain lagged behind America in establishing the genre of the short story – and Barbara Korte's counter-argument – that English short fiction can be traced smoothly back to six-teenth-century 'coney-catching' tales – radically underestimate the Scottish romantic-era experimental short fiction that explored the widest register of naive and sentimental effects, and derived its claims for literary authority from as wide a range as did the poetry of the day.[7] Perhaps it will soon be possible for critics and theorists of the short story to attempt a 'loser's history' of the genre, told by way of the evanescent experiments and unreprinted forays of the past two centuries. In that context, Hogg's star may rise again: not simply as another example of the 'tangled bank' of experiments in the generation before Poe's code took hold, but also as the descendant of certain of the most devilish, perversely complicated and narratively complex tricks of earlier short fiction. 'The Ettrick Scheherazade' would, after all, be no more outlandish a title than others Hogg bore.

In the postmodern era, Hogg's stories may yet come to be valued for their affinity to certain strategies that have altered, if not yet fundamentally reshaped, the short story's remit: pastiche, parody, frame-shifting, editorial games, polyglot puzzles, and various of the other formal tricks sometimes now credited to 'minor' literature (in the sense mapped out by Deleuze and Guattari).[8] Just as André Gide championed *The Private Memoirs and Confessions of a Justified Sinner* at a crucial late Modernist moment, the ghostly frisson of 'Cousin Mattie' and the ingenious troubling of animal–

human boundaries in 'The Pongos' may yet spark a twenty-first-century recrudescence for Hogg's short fiction.

Hogg's work is, nonetheless, anchored very firmly in the debates about the textuality, fictionality and literary authority of his own day. Hogg's response to those debates, this chapter argues, propelled him towards a kind of fiction that was distinct from that of his peers and fundamentally incompatible with the post-1830 critical consensus that began with Poe and was codified and promulgated by Brander Matthews and his successors down to the present day. In fact, Hogg is almost an anti-Poe, a writer dedicated to demonstrating the impossibility of singleness of effect. Hogg's quarter-century of fiction writing began in 1810 with *The Spy* and eventually spread to the scores of tales, stories, elaborated jokes, sketches, records of local customs, melodramatic vignettes and linked story cycles that in diverse ways constitute the core of such books as *Winter Evening Tales*, *The Shepherd's Calendar*, *Altrive Tales*, and *The Three Perils of Man*. Robert Crawford has made a persuasive case that *The Spy* is 'one of the places the modern short story was born'.[9] However, Hogg's commitment to the staging of conflict between narrative frames – not simply shifting focalisation, but actively disrupting it – makes his fictional experiments fundamentally different from Poe's. Hogg produced texts with central mysteries that lend themselves to various sorts of explanation – Satanic possession, individual madness, collective delusion, or simply the distorting lens of history – but which finally resist the triumph of any one explanatory schema over its alternatives. Hogg practised what could be called (on the model of Bakhtin's 'polyglossia') *polydoxy*, which stages the intersection of profoundly disjunctive belief systems within a single piece of fiction.

To understand what Hogg's short fiction is, it may help to begin with what it is not. Walter Allen once declared Scott's 'The Two Drovers' 'the story that I recognise as the first modern short story in English'.[10] David Cecil, praising Scott's short stories over his novels, revealingly claimed that Scott lacked the 'sense of form' but was saved in such short works as 'Two Drovers' because '[a] short story is by definition the record of an isolated incident'.[11] Both critics understand Scott's mastery of short fiction to consist in the gradual winnowing out of alternative possibilities for understanding a given incident, until what stands revealed is what Poe called 'the single effect'.

In 'The Two Drovers' the murder of an Englishman by a Highlander and the latter's execution at the Carlisle Assizes serve to reconcile all divergent world views under a single, universally acknowledged justice – a justice that is recognised by the man doomed to die under it: '"I give a life for the life I took," he said, "and what can I do more?"'[12] 'The Two Drovers' highlights in Scott's short fiction what might be called a gathering effect. Franco Moretti proposes dividing the *Bildungsroman* into 'classification' and 'transformation' novels. In the former 'events acquire meaning when they lead to *one* ending and one only' while in the latter 'what makes a story meaningful is its narrativity, its being an open-ended process'.[13] In such works, 'the ending, the privileged narrative moment of taxonomic mentality, becomes the most *meaningless* one'. 'The Two Drovers' underscores the strong affinity between Moretti's mode of 'classification' and the 'singleness of effect' that since Poe has been so central to the formal requirements of short story. For Scott the crucial authenticating move, in works that are densely historically mediated and tied to claims of cultural authenticity, is that the fictive pay-off be evident in the judicial ending of the story – the ruling that puts every character into a single interpretive frame and thus secures the narrator's footing, like the thief who says on his arrest, 'It's a fair cop, guv.'

In Hogg's fiction, however, there are no fair cops. What we principally encounter at the story's end are sudden dilations, shifts in speech, and closing paragraphs that shift (like *The Thousand and One Nights*) to other forms entirely: 'An Old Soldier's Tale' for example, ends with a stanza of a Scots song.[14] There is always one further document to be unearthed, one further mystery to puzzle out (no matter if the gravestone be indecipherable or the sources partially suspect), and one further genre to be dropped onto the page. Inescapable variability – in focalisation, in form of address, in dialect, and in epistemology – is precisely the point of many of Hogg's stories.

Critics have noted Hogg's attachment to disputation and undecidable problems. Douglas Mack has pointed out that Hogg does his best to balance the necessity and absurdity of supernatural beliefs, and Tim Killick has spoken of his predilection for a 'zone of dispute'.[15] If Hogg was haunted by '[John] Wilson's syrupy stories of benign Providence',[16] as well as by Scott's forceful accounts of a distinctively Scottish past, his response was not to pick sides in a battle between local tradition and onrushing modernity but rather to thematise and foreground both the necessity and the impossibility of choosing sides in that battle. Despite his ear for dialect and his passion for charting ethnographic variation, Hogg's commitment to polydoxy does not primarily consist in registering sociolects. In Hogg's fiction, divergence in belief does not solely or inevitably occur at the level of speech itself, but may also be found at the level of incident, plot, character or motive – in the question of what makes a given occurrence into a story at all.

In 'An Old Soldier's Tale', for instance, rival interpretive communities (Highland rebels and Lowland loyalists) can occupy the same space without acknowledging one another's existence – or they can decide to duel about what sorts of tales will survive from a particular period of war. A Lowland Scots soldier who claims to have done great duty for the government forces at Culloden is 'drowned' (shouted down) and 'overpowered' by a Jacobite loyalist who gives him hospitality for the night.[17] Yet when his hostess has outsung him, as compensation for his defeat she lets him turn the tables and embark on a gory and largely incredible tale: how he was besieged, bungled his use of civilian hostages, and used a heroic handcuffed backflip to throttle his would-be executioner and win the admiration of his enemies. And that plot, convoluted as it may sound, is far easier to follow than the stylistic and linguistic gyrations of the story itself, which features Lowland Scots, Highlanders speaking garbled English, Lowlanders speaking garbled Gaelic, and not-quite translations of diverse Scottish speech into 'proper' English.

In this story and others, Highland and Lowland Scots fail (and pretend to fail, and fail to pretend, and even fail to pretend to fail) to understand one another's words. Meanwhile, bemused or smugly obtuse outsiders, English tourists or stuffed shirts, keep popping up, presenting themselves as authoritative voices explaining rural phenomena that the natives have long given up on understanding. Paranormal and dryly scientific accounts of lightning strikes may coexist, or a community's shared understanding of why a given event occurred may be regarded by a narrator endowed with other foibles and values as impossible – yet irrefutable.[18]

One way to understand Hogg's commitment to shifting frames of believability is to consider Maureen McLane's recent anatomy of 'Seven Types of Poetic Authority circa 1800'. Building on work by Margaret Russett, Ian Duncan, Penny Fielding, Ina Ferris and others, McLane rejects a stark division between 'the radical authority of deep extended "Authentic" subjectivity' and 'the elaborated authority of editorial objectivity'.[19] Instead, she argues for seven often overlapping ways in which poetic authority can be generated: authority of inspiration, authority of anonymity, authority of imitative authorship, authoritative translation, editorial authority, ethnographic authority, and experiential authority.[20] All seven of McLane's categories undergird Hogg's tales, in which multiple ways of eliciting the reader's belief or acquiescence rapidly succeed or even overlap with one another. Consider, for instance, the variety of authoritative claims embedded in just the title for one of Hogg's volumes of stories – *Altrive Tales: Collected among the Peasantry of Scotland and from Foreign Adventurers By the Ettrick Shepherd* – in which the 'by' does double duty as a claim to have collected and to have composed the tales.

Hogg's attraction to stories with incompatible beliefs about seemingly straightforward events frequently means that demonic intervention emerges as the only explanation left standing that seems to cover all the facts. Accordingly, supernatural explanations are often offered to the reader with a shrug of disbelief, because the most reasonable interlocutors within the stories are dissatisfied with their veracity, but can find no alternative ground from which to deny them. A line describing the Devil's presence at the death by lightning of 'Mr. Adamson of Laverhope' – 'It was asserted and pretended to have been proved' – might be taken as the key to all Hogg's mythologies.[21]

Sometimes the shifts are overtly marked. 'An Old Soldier's Tale' closes with a poem about food that silences all debate (as similar lyric interludes do in *The Thousand and One Nights* or *The Decameron*). But at other times the substitution of one grounding for a story's credibility with another can be subtler. In 'The Lasses' (*The Shepherd's Calendar*) a ruse whereby the best man cannily abducts a bride-to-be is explained by the assertion that it is a time-honoured local custom that the bride should ride to her wedding on the best man's horse. That the bride in question is eloping across a moor at midnight does not, Hogg insists – in a tone half stern and half tongue-in-cheek – affect the deep-seated cultural necessity of that arrangement. The reader, well ensconced in a Chaucerian fabliau, is suddenly also a bemused outsider receiving an ethnographic education on the fly.

McLane's work on the ways that the various sorts of poetic authority interact resonates with recent investigations of the ways in which Victorian narrative strategies depend on a kind of magisterial 'ethnographic authority'.[22] James Buzard has focused on the 'self-interrupting' narrator, a voice that creates a sense of movement between the reader's world and a 'knowable community' made up of the ethnographically grounded but quaint beliefs of various characters.[23] Buzard sees such self-interruptions working in Victorian realist novels, much as free indirect discourse may, to fortify an ultimately seamless sense of realist authority. In Hogg's stories the shifts are sudden, striking, and seem designed to alert the reader to the fact that the grounds for trust in the narrative's reliability have shifted.

Such games are everywhere in Hogg's oeuvre, an irrepressible habit or imp of the perverse that sends his fictions teetering sideways into a condition of suspect textuality. Mimetic propulsiveness is replaced by a diegetic excess in which every line needs to be read for the narratorial presence encoded in it, as well as the dialectic it points back to, as well as the authoritative (or dubitable) 'authentic' character – as when Hogg ends an early story about a ruined maid (M.M.) in *The Spy* with a plaintive note, '*The SPY sends his kindest respects to M.M. and requests to be favoured with a continuation of her correspondence.*'[24]

I describe Hogg's central strategy as polydoxy as a way of getting at the most distinctive way he has of offering multiple grounds for textual authority: the strikingly disruptive juxtaposition of plausible alternative schema to interpret a single set of events. Time and again in these stories a fully coherent account of events is replaced, in the final page or so, with an entirely plausible recasting. In 'Mr. Adamson of Laverhope' we are led to entertain the notion that lightning and a flood killed a proud farmer because he mocked an agent of the Devil. But perhaps it was ball lightning, after all, the narrator concludes; and in any case this story is not well attested, and may be explained instead as a garbled version of another old legend. There is no 'degree zero' in Hogg's stories.

One solution we might expect to find to this perpetual war of interpretations is violence, which pervades Hogg's stories. After all, death by lightning, the drowning of sheep in a flash flood, or even a fatal swordfight would seem to remove all uncertainty. Far from doing so, each blow, each fire, each death only generates more images, and more stories.

Consider the reiteration of violence in 'Mr. Adamson of Laverhope', which requires that the story not end with Adamson's death by lightning, but instead detour fifty-one years forward to another death by lighting, that of Adam Copland of Minniness. Although this second death occupies only about a twentieth of the story as a whole, the narrator's explanation for it – no moral element at all, simply a common man at the wrong place at the wrong time, when electrical fire seemingly came out from the ground itself – initially appears to be definitive and objective, undermining the suggestion that it was the Devil who used lightning to slay Mr Adamson. But that calm, linguistically neutral (even drab) account is itself immediately undermined in a variety of ways. The one witness present cannot actually remember the actual moment of the strike; even the narrator cannot provide the moral exhortation that is to be found carved on Copland's tomb; and so on.

Why would Hogg attach this odd demi-quaver of a tale to the vivid account of how Adamson's sins against his neighbours – recollected with crystal clarity seventy years later – brought about his doom? He is experimenting with what it might mean to achieve what he knows to be impossible: a neutral ground where various possible explanations hang in equipoise with one another. And thus this story, like other such balancing acts as 'An Old Soldier's Tale', ends with some apparently unrelated detail (the unrecollected epitaph, the poem about dinner) which serves to embed the entire tale within a universe where stories, poems and inscriptions, each equally unlikely, compete for the same scarce conversational space.[25]

By the same token, 'A Singular Dream, From a Correspondent' detours away from its ostensible protagonist, 'Mr A. T. philosopher, and teacher of the science of chance', to close with two paragraphs on 'an old man named Adam Bryden, whose disposition and rule of behaviour were widely different from those of the philosopher above mentioned'.[26] Like the scientifically described death by lightning of a man whose actions merited no divine punishment, Adam Bryden's benevolence is brought in as a counterweight to the multiple 'dangerous errors' of judgement that dog the characters of 'A Singular Dream'.

Such turns towards irrelevancy mean that even the events, persons, causes and effects in any story – the very components that allow it to appear to be a story at all – are perpetually at issue. It is often unclear why a given piece of prose ends where it does, whether the last few pages were an afterthought, the motive for the whole piece, or simply the gateway to another tale told from a different perspective. The sort of *in medias res* that Hogg pursues, rather than gesturing at an Auerbachian epic totality, lends to his stories the feel of deliberate fragments, made to be appreciated precisely for their fractured, and their fractal, quality.

Even when Hogg's stories seem to aim for the complete package, the full-throated comprehensiveness that a *Spectator* tale (or a Sketch by Boz) manages effortlessly, the effect is oddly laboured. 'The Long Pack', for instance, is a perfectly self-contained squib about a pedlar's pack that bleeds when fired on (because a thief is tucked inside, waiting for nightfall). Hogg centres the story on Edward, who becomes a hero by firing into the pack (as he does many other things) 'without hesitating one moment'.[27] This is a Poe story in the making: Edward's nature is perfectly unfolded in the action itself: he is the ardent defender whose unthinking action saves the day. Why then does Hogg end the story, a good two thousand words further on, by running through Edward's later life, from his career in the army to his death?[28] There is some undercurrent of what McLane calls 'experiential authority' here, as the narrator reveals that he had heard the story from this same Edward. But the detour to that effect away from the focused sensation of the original instance is deliberately odd. Hogg's endings are memorable for the ways in which they deny or undo the potential energy that by Poe's logic should be accumulating towards a final climactic discharge. His stories linger in the mind as much for the effects they refuse as those they produce.

Hogg is in some revealing ways like his contemporary Heinrich von Kleist, whose formal gyrations are on display in the deliberate irresolution and the teasing half-turns towards magical explanations in works such as 'Michael Kohlhass' and 'The Beggarwoman of Locarno'.[29] Both Hogg and Kleist succeed by generating an often uneasy sense of between-ness: a solution between magic and science, a world between our own and the past, a character between rationality and inexplicable depths. As Gillian Hughes puts it, 'Hogg's passage from primitive bard to professional literary man' is always partially performance, and dependent upon an audience that is hoping for various versions of authenticity at various points in his career.[30]

The point might even be taken slightly further. Unlike Hogg, Scott's success lay in mastering the footing that allowed him confidently to direct the reader to the moment where the view of the law, the guilty party, and the reader all find themselves in agreement on the events that have just transpired: all end the story, we might say, on the same page.[31] Hogg's fiction, by contrast, aims at disrupting the smooth fit between frames of reference within the story – and, accordingly the fit between viewpoints expressed within the story and the stance towards the story that the reader can be expected to take. Hogg has often been understood as striving to master one role or another, or to manage his transitions from one kind of authority claim to another.

However, a great deal of his work strives not to paper over or to excuse a given story's between-ness (between groups, between dialects, between forms) but to celebrate it. Hogg's notion of success in his short fiction is to create a repository that fails to contain the voices that populate it, that ultimately resigns the task of uniting the divergent forces within it into anything resembling an agreeable and agreed-upon outcome.

CHAPTER FOURTEEN

Hogg and the Novel

Graham Tulloch

James Hogg had a problem with novels, and yet he wrote one of the greatest novels of the nineteenth century. He essayed the popular genres of his time – sentimental novel, Gothic fiction, historical novel, national tale – but always produced something rather different from the way these genres had defined themselves. In a broader sense, too, Hogg did not conform to the conventions of novelistic decorum prevailing at the time. His habitual tendency to mix different modes of writing, such as tragedy and farce, disturbed his contemporaries, as did his willingness to deal overtly with sexuality. He never really succeeded in writing a novel in the dominant form of the age, as exemplified in the work of Walter Scott: a long narrative built around a central, unifying plot and published in the three-volume format preferred by booksellers and circulating libraries. By contemporary standards he was a failure as a novelist, and his contemporaries felt they understood why: for them Hogg was a poet, even a peasant poet, the 'Ettrick Shepherd'. The modern reader is not bound by these expectations. We are ignorant of, or indifferent to, the generic conventions of the time; we are accustomed to novels of sharply varying length; we accept the joining together of contrasting elements and the frank discussion of sexual matters. For us Hogg has become best known as a novelist; we no longer judge him primarily as a poet.

Because we do not share early nineteenth-century attitudes, we are perhaps more open to appreciating certain aspects of Hogg's work, such as the extraordinary psychological insights of A Justified Sinner. It would be a mistake, however, to think that we can fully appreciate Hogg's successes without reference to those attitudes. This chapter considers Hogg's work against the expectations of his own time in order to show how far he rejected or transcended them in order to give scope to his particular strengths. In this light, instead of being a record of failure, Hogg's career as a novelist includes successful innovation in ways that look forward to the future development of the form. At the same time we should not, by seeing his novelistic career as an uninterrupted record of success, compensate too much for his contemporaries' unfavourable judgement. Hogg worked hard to establish himself as a novelist, but the conventions prevailing in his time resisted him in many ways, and it was only with his last novel, *The Private Memoirs and Confessions of a Justified Sinner*, that he found a novelistic form that fully matched its content. This chapter traces the path towards this success by considering first the genres and then the structures that Hogg adopted and adapted. Before that, however, it is worth considering why Hogg wanted to become a novelist.

Hogg's first experiments in prose fiction appeared in his weekly magazine *The Spy* in 1810–11. However, it was with a collection of poems, *The Queen's Wake*, that he achieved a measure of fame and success comparable to that which his patron and rival Scott enjoyed through his poetical romances. The poetic contest that provides the framework for the poems allowed Hogg important creative freedoms. Although he had moved from a peasant world dominated by oral tradition to the literary culture of Edinburgh, he had not abandoned the interests and attitudes of his earlier years. In particular, he had grown up in a world into which Enlightenment scepticism about the supernatural had scarcely penetrated. Using the poetic personas of contending bards in a sixteenth-century setting, Hogg presented unquestioned stories of the supernatural, including the two most highly regarded poems of the collection, 'Kilmeny' and 'The Witch of Fife'. He also adopted a folk voice in the ballad 'Mary Scott'. Hogg was thus able to represent two important aspects of his background and beliefs within the poetic conventions of his time.

Just as Hogg was winning success as a poet, his great model, Scott, moved on to achieve even greater fame and fortune as a novelist. Very quickly Scott established the novel as the dominant genre of Scottish Romanticism. Hogg was eager to follow in his footsteps, even though the novel was a form less well suited to his concerns. As a product of Enlightenment scepticism and literary realism the novel was inimical to the supernatural, and as a middle-class genre it could not easily accommodate the voice of the peasantry, except when confined to dialogue enclosed within the narrative. Similarly, the language of Scottish Presbyterianism, another crucial strain of Hogg's cultural heritage, was alien to the novel's discourse, beyond a limited use in dialogue.

Some kinds of novel were more productive for Hogg than others. On the face of it a writer like Hogg, who characterised one of his novels as 'replete with horrors', might find Gothic fiction congenial, and Gothic certainly accommodated a range of novelistic concerns in ways that helped him.[1] Yet, in the end, it offered less than we might expect. Well stocked with castles and captive maidens, and thus potentially the most 'Gothic' of Hogg's novels, *The Three Perils of Man* is nevertheless not a Gothic romance. The comic treatment of the dead horseman with his head cloven through subverts the sublime expectations that such an image arouses. Similarly, the Gothic figure of the captive maiden receives unorthodox treatment in *Perils of Man*.

While Lady Jane Howard is imprisoned Hogg turns the spotlight away from her onto her counterpart and rival, Princess Margaret, who, far from being locked up is almost preternaturally mobile. The maid Delany's captivity receives no special attention. Even the threat of rape hanging over Lady Jane, a commonplace peril in Gothic fiction, is quite differently handled – its circumstances of public exhibition and atrocity far exceed the usual Gothic limits. Ultimately, although there are some horrific images in the novel, the sensations of terror, panic and claustrophobia that characterise Gothic fiction are absent or incidental.

Even more importantly, the Gothic does not offer Hogg an outlet for the supernatural, at least not for the kind of supernatural that fascinated him. Hogg's supernatural came from folk tradition: stories of fairies, ghosts and the Devil. Famously, the first Gothic novel opens with a supernatural event – the fall of a colossal helmet into the courtyard of the castle of Otranto. This is, however, a self-contained, literary supernatural. It does not require acceptance outside the literary experience; nor does it appeal to the modes of popular belief, such as belief in fairies or in the corporeal presence of the Devil, which the Enlightenment had dismissed as 'superstition'. As the Editor of *Confessions of a Justified Sinner* (a man of the Enlightenment) points out, 'in this day, and with the present generation it will not go down, that a man should be daily tempted by the Devil, in the semblance of a fellow-creature'.[2] Other Gothic novels (e.g., by Ann Radcliffe) feature apparently supernatural phenomena only to explain them away. This strategy does not work for Hogg, who habitually writes as though the supernatural is real, an aspect of common life.

A second genre developed in the later eighteenth century, the sentimental novel, offers Hogg different opportunities. Despite the homage paid to Henry Mackenzie, its great Scottish exponent, in the last chapter of *Waverley*, Scott appears to have much less interest in the sentimental than Hogg. The exploration of fine and delicate feelings plays a large part in the first and longest story in *The Three Perils of Woman*. Nevertheless, this is not a sentimental novel. The Richard Rickleton companion plot, treated largely in comic terms, despite its serious implications, resists the manners associated with the genre as well as its prevailing mood. By shifting the focus in the latter part of the tale away from Gatty's feelings to those of her Scots-speaking father, who connects strongly with the labourers around him and rejects the middle-class pretensions of his wife, Hogg does not so much undercut the sentimental novel as expand its possibilities. Typically sentimental fiction is attuned to middle- and upper-class sensibilities, and these do not express themselves in broad Scots. Hogg thus moves the sentimental novel's concerns beyond the social and linguistic limitations that it had previously adhered to. In the end, however, the genre cannot accommodate his interest in the horrific and the absurd. Hence the final tale of *The Three Perils of Woman* breaks decisively away from sentimental fiction by offering a horrifying account, shot through with grim humour, of the terrible aftermath of Culloden.

Another genre had made its more recent (and flamboyant) debut in Sydney Owenson's *The Wild Irish Girl* (1806), which provides a blueprint for the 'national tale'. An English traveller arrives in Ireland expecting to find it a cultural desert but comes to appreciate the richness of Irish culture, thanks to a series of encounters with Glorvina, Princess of Inismore, whom he eventually marries, in a symbolic union of England and Ireland. An Anglo-Irish invention, the national tale was taken up by Scottish authors, such as Elizabeth Hamilton in *The Cottagers of Glenburnie*, and it influenced the novels of Scott. No less Scottish in his interests than Scott, Hogg handles the issues raised by the national tale quite differently. As Ina Ferris points out, the romantic national tale 'articulate[s] the grievances [. . .] of small European nations that stand in a certain relation of hostility to a larger and oppressive nation'.[3] In Hogg that sense of national grievance, which Ferris sees as essential to the genre, is largely absent.

His most overt treatment of a Scottish–English confrontation is to be found in *The Three Perils of Man*, set during the medieval Scottish Wars of Independence; however, the novel represents the English as fundamentally the same as the Scots, whether they are high-born knights driven equally crazy by chivalry, or Border raiders differing only in the direction in which they cross the frontier. The characteristic tropes of the national tale fail to materialise: we find neither the dirt and squalor that Ian Duncan traces as signifiers of regional identity in Edgeworth and Hamilton, nor the transformation of the English traveller in Scotland (Lady Jane is apparently unchanged by her journey), nor the symbolic marriage of nations (Lady Jane in marrying Charlie Scott represents beauty and wealth rather than Englishness).[4] Opposition of national cultures is apparently of less interest to Hogg than the recognition of cultural diversity within Scotland and, indeed, northern England. Not for nothing did Hogg call himself the Ettrick Shepherd: his sense of Scottishness is deeply rooted in the local.

Although born in Ettrick Forest he knew and appreciated many parts of Scotland. Hence the multiplicity, even cacophony, of voices in *The Three Perils of Man* – Border voices, Highland voices, Aberdeen voices, Galloway voices. Alongside these the northern English voice of Heaton (registered, like those from Aberdeen and the Highlands, in comic terms) contributes just another noise to the cacophony. Rather than representing a shared culture, these competing voices seem to suggest mutual cultural incomprehension – if there is any unity, it lies in diversity. Rather than realising an English-Scottish union, the most symbolically charged marriage in all of Hogg's novels joins the Lowlander Gatty with the Highlander M'Ion in *The*

Three Perils of Woman. Hogg uses the device to unite elements within the nation rather than to unite the former nation with another, more powerful nation in the mode of the national tale.

Of all the genres available to Hogg the most important was the historical novel, for two reasons. First, if Hogg was to emulate Scott as a successful novelist, he had to adopt the form which Scott had made peculiarly his own. Second, if he was to be a Scottish writer, he had to confront the fact that Scott had located Scottish identity in its past. However, Hogg faced a major hurdle in coming to terms with the historical novel as defined by Scott. For Scott, moulded as he was by Enlightenment historiography, history was progressive – it traced a movement from more primitive to more developed forms of society. By contrast, Hogg's view of history was cyclical, attentive to the endless repetition of the same human behaviour and emotions. Structurally, this is made most obvious in *The Three Perils of Woman*, in which the component stories belong to different historical settings but nevertheless depict a consistent intensity of female suffering. The treatment of chivalry in *The Three Perils of Man* provides another example. Regarding Douglas's declaration of love for the princess, the narrator comments: 'Women love extravagance in such matters, but in those days it had no bounds.'[5] Although these are the words of Hogg's narrator, Isaac the curate, he is so ill-defined that it is hard to separate his views from the author's own. Such comments suggest that Hogg understands chivalry in terms of perennial human feelings and that the closest he comes to a sense of the otherness of the past is to imagine it as a more extreme expression of what he knows from his own days. Scott understands chivalry differently, as the product of a particular past, the Middle Ages. In *Ivanhoe* and in his *Encyclopaedia Britannica* essay on 'Chivalry' he represents it both as expressive of perennial human passions (evil as well as good) and as embedded in the institutions of medieval knighthood. For Hogg, however, the perennial passions dominate his view, not historical context.

Partly because of his way of understanding chivalry, Hogg's most overtly and ambitiously historical novel is in many ways his least historical. Not only does Hogg view the chivalric material out of its historical context, he also eschews the opportunity to present an Enlightenment historical perspective on the other great theme of the novel, the supernatural. Rather than offering us the supernatural as something that people in the past believed in, although not empirically real – as Scott does with the stories told about Rebecca at her trial in *Ivanhoe* – Hogg presents it to us as fully real. In describing the uncanny phenomena experienced by the peasants living around Aikwood he does not say that they 'believed' these things happened but that they 'knew' they did.[6] The novel escapes from history in other ways too. In the tale-telling contest the two stories about Marion's Jock move out of their ostensible period setting into a timeless rural Scotland: the first in particular has no historical markers and draws heavily on Hogg's own childhood experiences. Similarly, the Poet's tale is legend rather than history.

Of course, Hogg's failure to produce a historical novel à la Scott does not mean that the novel was a failure by other standards. Indeed it could be argued that Hogg's ahistorical treatment of chivalry allowed him freer rein to present a satirical account and permitted him to link chivalry and violence more explicitly than Scott was willing to do. Equally, the refusal of Enlightenment scepticism gave Hogg's imagination more exuberant scope in the Aikwood parts of the novel. At the same time, the analysis of Hogg's failure to produce a historical novel of a particular kind can help us under-stand his successful achievement with other models of historical fiction. For Hogg did, indeed, have considerable advantages as a historical novelist in a non-Scottian mode. For certain kinds of historical writing his background provided valuable material and modes of understanding. His profound inti-macy with Border oral tradition gave him a direct link to events of the past, while his Presbyterian upbringing gave him command of the language and thought of the dominant national religious tradition, as distilled in particular in the Shorter Catechism. These two traditions interacted: many of the local oral tales were concerned with the 'Killing Time', the late seventeenth-century persecution of the Covenanters, while the Covenanting tradition itself cannot be understood without some appreciation of Calvinist resistance to the authority of the state over the church. Similarly, Covenanting stories of the appearance of Satan on earth were more fully accepted in a world that gave credence to a whole range of other stories about the Devil. Most useful of all, these traditions gave Hogg an alternative view of the world and of Scottish history to that accepted by Scott.

Hogg himself claimed that he had written his Covenanting novel, *The Brownie of Bodsbeck* (1818), before Scott published his, *Old Mortality* (1816). Whether or not this is true, Hogg is certainly able to take a much more sympathetic view of the Covenanters than Scott. Hogg wrote later of *The Brownie* that 'the general part is taken from Wodrow, and the local part from the relation of my own father, who had the best possible traditionary account of the incidents', a useful reminder that his sources were written as well as oral, although he drew particular strength from the oral sources.[7] Robert Wodrow's *History of the Sufferings of the Church of Scotland* was sympathetic to the Covenanters and evidently consonant with Hogg's father's traditional account. Popular oral tradition, entering the novel directly through the voice of the farmer of Chapelhope, as he relates much of the story, ensures that the novel provides an authentic voice for a more democratic and grass-roots view of the controversial royalist leader, Claverhouse, than Scott, with his aristocratic leanings, could afford. As Duncan points out, 'The compassion

Hogg's farmer hero feels for the persecuted Covenanters suggests an alliance against oppressive government based on a nascent class sympathy rather than on religious or political ideology.'[8] However, the voice of the peasant always threatens to become comic; Hogg's ambivalent attitude to Scots vernacular prayer, a feature of several of his novels, is a symptom of this.

This difficulty did not arise with the language of religion. Hogg's command of the language of Scottish Presbyterianism, with its privileging of divine over secular authority, allows him to give Robert Wringhim's memoir, in *Confessions of a Justified Sinner*, an effect of authenticity similar to that provided by the Scots peasant voice. The memoir also, in a different way, undercuts the discourse of contemporary Tory cultural and political dominance. This is not to say that Hogg endorses the Sinner's views, merely that he understands the language and the theology, however perverse. The irony that envelops the memoir is not directed at Presbyterian doctrine but at Robert's failure to see his total misapplication of it. Everything suggests that Hogg rejected fanaticism such as Robert's, but, because he understood the language and even the mindset of Presbyterian extremism, he could authentically represent it. Hogg's religious upbringing thus provides one of the key elements in the success of *Confessions of a Justified Sinner*. When he could draw on the culture in which he had grown up to help understand the past he was able to achieve success as a historical novelist.

Turning to form and structure, we immediately note that none of Hogg's novels conforms to the dominant contemporary model of a single narrative extending over three volumes. It seems that shorter narratives suited Hogg best, including the fictional memoirs that he collected late in his life in *Tales of the Wars of Montrose*. Nevertheless, after his first long tale, *The Brownie of Bodsbeck*, which occupies one and a quarter volumes of a two-volume set, he experimented with the three-volume format in the two *Three Perils* novels, before alighting on a format that suited him really well in *Confessions of a Justified Sinner*, where he was able to adopt what Garside describes as being 'at that precise moment a fashionable vehicle for new fiction'.[9]

In *The Three Perils of Man* Hogg does extend a single tale to three volumes but by splitting the narrative between the very different domains of chivalric romance and the supernatural tale, and by interpolating a storytelling contest. Hogg's uneasiness with the complexities of two parallel narratives shows in his constant recurrence to the image of the wagoner obliged to separate his load into parts in order to carry it up a hill.[10] Introducing a series of full-blown supernatural events into a historical novel is risky but Hogg largely succeeds in his endeavour by locating the two different domains in two different castles, keeping them apart and offering them as contrasting kinds of 'peril'. The strategy only falls down when the two domains come together at the end: the queen's coy fascination with Charlie

Scott's hints of diabolic encounters leads uneasily into the supernatural finale. Nevertheless, with the intrusion of the supernatural into historical fiction, Hogg, as Duncan notes, 'rebuts Scott's brilliant antiquarian fictions (*Ivanhoe*, *The Monastery*) with a ferociously comic performance of what can only be called a proto-postmodern magic realism'.[11] Hogg explodes Scott's model of the historical novel without as yet creating a fully satisfactory alternative.

Embedding individual tales within a novel was a longstanding convention, but Hogg's introduction of five stories into *The Three Perils of Man* exceeds contemporary novelistic conventions even though they are ingeniously, if somewhat artificially, connected to the main plots. However the storytelling contest, while formally a return to much earlier models of prose fiction, such as Boccaccio's *Decameron*, also offers Hogg the freedom he had enjoyed with the poetic contest in *The Queen's Wake*, enabling him to adopt quite different personas in stories of widely varying style and content. By contrast, *The Three Perils of Woman* adopts the different strategy of breaking the text into three successive narratives, with the first extending to two volumes and the others, linked in plot to each other but not to the first, filling the third volume. All three are presented as depicting different 'perils of woman' and all three are effective and well-controlled narratives. It seems that, for novels, a length of between one and two volumes suits Hogg well.

As Katie Trumpener has noted, even by 1760, 'the British novel already had a long history of pseudodocumentary fictions framed, in their prefaces, by pseudoeditorial authenticating devices', and the practice continued apace into the Romantic period.[12] Scott used such devices in his *Tales of My Landlord* series and in *Ivanhoe*, and Hogg experiments with them in 'An Edinburgh Baillie' and *The Three Perils of Man*. However, neither the low-key use in *Perils of Man* of the narrator Isaac, the curate (whose voice seems to disappear much of the time), nor anything Scott had done prepares us for Hogg's brilliant exploitation of the authenticating narrative in *Confessions of a Justified Sinner*. In making the 'Editor's Narrative' (68 pages of text in Garside's edition, excluding Hogg's embedded *Blackwood's* letter) two-thirds of the length of the Sinner's own central narrative (98 pages) Hogg hugely expands its size and significance. The Editor furnishes us with a full alternative account of the Sinner's life (and afterlife) and a Tory viewpoint set against the Whig viewpoint of the Sinner himself.

Critics have rightly pointed out that the Editor is not Hogg and that his narrative is not intended to provide an impartial and 'correct' interpretation of events.[13] Nevertheless, it is important to realise that there was a part of Hogg that identified with the Editor. Indeed Hogg appears in many guises in the novel. Apart from his two named appearances as the author of a letter to *Blackwood's* and the uncooperative shepherd with his 'paulies' at

the market, aspects of Hogg appear in both the Editor and the Sinner. The
Editor represents the Tory man of letters, a role to which Hogg in some ways
aspired although he never comfortably inhabited it, either in his own eyes or
in those of his contemporaries. The Sinner, though very different from Hogg,
is like him steeped in Scottish Presbyterianism and biblical language, even if
he interprets them quite differently. Furthermore, as he descends the social
scale during his flight at the end of his life he reaches the point at which Hogg
began, as an agricultural labourer of the lowliest kind.

What makes the combination of the Editor's and Sinner's narratives so
effective is that it embodies a division within Hogg and allows him, in modi-
fied fashion, to express both sides. In particular, by enclosing a supernatural
narrative within a sceptical framework Hogg can have it both ways – giving
expression both to scepticism and to belief. Precisely because it is enclosed
within a sceptical framework the Sinner's memoir is entire unto itself – there
is no need to intrude any scepticism into the memoir itself and Hogg can
give full expression to a combination of Scottish Christianity and folk belief
in the Devil's physical appearance in this world. In *The Three Perils of Man*
Hogg had not found an entirely satisfactory way of presenting the supernatural within the conventions of the novel. Indeed, he came to believe that the
'mass of diablerie' had spoilt his tale, although that is not necessarily the
view we might take of it today.[14] The other Hogg, the non-sceptic who in
some part of his mind believed in the supernatural, finally finds its unin-
hibited novelistic expression in the Sinner's narrative. What is more, Hogg
also manoeuvres the reader into becoming complicit in that belief. Robert
Wringhim's own failure to recognise the true nature of Gil-Martin forces the
reader into being the one who knows the truth – that Gil-Martin is the Devil.
We cannot read the novel without recognising this 'truth' and thus placing
ourselves alongside the non-sceptical Hogg.

The Sinner's memoir also allows Hogg in the end to produce a new model
of historical novel, quite different from Scott's. Its very enclosure within the
modern, antiquarian Editor's narrative emphasises its pastness. Robert lives
fully within a past that for him is the present. The Editor's narrative identifies the date of the novel's key events at Edinburgh only allusively, as that of
'the famous session that sat at Edinburgh when the Duke of Queensberry was
commissioner, and in which party spirit ran to such an extremity'.[15] Robert
does not specify it at all. When he does mention dates they have purely
personal significance: he has no historical sense of his own time and does
not see it from outside as Scott's narrators do. Yet it is this total immersion
in the world of early eighteenth-century Scotland that makes this, in a quite
different way to Scott's work, a historical novel. Through his understanding
of Scottish religion and popular supernatural lore Hogg was able to think
himself into Robert and live in his past world. Hogg had discovered how to

write a non-Scottian historical novel. Looking at his novels as a whole, we can see that the outstanding success of *Confessions of a Justified Sinner* was not an accident but the result of Hogg's finally finding the solution to the problems of form, genre and content with which he had contended over the years.

CHAPTER FIFTEEN

The Private Memoirs and Confessions of a Justified Sinner: Approaches

Penny Fielding

'And to what I am now reduced, let the reflecting reader judge', declares Robert Wringhim a few days before his suicide.[1] These words have proved prophetic, as different approaches to this most multifarious of novels have found their own reflections within it. Like Gil-Martin, master of 'the came-leon art of changing [his] appearance' (p. 86), *Confessions of a Justified Sinner* seems to adapt itself to whomever is looking at it at the time, although the reflections are often unstable. One does not have to read far in the novel to realise that the conventional terms of literary analysis – 'author', 'reader', 'narrator', 'plot', 'history' – are not going to be helpful in any straightforward sense. Attempts to reconcile the conflicting evidence of the novel's narrators under the controlling intelligence of 'James Hogg' have proved difficult in the case of a figure who jumps in and out of his authorial and fictional status with abandon. Readers are given conflicting information, versions of the plot do not add up, historical references tantalise rather than confirm. As Susan Manning neatly puts it: 'Every exegetical attempt leads straight into a cul-de-sac.'[2] All this, needless to say, has proved both fecund and frustrating for readers: the novel does much to show us how literature works, but no context in which we read it can exhaust its meanings.

After the French novelist André Gide's rediscovery of *Confessions* in the 1940s, literary criticism alighted early on the novel's Gothic qualities and the ways in which these could be understood through psychoanalysis, par-ticularly through the figure of the double.[3] As infants, we have to learn how to see ourselves, a process fraught with potential anxiety. Freud argues that doubles are part of the difficult growth of the psyche in childhood that returns to haunt us in later life in a process that he calls 'the Uncanny' (in German *das Unheimliche*). As infants we see ourselves in imaginary doubles, in a form of narcissistic identification that seems to ensure our continued existence. But the double also can become a projection of our conscience (Freud's 'superego'), which we suppose to be censoring or criticising us. '[T]hat man is capable of self-observation', writes Freud, 'renders it possible to invest the old idea of a "double" with a new meaning and to ascribe a number of things to it – above all, those things which seem to self-criticism to belong to the old surmounted narcissism of earliest times.'[4] We can detect both these forms of the double in Robert's relation to Gil-Martin. At first Robert experiences thrilling, pleasurable sensations on meeting his double. Yet soon he finds himself directed and dominated by him in ways that he cannot understand: 'he either forced me to acquiesce in his measures, and assent to the truth of his positions, or he put me so completely down, that I had not a word left to advance against them' (p. 88).

Some readers have identified in Robert the conditions of a modern patho-logical diagnosis, such as paranoia or schizophrenia. Others point out that the early nineteenth century was not short of interest in abnormal psychology or in 'double consciousness'. Psychoanalytic criticism, however, can do more than analyse the imagined psyche of fictional characters, and some of the most interesting readings of *Confessions* show how the novel's complex psycholo-gies are part of wider social and historical patterns. Eve Kosofsky Sedgwick looks at the 'homosocial', a term that cannot be separated from misogyny and homophobia. Interpersonal subjectivity tends to fall into gendered triangles in which men negotiate power by using women as tokens of exchange (most obviously in the marriage ceremony where one man 'gives away' a woman to another). Sedgwick suggests that this is an unstable arrangement in which the mutual respect and confirmation of male power structures depends on the repression and demonisation of same-sex desire. Sedgwick uses this idea to show how the psychic entanglements of *Confessions* express fluid social identities: 'the proliferation of faces, identities, paranoias, families, overlap-ping but subtly different plots [. . .] requires a move away from the focus on intrapsychic psychology, and back towards a view of the social fabric'.[5] She traces this shifting set of relationships to show how such forms of sexualised and gendered power work not as essential identities but as subject positions. George conducts a strapping homosocial lifestyle with his male friends, sharing – it is implied – women in their visits to the bagnio. Robert finds it much harder to triangulate his desire in this patriarchal society, feminises himself (in social terms) as an abject figure to gain the attention of the domi-nant male group, and is then seduced by the dominant figure of Gil-Martin, whom he both loves (as another male) and fears (as a more powerful male), resulting in 'an uncrystallizable, infusory flux of identification and desire'.[6]

As well as exemplifying psychic processes, the novel's Gothic qualities express the structural conditions of Scottish cultural history. Ian Duncan has argued that late eighteenth- and early nineteenth-century Scotland, even as it generated the terms for a modern, enlightened society regulated by science, law, and urban living, was, at the same time, imagining and defining itself against another version of Scottish national experience – one that it viewed as 'organic', irrational, and rural. This structuring of national identity is analogous to Freud's Uncanny, where a developmental stage that should have been superseded irrupts into the rational order of adult life. 'Primitive', wild, superstitious, this Scotland refused to remain isolated in its designated past. Attuned to the burgeoning contemporary interest in folk tradition, romance revival, and the ethnography of 'the peasantry', Hogg's work shows with exceptional vividness how a Gothic premodernity bubbles up through the Edinburgh New Town pavements that invented it in the first place. Many readers have noted that the 'Editor' of *Confessions of a Justified Sinner* is as prejudiced as the 'fanatics' he condemns. In the closing section of the book he describes the exhumation of Robert's memoir along with his corpse, in a parody of the antiquarian project of '[resurrecting] a buried and dismembered national culture, associated with a textual corpus [. . .], [so as] to replenish the ruined imaginative life of modernity'.[7]

In another use of psychoanalytic theory to interpret cultural phenomena, Scott Mackenzie develops a line of argument first identified by Duncan, according to which Hogg's text represents a type of incomplete, obstructed or insufficient mourning, called 'incorporation' by the psychoanalytic theorists Maria Torok and Nicholas Abraham. In the normal or healthy work of mourning, the psyche works through loss by expressing the lost object symbolically though language and thus 'introjecting' it, or locating it as an object outside oneself that can be addressed and understood. But in the case of incorporation, loss is concealed within the psyche as if in a crypt, kept artificially alive but not accessible through language or representation.[8] Mackenzie reads in Robert Wringhim's unceremonious death and burial the allegory of a Scottish culture that is unable to come to terms with its own past: 'Secret nationality for Hogg equates to buried histories of dispossession and suppressed tales of expulsion from home. [. . .] Scottish space will not function here as a coherent field of aesthetic experience.'[9] So far from the Editor's initial confidence that the events of the story can be recovered from history and tradition and made available to the reading public, the novel refuses to mourn Robert by refusing to provide a unified story that makes sense of his life and death. He remains unassimilated by the national psyche, cast out from society and its norms, a monster or freak that cannot be accounted for.

This does not mean, of course, that the novel is impervious to historicist approaches. Douglas Mack draws attention to the 'subaltern', socially marginalised voices within the text – the prostitute Bell Calvert, the servant Samuel Scrape – who challenge the dominant voices both of the seemingly enlightened Editor and of Calvinist orthodoxy.[10] Murray Pittock goes further in seeking to retrieve the traces of an authentic, pre-Union Scotland in the Scots-speaking characters. He reads *Confessions of a Justified Sinner* as a threnody for '[t]he death of Scotland at the hands of extremist Presbyterianism'.[11] The novel also strikes some very contemporaneous resonances. It was written immediately after a period of radical activity and a government crack-down that gave rise to a widespread fear of spies, causing the newly-founded *Scotsman* newspaper to denounce the culture of espionage: 'does not the mere acknowledgment of employing spies generate a feeling of distrust and insecurity? This may be limited at first; but in the end it will spread through the whole of society.'[12] *Confessions* is shot through with references to spying: Gil-Martin acts as an agent provocateur, and Robert believes that he is being secretly watched and followed: 'It seems, that about this time, I was haunted by some spies connected with my late father and brother' (p. 141). In an attempt to find out what people know about his crimes, Robert assumes the role of spy as he '[mixes] with the mob to hear what they were saying' (p. 144).

But Hogg warns us to tread carefully in the historical field. John MacQueen has pointed out that the events in the novel seem to be dated very precisely, as if tempting us to anchor it in 'actual' historical occurrences. On closer inspection, however, the dates turn out to be inconsistent both against each other and with recorded history.[13] Hogg poses the question: 'What is history'? Cairns Craig argues that the Editor and Robert are not merely different narrators but competing versions of historiographic authority, which the novel inextricably links. The Editor represents the progressive history of the Scottish Enlightenment in which society gradually improves from irrational fanaticism to rational objectivity. Yet this narrative is overtaken by the cyclical time of Robert's memoir, bound by 'the eternal conflict of God and Devil'.[14] More recently, Ina Ferris looks at the novel's establishment and dissolution of an opposition between conjectural history, which adduces a coherent narrative of the past from ideas of what is likely to have happened, and antiquarianism, which stitches together a past that *did* happen from the material evidence that survives in the present (in this case Robert's book and his corpse):

> On the one hand [. . .] the novel undermines the mediating concepts through which a modern mind makes sense of and surmounts the past to produce the kind of synthesis exhibited most famously in the period by Scott's Waverley novels. On the other [. . .] it places in question the antiquary's conviction that [. . .] the past can be authentically approached through the concreteness and intimacy of its fragmentary 'remains'.[15]

Ferris situates the novel in the early nineteenth-century debate about what should constitute historical evidence.

Confessions' remarkable attention to its own status as a text has attracted a variety of readings attentive to the ways in which a book is both literally and figuratively bound up with its own processes of writing and publication.

Peter Garside's edition and numerous articles, by Garside, Gillian Hughes, Douglas Mack and others in the journal *Studies in Hogg and his World*, have documented the novel's coming into being in the bibliographical milieu of the 1820s.[16] Its elaborate fictionalisation of its own production has made *Confessions* a rich source for historical criticism that explores the social implications of literary work. The sociological thinker Pierre Bourdieu gives us a way of seeing the literary (or any other) text as a symbolic object in a network of cultural practices, exchanges, and competitions:

> The public meaning of a work [. . .] originates in the process of circulation and consumption dominated by the objective relations between the institutions and agents implicated in the process. The social relations which produce this public meaning are determined by the relative position these agents occupy in the structure of the field of restricted production. These relations, e.g. between author and publisher, publisher and critic, author and critic, are revealed as the ensemble of relations attendant on the 'publication' of the work, that is, its becoming a public object.[17]

Hogg is an especially striking example of an author who reflects upon his position at the intersection of these relations. His own self-performance as the faux-naïf, the 'Ettrick Shepherd', his relations with the judgemental *Blackwood's* set, his struggle to adapt to the changes in the literary field forged by Scott's Waverley Novels, and his continual experimentation with different genres – all of these inform *Confessions of a Justified Sinner* and have stimulated some of the most important work on Hogg. Rather than simply being produced by these forces, as any work must be, *Confessions* conspicuously announces its own engagement with them in the competitive world of Edinburgh publishing. David Groves makes the point that a 'justified' sinner is one who has gone through the typographical process of 'justification',[18] set within the confines of a printed text, while Mark Schoenfield has shown how 'Hogg dissolves the margins of his fiction by marshaling procedures usually *about* a novel, including its typesetting, advertisement, and review, as part *of* the novel.'[19] Many critics have been drawn to the way the novel leaps in and out of 'fact' and 'fiction', with its reproduction of Hogg's letter about the suicide's grave first published in the August 1823 number of *Blackwood's Magazine*, or the various social significances of the different literary forms which compete for the status of 'last word': letter, editorial commentary, manuscript diary, privately-printed memoirs and confessions, published novel.

All the criticism of *Confessions of a Justified Sinner* arrives at the apparently unavoidable conclusion that meaning itself is elusive in Hogg's text. Points of view compete for the reader's faith without offering confirmation, evidence remains incomplete, and language itself slips between punning or contradictory meanings. The novel abounds with examples, but the most audacious is perhaps Robert's complaint of 'the singular delusion that I was two persons' (p. 106). We have already seen how the work generates multiple meanings for itself as a literary text. In addition to Robert's and the Editor's narratives, there is another book in *Confessions*: Gil-Martin's own mysterious Bible, upon seeing which Robert experiences something like 'a stroke of electricity' (p. 85). It is as though he views the material fact of the book itself, underlying and undermining the literary text and all the cultural meanings that might be found in it, as Ian Duncan has suggested:

> Illegibility is the point, the effect of writing viewed from outside itself. The electric shock Wringhim feels is the charge of an abstract textuality, a printed sign system unattached to human hand or voice. The Devil's book is a text for one reader only – it does not circulate in an economy, it does not constitute a culture.[20]

The theorist who has most closely examined this way of thinking about language is Jacques Derrida, who shares one of Hogg's most abiding interests: the problem of singularity. 'Singular' appears in the novel nineteen times, in which its meaning of 'unaccountable' (another of Hogg's favourite terms) or 'strange' comes up against its meaning of 'unique'. Derrida shows us that there is nothing more unaccountable than the singular. He addresses the same question that confronts Robert Wringhim in *Confessions*: how do I truthfully tell the unique account of what happened to me in a specific time and place? Derrida writes: 'In essence a testimony is always autobiographical: it tells, in the first person, the sharable and unsharable secret of what happened to me, to me alone, the absolute secret of what I was in a position to live, see, hear, touch, sense, and feel.'[21] Testimony is sharable, since it must be communicated and repeated; an experience that only made sense in the moment in which it happened would, perversely, be nonsense. But the great pressure that comes to bear on someone making a testimony is that its 'truth' must be guaranteed by the fact that it did only happen to the testifier, and in this sense it is 'unsharable'. Once the experience is recounted in other contexts, as it must be to be intelligible, it is torn away from its originary moment. Hogg's novel dramatises this problem. Despite the increasing urgency and desperation with which Robert seeks to relate exactly what happened to him, right down to his curse on any future reader 'who trieth to alter or amend' (p. 165), his text will always be interpreted differently, in different cultural contexts, from the Editor, through the novel's first reviewers, to the modern theoretical approaches discussed here.

Robert's testimony is also a 'Confession', both a religious and a legal concept. The form of Calvinism represented in the novel is sometimes called 'antinomianism', meaning 'opposition to the law', or the belief that religious salvation comes from divine grace rather than from adherence to the moral law.[22] Looking outwards from doctrinal to general principles of law, the novel traces a violent collision between two forms of compulsion: a modern, legal, civic order versus a religious conviction that takes no heed of historical variation. (These two forms do not, of course, fit neatly into the novel's two narratives.) *Confessions* addresses the problem of right action. Should we act from inner conviction? From precedent? Or according to an agreed code? These ideas had been much discussed as political questions in Britain following the French Revolution, and had more recently surfaced again in Scotland in the trials for sedition from 1815–20. Radical thinkers like Tom Paine had insisted that a government cannot be trusted to rely on precedent, but should follow a set of modern constitutional rights, to be negotiated and agreed upon by the people as a body. This seemed a very dangerous idea to those who believed that the hierarchal laws of society had settled organically over time, in a process that seemed to lie almost outside history itself: in Edmund Burke's use of a well-worn phrase, in 'time out of mind'.

Resisting direct political analogies, Hogg's novel complicates the general question of how we are subject to law, and whether a society should work out a set of agreed laws applicable to everyone or whether, as Robert comes to believe, right is the issue of an incalculable, barely describable state of affairs that pre-exists any decision in the present. Ian Duncan argues that the division of narratives in the novel maps the conceptual antagonism between civil society and fanaticism upon which the liberal political imagination is founded. The Scottish Enlightenment philosophers did not always acknowledge the ideological idealism that underlay their own discussions of civil society and the ways in which it might be structured and managed. *Confessions* imagines the return of this repressed absolutism in the mode of fanaticism, or 'political reason moved by ideology in its pure, absolute, metaphysical form – the form [. . .] of religion: a revenant by which modern thought keeps finding itself surprised'.[23]

These were also questions that informed moral philosophy in the late Enlightenment. Kant's famous 'categorical imperative' argues that moral action should be unconditional and should apply to all circumstances. In deciding on right action we should not make a calculation of likely outcomes but should follow our innate reason. Utilitarian philosophers, most famously Jeremy Bentham, argue to the contrary that it is precisely this sort of calculation that should construct a set of moral laws all subjects can follow. Meredith Evans has shown how *Confessions* makes these distinctions very difficult to understand in terms of coherent moral action. Robert rejects external or given laws, and believes that his actions are right, or 'justified' in themselves. For him virtue is not describable as a set of principles but is simply given.

Yet from what, Hogg asks, does this 'justification' proceed? From God? From Gil-Martin (whose own agency is both internal and external)? From conscience? Robert asks himself a question to which the novel does not provide an answer: 'I tried to ascertain, to my own satisfaction, whether or not I really had been commissioned of God to perpetrate these crimes in his behalf, for in the eyes, and by the laws of men, they were great and crying transgressions' (p. 108). As Evans notes, the novel dramatises in Robert the collapse of 'the modern distinction between law and morality'.[24]

Confessions of a Justified Sinner was difficult for readers to gauge on its first publication. But it has proved a remarkably resonant text for later generations, one on which critics have plotted ideas about internal psychic life, social organisation, political ideology and language. All of these testify not only to the novel's complexity but also to its importance for modernity, with its recognition of repression, its atomised subjects, and its fractured historicism. Among the editor's last observations is that the novel's import is both 'scarcely tangible' and of 'great weight' (p. 175): a paradox that suggests that interpretation of the novel, at once frustrating, fascinating, and inexhaustible, is not over yet.

CHAPTER SIXTEEN

The Private Memoirs and Confessions of a Justified Sinner: Afterlives

Gillian Hughes

On first publication in 1824 Hogg's *The Private Memoirs and Confessions of a Justified Sinner* could hardly be described as a popular novel. It sold so badly that the bulk of the thousand copies was remaindered and the author's half-share of profits two years subsequently was roughly £2.[1] It was not until the appearance of an edition bearing the imprimatur of André Gide in 1947, and subsequent wide circulation in Britain and the USA in the 1970s, that the book's direct effect on other writers can easily be demonstrated, and yet the water of *Confessions* seems part of certain streams of Scottish, English, German, and even perhaps Russian fiction written much earlier, from the detective story to the Gothic to the *Bildungsroman*.

The young Brontës were avid readers of *Blackwood's Edinburgh Magazine*, in which 'A Scots Mummy' first appeared, with Branwell hoping to succeed James Hogg as a contributor. Emily's *Wuthering Heights* (1847) is the story of a cuckoo in an old family, a wild north pictured through harsh religious imagery, the exhumation of a grave, and a mysterious evil stranger whom Cathy describes as 'my own being'.[2] Stevenson, though more dismissive of Hogg's achievement, created in *The Master of Ballantrae* (1889) a multiply narrated tale of the inter-related fate of two brothers, one Jacobite and attractive, one Hanoverian and repellent. There is a night-time duel between them, and the one seems devilish while the other loses his better self in his murderous pursuit. The novel closes with an uncanny exhumation scene.[3]

Dr Jekyll and Mr Hyde (1886) also concerns a self-division reflected in a multiple narrative, Jekyll seeking to escape from the social repression that has committed him to a profound duplicity of life by freeing the worse part of himself with a chemical potion. As Jekyll he remains a mixture of good and evil, but as Hyde is solely wicked and in refusing to accept his responsibility for Hyde's acts Jekyll eventually destroys both. There is also a thematic link between *Confessions* and Conrad's *The Heart of Darkness*, pointed by the publication of the first of three parts of Conrad's tale in a commemorative thousandth issue of *Blackwood's Edinburgh Magazine*, in which Hogg features in Andrew Lang's nostalgic poem 'Our Fathers' as one who 'taught how dreadfully he died, | The Sinner, Lost and Justified'.[4]

The influence of Hogg's *Confessions* on classic detective fiction as well as on the Gothic must be suspected. G. K. Chesterton mentions 'Kilmeny' in his sceptical 'The Blast of the Book' (1935), but an earlier 'Father Brown' story 'The Hammer of God' (1911) focuses on a puritanical clergyman who, in seeing other people as insects crawling beneath him and himself as an agent of God, falls into mortal sin and murders his free-living elder brother.[5] Conan Doyle's doubles, Sherlock Holmes and Professor Moriarty, though not actually brothers, mirror one another: the pre-eminent detective needs a pre-eminent villain to engage his energies fully, and in 'The Final Problem' (1894) the two fall into the tremendous abyss of the Reichenbach Falls, locked in one another's arms.[6]

Hogg's *Confessions* is partly a grim parody of the German *Bildungsroman*, in which the chief character after a number of hesitations is led to follow the right path and fully develop his true nature. Hermann Hesse's *Demian* (1919) has striking affinities with it. The name of Hesse's title character, Max Demian, reflects the Greek origins of demon/Dämon as a person's genius as well as the Christian evil spirit. Does this mysterious friend of the narrator Emil Sinclair (to whom the book was attributed on first publication) really exist or is he a symbolic representation of a dark side of Sinclair's nature that he initially wishes not to recognise? Like Gil-Martin, Demian seems a superior being, he is able to read the thoughts and anticipate the actions of others, and is drawn to Sinclair because both bear the mysterious mark of the biblical evil brother Cain. Apparently supernatural events occur, so that Sinclair is mysteriously drawn to the scene of a schoolfellow's attempted suicide and a letter of advice from Demian uncannily appears tucked into a textbook one day. The language of Hesse's book is tensely held between the biblical scheme of his religious upbringing and the enlightenment of Jungian analysis, just as Hogg's novel operates between the spiritualism of Calvinism and the rationality of the Enlightenment.[7]

Karl Miller has remarked on the astonishing similarity between Hogg's *Confessions* and Vladimir Nabokov's *Despair*, originally written in Russian in 1932 but now existing in the version the author rewrote in English in 1965.[8] It takes the form of a memoir, falling into a diary as the narrator's mental state deteriorates, and opens with his taking a walk into the country and recognising his double in a tramp named Felix: 'Slowly I raised my right arm, but his left did not rise, as I had almost expected it to do.' His pose of superior acuteness is betrayed by his ignorance of what is obvious to his reader, for instance, his wife's affair with her cousin Ardalion; and he constantly draws attention to his own unreliability. After shooting Felix, the narrator remarks, 'our likeness was such that really I could not say who had been killed, I or he'.

Among the titles Nabokov jests are suitable for his work are '"Memoirs of a" [. . .] "The Double" [. . .] "Crime and Pun" [. . .] "Justification of a Likeness"', surely referencing Hogg as well as Dostoevsky.

Hogg's *Confessions* also has its jokes and, somewhat surprisingly, is the model for two modern comic novels. In *Two to Tango* (1998) Peter Guttridge's music journalist protagonist Nick Madrid trails a Rock Against Drugs tour in South America. Ageing megastar Otis Barnes, his career recently revived by two hit songs, featured in a film version of Hogg's book, 'Sinner Man' and 'Dark Friend', turns out to have his own murderous double, finally destroyed in a hilarious slow-motion chase in the high altitude of Machu Picchu. Otis's double claims his identity, evoking from Nick the comment, 'You're a bit too post-modern for me.'[9] The protagonist of James Hynes's comic take on the American campus novel, *The Lecturer's Tale* (2001), is a Hogg scholar battling for tenure in a Faustian legend of Gothic encounters that ends with the destruction by fire of a famous research library, now become the gate to hell, and of which the chief survival is a collection of the works of James Hogg. James Lasdun's *The Horned Man* (2002) is a more straightforward attempt to remake Hogg's *Confessions* as a bizarre American campus novel.[10]

Confessions's most vigorous afterlife has undoubtedly been in Scottish fiction. A recent advertisement notes that Ian Rankin 'along with almost every other Scottish writer of any note' cites it as a major influence.[11] John Rebus's evil counterpart Cafferty proves in the final novel in the series, *Exit Music* (2007), to be as necessary to his existence as Gil-Martin is to Robert Wringhim's, with the newly retired Rebus frantically trying to resuscitate the arch-villain who has provided meaning in his working life. Rankin's division of Edinburgh into respectable overworld and dark underworld is Hogg's, so that when Rebus walks beside museum curator Jean Burchill in *The Falls*, 'Although they were walking the same path, he knew they were in different places.'[12] *Black Book*, with its epigraph from *Confessions*, casts Cafferty as the Gil-Martin to the young brewing heir Aengus Gibson's Robert Wringhim, a personality 'just barely in control of himself'. Cafferty had held Gibson's hand, and perhaps pressed the trigger of the gun, when Gibson had years earlier shot his opponent in a poker game before starting a fire to cover the murder, and has since protected him from justice, waiting for the day when the young man would take over the brewery. Aengus Gibson escapes him only by suicide.[13]

John Herdman's *Pagan's Pilgrimage* (1978) is a straightforward, if slight, transference of Hogg's work into an allegorical twentieth-century Edinburgh. The son-of-the-manse, a would-be murderer who yearns for 'some God-given, exalted destiny which would lift me far above the inherent limitations of my talents and personal attributes' is called Horatio Pagan. Pagan has a mysterious friend and co-conspirator who bears an uncanny physical resemblance to him, is named Raith, and urges him to destroy aristocratic Viscount Gadarene of Teuchtershards. Pagan, however, repents at the eleventh hour and settles into the quiet life of an antiquarian bookseller.[14] Stuart Hood's *The Upper Hand* (its title taken from Nöel Coward's song 'The Stately Homes of England') also picks up the thread of class envy implicit in Hogg's novel, but with a looser relationship to the original plot. John Melville, another son of the Manse, opens his first-person narrative with his adolescent encounter with Colin Elphinstone, the privileged only son of the local landowner, who crosses his path again at the University of Edinburgh as part of a group of left-wing students whose birth and breeding, he declares, 'had allowed them to play at politics like Marie Antoinette playing at dairy-maids'. Meanwhile, Melville supplements his inadequate bursary by reporting on student politics to a mysterious Mr Halcro, and feels that he has been granted 'a glimpse of a current of power running beneath the surface of everyday life'. Attracted to Elphinstone and eager for his friendship, Melville's career is a dark counter-part to his, and eventually he betrays Elphinstone by taping his reminiscences for the benefit of a journalist named Gilchrist, 'with his fox's face, a prince of darkness and of paranoias' to whom, Elphinstone declares, he is 'some sort of *famulus*'.

The paranoia of the Cold War suits Melville's personality as much as that of extreme Calvinism does Robert Wringhim's, whereas Elphinstone may simply have been blundering through it unthinkingly. In the third part of the novel, in which Elphinstone becomes the narrator, he describes Gilchrist's accusations 'that he was an undercover member of the CP [. . .] that he acted as a courier [. . .] that he had betrayed some tunnel in West Berlin to the East German authorities' as having 'the plausibility of a dream from which I do not know how to escape, for I have the feeling of being caught – as the saying is between the devil and the deep blue sea'.[15] Elphinstone, rather than Melville, commits suicide.

James Robertson's *The Testament of Gideon Mack* (2008) formally adheres closely to Hogg's fiction, with an editorial account of events introducing Mack's testament and a puzzled editorial epilogue that also opens, 'What can this work be?' There are numerous pointers to Hogg's work, from the devil's own recollection of the Auchtermuchty preaching, to the initials G. M. that he as Gil-Martin shares with Mack himself. A strong element of pastiche is also reflected in the interpolated documents, such as the Monimaskit entry in the Gazeteer of Scotland or 'The Legend of the Black Jaws' from a local work of history written by Mack's Victorian predecessor. (The provision of explanatory footnotes and references to academic expertise from Stirling presumably alludes to the accelerating revival of interest in Hogg since the early 1990s.) Robertson, like Hogg, understands the universal appeal of tales of the supernatural: a journalist on hearing that there is a rational alternative story to Rev. Robert Kirke's reputed translation to fairyland retorts, 'Well, don't tell me that one!' Mack lacks Wringhim's desperate religious earnestness, though not his hypocrisy, in choosing to become a Church of Scotland minister despite a complete lack of faith. Robertson's rational world is further away from the supernatural world than Hogg's was. As Mack remarks, 'In the seventeenth century a minister who claimed to have seen and spoken with Satan in the flesh would have been not only believed, but, assuming he had given a good account of himself, hailed a hero. In the twenty-first century such a minister is simply an embarrassment.' Mack's devil is actually less frightening than the childhood Jesus of whom he was taught, 'Always there was one who walked beside me.'[16] Since Mack encounters the devil without real terror of hell or murderous crime, the narrative tone is predominantly playful: Robertson cannot draw the reader in to share the protagonist's paranoia as Hogg does.

Emma Tennant's *The Bad Sister* (1978) is a grippingly direct transference of Hogg's work, its energy deriving partly from its radical feminist ideology, which as a cultural disturbance substitutes admirably for Calvinism. Illegitimate Jane Wild, raised in a feminist commune, envies her legitimate and conventional half-sister Ishbel Dalzell, daughter of a Borders landowner, and eventually murders her and probably their common father too. A mysterious woman, Meg Gil-Martin, initiates her as a vampire and feeds her yearning for a mysterious male demonic power called 'K' or 'Gil-Martin'. *The Bad Sister* pays tribute to *Confessions* structurally as well as thematically, Jane's first-person account succeeding to an Editor's narrative, and being followed by an editorial note recounting the exhuming of her body in the hills above St Mary's Loch and issuing a warning against 'the increasing dangers of fanaticism'.[17] Although the city scenes of Tennant's work are located in London rather than in Edinburgh, Ettrick Forest is vividly realised in the coda to the work, close to the family home of the author herself. *The Bad Sister* is a fiction of extraordinary power, not too taken up with and distanced by ludic post-modernism, and in its way a love letter from Tennant to Hogg as an overwhelming local literary influence.

In *Engleby* (2007) Sebastian Faulks shows the general influence of Hogg's *Confessions* on the murder mystery and upon fictions focusing on time and unreliable narration. When Jennifer Arkland disappears from Cambridge, Mike Engleby at first seems as shocked as his fellow students, though gradually a damning body of evidence builds up to indicate that he is in fact her murderer, and that he continues to murder women during his subsequent career as a journalist in London. Only after nearly three hundred pages is the reader made aware that the journal she has been reading was written after Engleby's arrest and conviction to promote his passage to a psychiatric hospital rather than a prison. Like Wringhim's narrative, framed as a puritan spiritual autobiography, it is a piece of special pleading and a palimpsest. In both cases the novel's centre is a desperately earnest negotiation, an attempted justification.[18]

Like Emma Tennant, the Canadian writer Alice Munro has personal as well as narrative connections to James Hogg: she shares his descent from Will Laidlaw, a member of Thomas Boston's Presbyterian congregations and also reputedly the last man in Ettrick Forest to be acquainted with fairies. In *The View from Castle Rock* Munro charts this legacy for a writer as 'a reality that was commonplace and yet disturbing beyond anything I had imagined'.[19] A disputed interpretation is at the centre of the title story of *Friend of My Youth* (1990). Flora Grieve from a Canadian community of Cameronians loses her lover Robert and her social importance firstly to her younger sister, Ellie, and then to the nurse who comes to nurse Ellie through her final illness. Like Robert Wringhim, Flora is in one view morally elevated by worldly abasement, for 'the elect are veiled in patience and humility and lighted by a certainty that events cannot disturb'. In another she is a 'Presbyterian witch', avoiding normal sexuality.[20] Annie McKillop of 'A Wilderness Station' has 'a waywardness about one eye' and her story is one of confused perspectives. She is taken from an orphanage as bride to a tyrannical backwoodsman, Simon Herron, who is subsequently killed, officially by the fall of a tree, liberating both his wife and his put-upon younger brother. The brother, George, marries happily into the family of a neighbour, while Annie appears to suffer a mental breakdown, seeking refuge in the county gaol. The reader attempts to filter the truth from a variety of competing accounts, that of the Presbyterian and misogynistic minister, a nostalgic and commemorative account by George in his old age of the early days of the settlement, products of story-loving Annie's strange mind, and the distanced perspective of her young employer. Did George kill his brother with an axe? The final word is Annie's admission, 'I did used to have the terriblest dreams.'[21]

The influence of Hogg's *Confessions* on Robertson Davies, greatest of Canadian novelists, is less easily demonstrated, but in *Murther & Walking Spirits* (1991) an examination of personality as the product of family history is viewed from beyond the grave. Connor Gilmartin is murdered in the novel's opening pages by his wife's lover, whom he subsequently haunts while intermittently watching film-like sequences of his ancestor's experiences. As the metaphysical Scot McWearie tells the murderer, 'there are a lot of mischievous things that are likely to happen when we step a little aside from the straight path of life'.[22] In America, Chuck Palahniuck's *Fight Club* (1996) opposes to a prevailing consumerist quiescence an anarchic world of male resistance expressed in physical and social violence, the destructive and radical Tyler Durden emerging from the disintegrating psyche of a corporate worker. Particularly in the popular film version starring Brad Pitt and Edward

Norton (1999), Durden, like Gil-Martin, is the secret friend become enemy who may after all be oneself.

Hogg's *Confessions* seems, however, to be particularly central to the Scottish psyche in other media, though its international appeal is evidenced by a film version by the Polish director Wojciech Has (1986). Within Scotland – as play, opera, radio drama, and soon film – *Confessions* is becoming an increasingly known story of a dark Scottish Everyman. In 1971 the Edinburgh International Festival presented the Edinburgh Royal Lyceum Company production, directed by Richard Eyre, of Jack Ronder's adaptation *The Sinner's Tale*. Starring leading Scottish actors including Andrew Keir and Russell Hunter, this marked in an international context a major discovery for the theatre of Hogg's work. Thomas Wilson's opera, commissioned by Scottish Opera and staged in 1976, followed and provided Philip Langridge with an early opportunity to create in the Sinner one of the dark roles for which he was best known.[23] There was a radio adaptation by Alexander Reid in 1983, and the Royal Lyceum Theatre in Edinburgh returned in 2009 to Hogg's text in a stage version written and directed by Mark Thomson.[24] Ian Rankin is currently working on a film treatment that may now pull Hogg's Justified Sinner from a cult figure to a common reference point in the popular culture of Scotland. The poor response received by Hogg's novel on first publication in 1824 seems perverse in retrospect, now that *The Private Memoirs and Confessions of a Justified Sinner* has achieved a polar position in Scotland and beyond – much read, greatly respected, and profoundly influential. Perhaps some decades from now the same feeling may exist with respect to other key Hogg works.

Endnotes

Duncan – Introduction

1. James Hogg, *Altrive Tales*, ed. Gillian Hughes (Edinburgh: Edinburgh University Press, 2003), p. 23.
2. Pascale Casanova, *The World Republic of Letters*, trans. M. B. DeBevoise (Cambridge, MA: Harvard University Press, 2005). On early nineteenth-century Edinburgh as a literary capital, and Hogg's career there, see Ian Duncan, *Scott's Shadow: The Novel in Romantic Edinburgh* (Princeton: Princeton University Press, 2007), pp. 3–45, 147–59.
3. Two full-length critical studies of Hogg's literary self-fashioning are Silvia Mergenthal, *James Hogg, Selbstbild und Bild: zur Rezeption des 'Ettrick Shepherd'* (Frankfurt-am-Main and New York: Peter Lang, 1990) and Valentina Bold, *James Hogg: A Bard of Nature's Making* (Oxford: Peter Lang, 2007).
4. For a vivid account of Hogg's relations with Wilson and the *Blackwood's* circle see Karl Miller, *Electric Shepherd: A Likeness of James Hogg* (London: Faber & Faber, 2003).
5. See my discussion in *Scott's Shadow*, pp. 150–73.
6. Hogg, *Altrive Tales*, p. 55.
7. See Douglas S. Mack, 'Hogg's Bardic Epic: *Queen Hynde* and Macpherson's *Ossian*', in Sharon Alker and Holly Faith Nelson (eds), *James Hogg and the Literary Marketplace* (Farnham: Ashgate, 2010), pp. 139–56.
8. See Mack's introduction, James Hogg, *The Bush Aboon Traquair and The Royal Jubilee* (Edinburgh: Edinburgh University Press, 2008), pp. xvi–xviii, xlii–xliii.
9. See Peter Garside, 'Hogg and the Blackwoodian Novel', *Studies in Hogg and his World* 15 (2004), pp. 5–20 (hereafter *SHW*).
10. See Hogg, 'The Honorable Captain Napier and Ettrick Forest', in *Contributions to Blackwood's Edinburgh Magazine: Volume 1, 1817–1828*, ed. Thomas C. Richardson (Edinburgh: Edinburgh University Press, 2008), pp. 96–137; 'On the changes in the habits, amusements, and condition of the Scottish peasantry', forthcoming, with notes and commentary by H. B. de Groot, in *Studies in Hogg and his World* 22 (2012).

11. See Hogg, *Contributions to Blackwood's Edinburgh Magazine: Volume 1*, ed. Thomas C. Richardson, p. lxix.
12. See Janette Currie, 'Hogg and the American Literary Marketplace', in Alker and Nelson (eds), *James Hogg and the Literary Marketplace*, pp. 219–34; and Currie's online bibliography of Hogg in American periodicals, www.jameshogg.stir.ac.uk/showbib.php?id=1 (accessed 18 September 2011).
13. See, for example, David Duff, *Romanticism and the Uses of Genre* (Oxford and New York: Oxford University Press, 2009); Andrew Piper, *Dreaming in Books: The Making of the Bibliographic Imagination in the Romantic Age* (Chicago and London: University of Chicago Press, 2009).
14. See Maureen N. McLane, *Balladeering, Minstrelsy, and the Making of British Romantic Poetry* (Cambridge: Cambridge University Press, 2008); Tim Killick, *British Short Fiction in the Early Nineteenth Century: The Rise of the Tale* (Burlington: Ashgate, 2008) and Anthony Jarrells, *The Time of the Tale: Romanticism, Genre, and the 'Intermixing' of Enlightenment* (forthcoming); Mark Parker, *Literary Magazines and British Romanticism* (Cambridge: Cambridge University Press, 2000) and Mark Schoenfield, *British Periodicals and Romantic Identity: The Literary 'Lower Empire'* (Houndsmills: Palgrave Macmillan, 2008).
15. Gillian Hughes, *James Hogg: A Life* (Edinburgh: Edinburgh University Press, 2007), pp. 303–4.
16. See Bold's linking of Hogg's experimentalism to his status as 'autodidact': *James Hogg: A Bard of Nature's Making*, e.g., pp. 191–200.
17. See James Hogg, *Winter Evening Tales*, ed. Ian Duncan (Edinburgh: Edinburgh University Press, 2002), pp. xii–xiii, 166–228.
18. Susan Stewart, *Crimes of Writing: Problems in the Containment of Representation* (New York: Oxford University Press, 1991), pp. 67–74, 86–8.
19. Duff, *Romanticism and the Uses of Genre*, pp. 165, 186–7.
20. Hogg, *Winter Evening Tales*, pp. xxx–xxxi, 3–74.
21. See Anthony J. Hasler, 'Introduction' to James Hogg, *The Three Perils of Woman; or, Love, Leasing, and Jealousy. A Series of Scottish Domestic Tales*, edited by Hasler and Douglas S. Mack (Edinburgh: Edinburgh University Press, 1995), pp. xxxiii–xxxix.
22. See Sharon Alker and Holy Faith Nelson, 'Empire and the "Brute Creation": The Limits of Language in Hogg's "The Pongos"', in Alker and Nelson (eds), *James Hogg and the Literary Marketplace*, pp. 201–18; Penny Fielding, *Scotland and the Fictions of Geography: North Britain 1760–1830* (Cambridge: Cambridge University Press, 2008), pp. 161–88.
23. See, e.g., Allan Beveridge, 'James Hogg and Abnormal Psychology: Some Background Notes', *Studies in Hogg and his World 2* (1991), pp. 91–4; Valentina Bold, 'The Magic Lantern: Hogg and Science', *SHW* 7 (1996), pp. 5–17; Katherine Inglis, 'Maternity, Madness and Mechanization: The Ghastly Automaton in James Hogg's *The Three Perils of Woman*', in *Minds, Bodies, Machines: 1770–1930*, ed. Deirdre Coleman and Hilary Fraser (Houndmills:

Palgrave Macmillan, 2011), pp. 61–82; Karl Miller, *Cockburn's Millennium* (Cambridge, MA: Harvard University Press, 1976), pp. 204–8; Meiko O'Halloran, 'Hogg's Kaleidoscopic Art: Identity, Tradition, and Legitimacy in the Work of James Hogg' (Oxford University DPhil thesis, 2004); Megan Coyer, 'The Modern Pythagorean and the Ettrick Shepherd: Science and Imagination in Romantic Scotland' (University of Glasgow PhD thesis, 2010).

Chapter 1 – Bold and Gilbert

1. Portions of this essay dealing with Ettrick life and Hogg's factual prose have appeared in Valentina Bold, 'James Hogg and the Traditional Culture of the Scottish Borders', unpublished MA thesis (St John's: Memorial University of Newfoundland, 1990).
2. See Thomas Johnston, *General View of the Agriculture of the County of Selkirk, with observations on the means of its improvement* (London: The Board of Agriculture, 1774).
3. See *The Exchequer Rolls of Scotland [Rotuli scaccarii regum Scotorum 1264–1600]* 24 vols (Edinburgh: H. M. Register House 1878–1908), 1499; J. M. Gilbert, *Hunting and Hunting Reserves in Medieval Scotland* (Edinburgh: John Donald, 1979).
4. James Hogg, *The Brownie of Bodsbeck*, ed. Douglas Mack (Edinburgh: Scottish Academic Press, 1976), p. 101.
5. See National Library of Scotland MS 5509, 36.
6. Robert Douglas, *General View of the Agriculture of the Counties of Roxburgh and Selkirk, with Observations on the Means of their Improvement* (Edinburgh: The Board of Agriculture and Internal Improvement, 1798), p. 222.
7. See Rev. Robert Russell, 'Parish of Etterick, County of Selkirk', and 'Parish of Yarrow, County of Selkirk', *The Statistical Account of Scotland*, vol. 3 (Edinburgh: Creech, 1791–99), pp. 294–7; pp. 500–12.
8. See the Buccleuch Muniments, held in the Scottish Records Office (SRO GD 224) and, in particular, GD 224/522/3 and GD 224/83/56; see too, Douglas, *General View*, pp. 128–42 and William Singer, 'Report of a Survey of Watered Meadows, situated on, or near the rivers Elk, Ewes, Tiviot, Etterick, and Yarrow. Made in 1804, 1805', *Prize Essays and Transactions of the Highland Society of Scotland* 3 (1807), pp. 257–338.
9. See Russell, 'Parish of Etterick', p. 731; Alexander Fenton, 'Early and Traditional Cultivating Implements in Scotland', *Proceedings of the Society of Antiquaries in Scotland* XVCI (1962–3); R. A. Houston, 'Women in the Economy and Society of Scotland 1500–1800', in R. A. Houston and I. D. Whyte (eds), *Scottish Society 1500–1800* (Cambridge: Cambridge University Press, 1989), p. 21.
10. See James Hogg, 'The Hon. Captain Napier and Ettrick Forest', *Blackwood's Edinburgh Magazine* 14 (1832), pp. 175–88.

11. 'The Crookwelcome Club of Ettrick', MS Book of 'Crookwelcome Club', Personal collection of the Mitchell family, p. 1.
12. See Elaine E. Petrie, 'Odd Characters: Traditional Informants in James Hogg's Family', *Scottish Literary Journal* 10:1 (May 1983), pp. 30–41; and Elaine E. Petrie, 'James Hogg: A Study in the Transition from Folk Tradition to Literature' (unpublished doctoral thesis, University of Stirling, 1980).
13. Petrie, 'Odd Characters', pp. 45–6.
14. See Kirsteen McCue's chapter in this volume.
15. J. G. Lockhart, *The Life of Sir Walter Scott, Bart.* (London: Adam & Charles Black, 1884), p. 145.
16. For details see Valentina Bold, *James Hogg: A Bard of Nature's Making* (Oxford: Peter Lang, 2007) and Bold, '"Nouther right spelled nor right setten down": Scott, Child and the Hogg Family Ballads', in Edward J. Cowan (ed.), *The Ballad in Scottish History* (East Linton: Tuckwell Press, 2000), pp. 116–41.
17. Hogg, *Anecdotes of Scott*, ed. Jill Rubenstein (Edinburgh: Edinburgh University Press, 1999), p. 38.
18. Hogg's anecdote appeared in 'Reminiscences of Former Days. My First Interview with Sir Walter Scott', *Edinburgh Literary Journal* (29 June 1829), pp. 51–2; in 'Reminiscences of Former Times' in *Altrive Tales* (1832); and (as quoted here) in *Familiar Anecdotes of Sir Walter Scott* (1834).
19. Quoted from *A Shepherd's Delight: A James Hogg Anthology*, ed. Judy Steel (Edinburgh: Canongate, 1985), pp. 41–2.
20. Ruth Finnegan, *Oral Traditions and the Verbal Arts: A Guide to Research Practices* (London: Routledge, 1992), p. 115.
21. John Miles Foley, 'Word-Power, Performance, and Tradition', *Journal of American Folklore* 105 (1992), pp. 275–301, 295, 277.
22. John Miles Foley, *Immanent Art: From Structure to Meaning in Traditional Oral Epic* (Bloomington: Indiana University Press, 1991), p. 7.
23. Hogg, 'Memoir of the Author's Life', in *The Mountain Bard*, ed. Suzanne Gilbert (Edinburgh: Edinburgh University Press, 2007), pp. 15–16.
24. Hogg, *The Mountain Bard*, p. 1.
25. See Suzanne Gilbert's appendix, 'The Popular Context', in Hogg, *Mador of the Moor* (Edinburgh: Edinburgh University Press, 2005), pp. 96–103.
26. Hogg, *The Queen's Wake*, ed. Douglas S. Mack (Edinburgh: Edinburgh University Press, 2004), p. 296, l. 1688.
27. Ibid., pp. 30, 37.
28. Ibid., p. xxvii.
29. Ibid., p. xxviii.
30. Hogg, *Queen Hynde*, ed. Suzanne Gilbert and Douglas S. Mack (Edinburgh: Edinburgh University Press, 1998), p. xxix.
31. Ibid., p. 16.
32. James Hogg, 'The Shepherd's Calendar. Class IV. Dogs', *Blackwood's Edinburgh Magazine* 15 (1824), pp. 177–83.

33. James Hogg, 'The Shepherd's Calendar. Class II. Death, Judgements, and Providences', *Blackwood's Edinburgh Magazine* 13 (1823), p. 632.
34. James Hogg, 'Storms', *Blackwood's Edinburgh Magazine* 5 (1819), pp. 75–81, 210–16.
35. James Hogg, *Selected Stories and Sketches*, ed. Douglas S. Mack (Edinburgh: Edinburgh University Press), p. 3.
36. Ibid., p. 4.
37. See NLS MS 3653, fos 147–8.
38. James Hogg, *The Shepherd's Guide* (London: Murray, 1807), p. 81.
39. Ibid., p. 91.
40. Ibid., pp. 15–16.
41. Ibid., pp. 17–53.
42. Ibid., p. 168.
43. Ibid., pp. 56–7.
44. Hogg, *The Brownie of Bodsbeck*, pp. 134–7.
45. Ibid., p. 7.
46. James Hogg, *The Brownie of Bodsbeck* (Edinburgh: Blackwood, 1818), vol. 2, pp. 336–9.
47. See Valentina Bold, 'Afterword', James Hogg, *The Private Memoirs and Confessions of a Justified Sinner* (Edinburgh: Merchiston, 1999), pp. 281–8.
48. Axel Olrik, 'Epic Laws of Folk Narrative', in Alan Dundes (ed.), *The Study of Folklore* (Englewood Cliffs: Prentice-Hall, 1965), pp. 129–41.
49. Karl Miller, *Electric Shepherd: A Likeness of James Hogg* (London: Faber, 2003), p. 223.
50. Thomas Craig Brown, *A History of Selkirkshire or Chronicles of Ettrick Forest*, 2 vols (Edinburgh: Douglas, 1886), vol. I, p. 337.
51. See R. S. K., *The Blanket Preaching. Being occasional sermons preached in St. Mary's Churchyard* (Galashiels: Stewart, n.d.).
52. Margaret Fletcher, 'Old World Superstitions and Stories of Ettrick and Yarrow', *The Border Magazine* 7 (1902), p. 168.
53. In the section which follows, all the quotations are from field recordings cited in Valentina Bold, 'James Hogg and the Traditional Culture of the Scottish Borders', chapter 5: 'Hogg in Tradition: the Ettrick Shepherd'. Valentina Bold would like to express her sincere and lasting thanks to the people she recorded in the 1980s, who are so stalwart in their support for research around Hogg, for permission to quote them: the late James Mitchell, Doreen Mitchell and their family, the late Walter Barrie and Mrs Barrie, the late Tibbie Shaw, in particular.

Chapter 2 – Garside

1. James Hogg, 'Memoir of the Author's Life', *Altrive Tales*, edited by Gillian Hughes (Edinburgh: Edinburgh University Press, 2000), p. 21 (hereafter *Altrive Tales*).

2. *Altrive Tales*, p. 21.
3. Hogg, *Songs, by the Ettrick Shepherd* (Edinburgh, 1831), p. 5.
4. *The Collected Letters of James Hogg*, ed. by Gillian Hughes and others, 3 vols (Edinburgh: Edinburgh University Press, 2004–8), I, p. 15 (hereafter *Letters*).
5. *Letters*, I, pp. 20–8.
6. Ibid., p. 39.
7. *Letters*, I, pp. 53–4; *Altrive Tales*, p. 22.
8. *Altrive Tales*, p. 23.
9. *Letters*, I, p. 166.
10. Ibid., p. 179.
11. *Altrive Tales*, p. 46.
12. *Letters*, I, p. 145.
13. Ibid., p. 153.
14. Ibid., p. 289.
15. Ibid., p. 423.
16. For an attempt to unravel this situation, see Peter Garside, 'James Hogg's Fifty Pounds', *SHW* 1 (1990), pp. 128–32; and the fuller account of Hogg's dealings in 'Three Perils in Publishing: Hogg and the Popular Novel', *SHW* 2 (1991), pp. 45–63. Fuller details for the novels mentioned can be found under 'Publishing' in the relevant records in the online *Database of British Fiction 1800–1829* at: www.british-fiction.cf.ac.uk.
17. *Letters*, I, p. 409.
18. *Letters*, II, pp. 91–2.
19. For further details, see Peter Garside, 'Printing *Confessions*', *SHW* 9 (1998), pp. 16–31. James Clarke had previously printed Hector MacNeill's *The Scottish Adventurers* (1812), evidently the first novel to be published by Blackwood, and one of the earliest new fiction titles to originate from the Scottish trade.
20. *Letters*, III, p. 70.
21. For a fuller account of Blackie & Son's operations, and its effect on Hogg's work, see Peter Garside and Gillian Hughes, 'James Hogg's "Tales and Sketches" and the Glasgow Number Trade', *Cardiff Corvey: Reading the Romantic Text*, 14 (Summer 2005), at: www.cf.ac.uk/encap/romtext/articles/cc14_n02.html.

Chapter 3 – Hughes

1. See Gillian Hughes, *James Hogg: A Life* (Edinburgh: Edinburgh University Press, 2007), p. 25 (hereafter *Life*).
2. For Laidlaw's letter, signed 'A Herd', see the *Edinburgh Weekly Journal* (30 June 1802).
3. Henry Scott Riddell, 'James Hogg, the Ettrick Shepherd', *Hogg's Weekly Instructor* (7 August 1847), pp. 369–74 (p. 372).

4. James Grant, *The Great Metropolis*, 2 vols (London: Saunders and Otley, 1836), II, pp. 252–3.
5. 'The Mistakes of a Night' is attributed to Hogg in 'Z.', 'Farther Particulars of the Life of James Hogg, the Ettrick Shepherd', *Scots Magazine*, 67 (July 1805), pp. 501–3 (p. 503); see also *The Mountain Bard*, ed. Suzanne Gilbert (Edinburgh: Edinburgh University Press, 2007), pp. 95–100.
6. Poetry in the *Universal Magazine* was sectioned as 'The British Muse'.
7. 'To Mr T. M. C., London', *Scots Magazine*, 67 (August 1805), pp. 621–2; 'Answer to the Ettrick Shepherd', *Scots Magazine*, 68 (March 1806), pp. 206–8.
8. Hogg to Janet Stuart, 10 October [1808?], in *The Collected Letters of James Hogg*, ed. Gillian Hughes and others, 3 vols (Edinburgh: Edinburgh University Press, 2004–8), I, pp. 94–6 (hereafter *Letters*). For Hogg's account of his first meeting with Allan and James Cunningham, the brothers of Thomas Mounsey Cunningham, see *Altrive Tales*, pp. 69–71.
9. Edith C. Batho provides details of early comment on Hogg as a poet and a chronological list of his known magazine publications before 1810 in *The Ettrick Shepherd* (Cambridge: Cambridge University Press, 1927), pp. 222–4, 183–8.
10. See James Hogg, *The Forest Minstrel*, ed. P. D. Garside and Richard D. Jackson (Edinburgh: Edinburgh University Press, 2006), pp. xli–xliv.
11. 'Memoir of the Author's Life', *Altrive Tales*, pp. 23–4.
12. See 'Notes on Contributors', *The Spy*, ed. Gillian Hughes (Edinburgh: Edinburgh University Press, 2000), pp. 557–71 (hereafter *Spy*).
13. *Spy*, pp. 333, 115–16, 185–91, 21–9, 32–43.
14. Gillian Hughes, 'A Tory Memorial for the Newspapers', *SHW*, 11 (2000), pp. 84–6, and 'Hogg's Poetic Responses to the Unexpected Death of his Patron', *SHW*, 12 (2001), pp. 80–9; *Letters*, I, 230; Gillian Hughes, 'James Hogg, and Edinburgh's Triumph over Napoleon', *Scottish Studies Review*, 4 no. 1 (Spring 2003), pp. 98–111.
15. Carol Polsgrove, 'They Made it Pay: British Short-Fiction Writers, 1820–1840', *Studies in Short Fiction*, 11 (1974), pp. 417–21.
16. *Letters*, I, pp. 300–1.
17. See 'Alarming Increase of Depravity among Animals', 'Sagacity of a Shepherd's Dog', and 'Further Anecdotes of the Shepherd's Dog', in *Blackwood's Edinburgh Magazine*, 2 (October 1817, January and March 1818), pp. 82–6, 417–21, 621–6.
18. James Hogg, *Contributions to Blackwood's Edinburgh Magazine Volume 1: 1817–1828*, ed. Thomas C. Richardson (Edinburgh: Edinburgh University Press, 2008), p. xiii.
19. J. H. Alexander, 'Hogg in the *Noctes Ambrosianae*', *SHW*, 4 (1993), pp. 37–47.
20. For a brief account see *Life*, pp. 213–15.
21. Hogg's account of the Carterhaugh cattle-show (National Library of Scotland

(NLS), MS 599, fols 281–2) was sent to Alexander Ballantyne, printer of the *Kelso Mail*, by the Duke of Buccleuch in a letter of 22 October 1818 (NLS, MS 580, fol. 123); see also 'The Young Buccleuch' in the *Edinburgh Weekly Chronicle* of 15 September 1830.

22. *Letters*, III, p. 256.
23. *Letters*, II, p. 456.
24. *Letters*, III, p. 283.
25. Gillian Hughes, 'The Importance of the Periodical Environment in Hogg's Work for *Chambers's Edinburgh Journal*', in *Papers Given at the First Conference of the James Hogg Society* (Stirling: James Hogg Society, 1983), pp. 40–8.
26. *Letters*, III, p. 190.

Chapter 4 – Gilbert

1. André Gide, 'Introduction' to James Hogg, *The Private Memoirs and Confessions of a Justified Sinner*, second impression (London: The Cresset Press, 1964), p. ix.
2. Ibid.
3. Hogg, *The Private Memoirs and Confessions of a Justified Sinner*, ed. Peter Garside (Edinburgh: Edinburgh University Press), 2001, pp. lxviii.
4. William St Clair, *The Reading Nation in the Romantic Period* (Cambridge: Cambridge University Press, 2004), p. 361.
5. *The Poetical Register* 6 (1807), pp. 548–9; see James Hogg, *The Mountain Bard*, ed. Suzanne Gilbert (Edinburgh: Edinburgh University Press, 2007), p. xlii.
6. Ibid.
7. *Literary Panorama* 2 (1807), cols 957–60; see Hogg, *The Mountain Bard*, p. xliv.
8. *The Annual Review and History of Literature* 6 (1807), pp. 554–7; see Hogg, *The Mountain Bard*, p. xliii.
9. *The Cabinet: A Monthly Magazine of Polite Literature* 1 (1807), pp. 332–3; see Hogg, *The Mountain Bard*, p. xliv.
10. James Hogg, *The Queen's Wake*, ed. Douglas S. Mack (Edinburgh: Edinburgh University Press, 2004), p. 394.
11. James Hogg, *Anecdotes of Scott*, ed. Jill Rubenstein (Edinburgh: Edinburgh University Press, 2004), p. 61.
12. See Hogg, *The Mountain Bard*, pp. 137–89.
13. James Hogg, 'Memoir of the Author's Life', in *Altrive Tales*, pp. 11–52 (p. 17).
14. See Hogg, *The Mountain Bard*, pp. 123–36.
15. Gillian Hughes, *James Hogg: A Life* (Edinburgh: Edinburgh University Press), p. 82.
16. Ian Duncan, *Scott's Shadow: The Novel in Romantic Edinburgh* (Princeton and Oxford: Princeton University Press, 2007), p. 148.

17. James Hogg, *The Spy*, ed. Gillian Hughes (Edinburgh: Edinburgh University Press, 2000), p. 514.
18. *Monthly Magazine* 35 (May, 1813), p. 501; see Hogg, *The Queen's Wake*, p. 1.
19. Ibid., p. li.
20. Ibid., p. l.
21. Ibid., pp. lii–liii.
22. Ibid., p. lxvii.
23. *New Edinburgh Monthly Review* 5 (June 1821), pp. 662–72 (p. 671).
24. James Hogg, *The Collected Letters of James Hogg, vol. 2, 1820–1831*, ed. by Gillian Hughes et al. (Edinburgh: Edinburgh University Press, 2000), p. 94.
25. Hogg, *Private Memoirs and Confessions of a Justified Sinner*, p. lxvii.
26. 'Noctes Ambrosianae' 8, *Blackwood's Edinburgh Magazine* 13 (May 1823), p. 599.
27. Duncan, *Scott's Shadow*, p. 174; 'Hogg's *Three Perils of Woman*', *Blackwood's Edinburgh Magazine* 14 (October 1823), p. 427.
28. Duncan, *Scott's Shadow*, p. 174.
29. J. G. Lockhart, *Peter's Letters to his Kinsfolk*, ed. William Ruddick (Edinburgh: Scottish Academic Press, 1977), p. 45
30. 'Noctes Ambrosianae' 20, *Blackwood's Edinburgh Magazine* 28 (October 1826), p. 624.
31. Hogg, 'Memoir of the Life of James Hogg', in *The Mountain Bard* (1821), p. 230.
32. James Hogg, *Queen Hynde*, ed. Suzanne Gilbert and Douglas S. Mack (Edinburgh: Edinburgh University Press, 1998), p. 176.
33. *Westminster Review* 3 (April 1825), pp. 531–7 (p. 537); see Hogg, *Queen Hynde*, p. 1.
34. Hogg, *Anecdotes of Scott*, p. xviii.
35. William Maginn, Review of *The Domestic Manners of Scott*, by James Hogg, *Frasers Magazine* 10:61 (August 1834), p. 125.
36. Hogg, *Anecdotes of Scott*, p. xxvi.
37. John Gibson Lockhart, *Memoirs of the Life of Sir Walter Scott, Bart.*, 7 vols (Edinburgh: Robert Cadell, 1837–38), vol. 1, p. 408.
38. Janette Currie, 'American Periodical Press', *James Hogg: Research*, www.james hogg.stir.ac.uk/showbib.php?id=1 (accessed June 2011).
39. Janette Currie, 'The Authorship of "Escape from Death – At Sea": A Literary Puzzle', *James Hogg: Research*, www.jameshogg.stir.ac.uk/showrecord. php?id=75&fulltext=1 (accessed June 2011).
40. Ibid.
41. See Andrew Hook, *Scotland and America: A Study of Cultural Relations 1750–1835* (Glasgow and London: Blackie, 1975); and *From Goosecreek to Gandercleugh: Studies in Scottish-American Literary and Cultural History* (East Linton: Tuckwell Press, 1999), pp. 116–34; see also Stephanie Anderson-Currie's *Preliminary Census of Early Hogg Editions in North American Libraries*,

South Carolina Working Papers in Scottish Bibliography (Columbia, SC: University of South Carolina, 1993), p. 3.

42. Hook, 'Hogg, Melville and the Scottish Enlightenment', in *From Goosecreek to Gandercleugh*, p. 128.

43. Hook, *Scotland and America*, p. 152.

44. *American Monthly Magazine*, 3 (1834), p. 177; see Hook, *Scotland and America*, p. 153.

45. John Wilson, *Noctes Ambrosianae*, ed. James Frederick Ferrier, 4 vols (Edinburgh and London: William Blackwood and Sons, 1864), vol. 2, p. ix

46. I am grateful to Janette Currie for this suggestion.

47. Extracted from *The American Monthly Magazine* (Boston: Pierce and Williams; N. P. Willis), 1 (November 1829), pp. 522–30. The magazine was edited by Nathaniel Parker Willis from April 1829 to July 1831. See Janette Currie, 'The American Reception of Hogg's Work', *James Hogg: Research*, www.james hogg.stir.ac.uk/showrecord.php?id=64&fulltext=1 (accessed June 2011).

48. See Hughes's chapter, 'Afterlives' (Chapter 16).

49. Edwin Morgan, 'The Stirling/South Carolina Edition of James Hogg', *Scottish Literary Journal*, Supplement 44 (Spring 1996), pp. 1–2.

Chapter 5 – de Groot

I thank Gillian Hughes for the helpful comments she made on an earlier draft of this Chapter.

1. In each case the dates given are those of the actual journeys. The travel accounts were published later, sometimes much later. On eighteenth-century travels to the Highlands, see Martin Rackwitz, *Travels to Terra Incognita: The Scottish Highlands and Hebrides in Early Modern Travellers' Accounts, c.1600 to 1800* (Münster: Waxman, 2007).

2. See Hogg, James, *Collected Letters*, ed. Gillian Hughes and others, 3 vols (Edinburgh: Edinburgh University Press, 2004–8), I, pp. 3–4.

3. All extant portions of Hogg's accounts of the 1802, 1803 and 1804 journeys have been brought together in Hogg, *Highland Journeys*, ed. H. B. de Groot (Edinburgh: Edinburgh University Press, 2010). Further references to this text are made in the body of this chapter. For earlier accounts of the *Highland Journeys*, see Silvia Mergenthal, *Selbstbild und Bild: Zur Rezeption des Ettrick Shepherd* (Frankfurt-am-Main: P. Lang, 1990): Antony J. Hasler, 'Reading the Land: James Hogg and the Highlands', *Studies in Hogg and his World* 4 (1993), 57–82; Gillian Hughes, *James Hogg: A Life* (Edinburgh: Edinburgh University Press, 2007), pp. 48–60.

4. See Janette Currie, Appendices III and IV in Hogg, *Highland Journeys*, pp. 231–45.

5. Hogg, 'Memoir of the Author's Life', in *Altrive Tales*, ed. Gillian Hughes (Edinburgh: Edinburgh University Press, 2003), p. 34.
6. Hogg, *Altrive Tales*, pp. 34–5; cited in Hogg, *Mador of the Moor*, ed. James E. Barcus (Edinburgh: Edinburgh University Press, 2005), p. xi.
7. Hogg to Alexander Bald, 14 November 1813 (*Collected Letters*, I, pp. 166–7).
8. James Barcus's comments on Hogg, *Mador of the Moor*, pp. xi–xii.
9. Hogg to Anne Bald, 1 June 1816 (*Collected Letters*, I, pp. 277–8).
10. Hogg, *Queen Hynde*, ed. Suzanne Gilbert and Douglas S. Mack (Edinburgh: Edinburgh University Press, 1998), p. 218.
11. Hogg, *The Spy*, ed. Gillian Hughes (Edinburgh: Edinburgh University Press, 2000), pp. 41–3, 397–402, 437–43.
12. Hogg, *Winter Evening Tales*, ed. Ian Duncan (Edinburgh: Edinburgh University Press, 2002), pp. 3–74, 98–106, 107–18; quotation from p. 104.
13. Hogg, *Tales of the Wars of Montrose*, ed. Gillian Hughes (Edinburgh: Edinburgh University Press, 1996), pp. 99–137.
14. Hogg, 'The Captain's Expedition', in *The Amulet: An Elegant Literary Present*, ed. Charles J. Cecil (London: R. A. Charlton; Dublin: J. Cumming; Glasgow: J. Campbell, n.d. [1846?]), re-edited by Thomas Richardson in *Studies in Hogg and his World* 20 (2009), pp. 100–26. Hogg also used his Highland experiences in several of his contributions to *Blackwood's Edinburgh Magazine*: 'Some Passages in the Life of Colonel Cloud', 'A Strange Secret' and 'The Stuarts o' Appin'. See Hogg, *Contributions to 'Blackwood's Edinburgh Magazine'*, Volume I, 1817–1828, ed. Thomas Richardson (Edinburgh: Edinburgh University Press, 2008), pp. 166–80, 315–45, 348–50. Two further contributions to *Blackwood's* ('Mona Campbell' and 'A Horrible Instance of the Effects of Clanship', later republished as 'Julia McKenzie' in *Tales of the Wars of Montrose*) will be included in the second volume of *Contributions to Blackwood's Edinburgh Magazine*. In 1829 Hogg published two articles in *The Edinburgh Literary Journal*: 'Anecdotes of Highlanders' and 'A Story of the Forty-Six' (2, pp. 293–95, 421–2). Both were reprinted in *Chambers's Edinburgh Journal* in 1834.
15. Hogg, *The Forest Minstrel*, ed. P. D. Garside and Richard D. Jackson (Edinburgh: Edinburgh University Press, 2006), p. 198.
16. William Donaldson, *The Jacobite Song: Political Myth and National Identity* (Aberdeen: Aberdeen University Press, 1988), pp. 105–6; Murray G. H. Pittock, *The Invention of Scotland* (London: Routledge, 1991), p. 94.
17. Hogg, *The Jacobite Relics of Scotland* [first series], ed. Murray G. H. Pittock (Edinburgh: Edinburgh University Press, 2002), p. v.
18. Hogg, *The Three Perils of Woman*, ed. by David Groves, Antony Hasler and Douglas S. Mack (Edinburgh: Edinburgh University Press, 1995), p. 407. See also Douglas Mack's comments in the paperback edition of this novel (Edinburgh: Edinburgh University Press, 2002), p. 427.

Chapter 6 – Alker and Nelson

1. Robert Crawford, *Scotland's Books: The Penguin History of Scottish Literature* (London: Penguin, 2007), p. 672.
2. Ian Brown, 'Staging the Nation: Multiplicity and Cultural Diversity in Contemporary Scottish Theatre', and David Hutchison, 'Theatres, Writers, and Society: Structures and Infrastructures of Theatre Provision in Twentieth-Century Scotland', in Ian Brown et al. (eds), *The Edinburgh History of Scottish Literature* (Edinburgh: Edinburgh University Press, 2007), vol. 3, pp. 283–94 (p. 286) and pp. 142–50 (p. 148).
3. Douglas S. Mack, 'Can the Scottish Subaltern Speak? Nonelite Scotland and the Scottish Parliament', in Caroline McCracken-Flesher (ed.), *Culture, Nation, and the New Scottish Parliament* (Lewisburg: Bucknell University Press, 2007), pp. 141–57 (p. 155).
4. 'Working Class', in John Scott and Gordon Marshall (eds), *A Dictionary of Sociology*, 3rd rev. edn (Oxford: Oxford University Press, 2009), p. 810. Pamela Sharpe, 'Population and Society 1700–1840', in Peter Clarke (ed.), *The Cambridge Urban History of Britain: 1540–1840* (Cambridge: Cambridge University Press, 2000), p. 521.
5. James Hogg, *The Collected Letters of James Hogg* (3 vols, Edinburgh, 2004–8), Gillian Hughes et al. (eds), vol. 3, p. 267.
6. Hogg to David Imrie, 23 February 1835, in Hughes et al. (eds), *Collected Letters*, vol. 3, p. 255.
7. Ian Duncan, 'Introduction', *Modern Language Quarterly* (2009), pp. 403–13 (p. 404).
8. See Ian Duncan, *Scott's Shadow: The Novel in Romantic Edinburgh* (Princeton: Princeton University Press, 2008), p. 149.
9. Simon White, 'Introduction', in Simon White, John Goodridge and Bridget Keegan (eds), *Robert Bloomfield: Lyrics, Class, and the Romantic Canon* (Lewisburg: Bucknell University Press, 2006), pp. 17–26 (p. 21).
10. Gillian Hughes, *James Hogg: A Life* (Edinburgh: Edinburgh University Press, 2007), p. 40.
11. James Hogg, *A Series of Lay Sermons*, ed. Gillian Hughes, with Douglas S. Mack (Edinburgh: Edinburgh University Press, 1997), p. 103.
12. John Barrell, *English Literature in History 1730–80: An Equal, Wide Survey* (New York: St Martin's Press, 1983), p. 179.
13. Ibid., pp. 196, 206–7.
14. James Hogg, *The Queen's Wake*, ed. Douglas S. Mack (Edinburgh: Edinburgh University Press, 2005), p. 367.
15. Hughes et al. (eds), *Collected Letters*, vol. 2, p. 185.
16. Luke Maynard, 'Hoddin Grey an' A' That: Robert Burns's Head, Class Hybridity, and the Value of the Ploughman's Mantle', in Aruna Krishnamurthy (ed.), *The Working-Class Intellectual in Eighteenth- and*

Nineteenth-Century Britain (Aldershot: Ashgate, 2009), pp. 67–84 (p. 75).

17. John Barrell, *The Dark Side of the Landscape: The Rural Poor in English Painting 1730–1840* (Cambridge: Cambridge University Press, 1980), pp. 2, 5.

18. Ibid., p. 9.

19. James Hogg, 'The Poachers', *Contributions to Annuals and Gift-Books*, in Janette Currie and Gillian Hughes (eds), (Edinburgh: Edinburgh University Press, 2006), pp. 241–9 (p. 241).

20. Ibid., p. 249.

21. James Hogg, 'Duncan Campbell', *The Spy*, ed. Gillian Hughes (Edinburgh: Edinburgh University Press, 2000), pp. 485–92, 504–13 (p. 491).

22. Ibid., p. 505 (lines 145–52).

23. James Hogg, 'Jock Johnstone the Tinkler', *A Queer Book*, ed. P. D. Garside (Edinburgh: Edinburgh University Press, 1995), pp. 69–76 (p. 73).

24. James Hogg, *The Brownie of Bodsbeck and Other Tales* (2 vols, Edinburgh, 1818), vol. 1, p. 3.

25. Ibid., vol. 1, p. 18.

26. Ibid., vol. 1, p. 36.

27. Ibid., vol. 1 p. 146.

28. Ibid., vol. 1, pp. 163, 230, 19.

29. Ibid., vol. 1, p. 19.

30. Ibid., vol. 2, p. 12.

31. Ibid., vol. 1, p. 49.

32. James Hogg, *The Forest Minstrel*, ed. Peter Garside and Richard D. Jackson (Edinburgh: Edinburgh University Press, 2006), p. 6.

Chapter 7 – Mack

1. James Gray, Hogg's close friend and relative by marriage, had been a member of Robert Burns's radical circle in Dumfries in the 1790s. Gray was an important contributor to Hogg's periodical *The Spy*. See Hogg, *The Spy*, ed. Gillian Hughes (Edinburgh: Edinburgh University Press, 2000), pp. 562–63.

2. From 'Superstition', in James Hogg, *The Pilgrims of the Sun* (Edinburgh: Blackwood, 1815), pp. 131–48 (p. 138).

3. 'On the Separate Existence of the Soul', in Hogg, *Selected Stories and Sketches*, ed. Douglas S. Mack (Edinburgh: Scottish Academic Press, 1982), pp. 180–95 (p. 181). This story was first published in the December 1831 number of *Fraser's Magazine* (4, pp. 529–37), having been rejected by *Blackwood's Edinburgh Magazine* in September 1831.

4. *The Private Memoirs and Confessions of a Justified Sinner*, ed. P. D. Garside (Edinburgh: Edinburgh University Press, 2001), p. 29.

5. *Confessions of a Justified Sinner*, ed. Garside, pp. 133–40 (pp. 134, 133).

6. From 'Anecdotes of Sir W. Scott', in Hogg, *Anecdotes of Scott*, ed. Jill Rubenstein (Edinburgh: Edinburgh University Press, 1999), pp. 3–30 (p. 3).
7. Scott, *The Life of Napoleon Buonaparte*, 9 vols (Edinburgh: Cadell, 1827), I, pp. 30–1.
8. Liam McIlvanney, *Burns the Radical: Poetry and Politics in Late Eighteenth-Century Scotland* (East Linton: Tuckwell Press, 2002), p. 7.
9. From 'Familiar Anecdotes of Sir Walter Scott', in Hogg, *Anecdotes of Scott*, ed. Jill Rubenstein (Edinburgh: Edinburgh University Press, 1999), pp. 50–2.
10. See *The Collected Letters of James Hogg*, ed. Gillian Hughes, 3 vols (Edinburgh: Edinburgh University Press, 2004–8), I, p. 136.
11. See Hogg, *Winter Evening Tales*, ed. Ian Duncan (Edinburgh: Edinburgh University Press, 2002: paperback reprint 2004), p. xiv.
12. Hogg, *Collected Letters*, ed. Hughes, I, p. 151. Like many letters written to Hogg at this unsettled period of his life, Scott's letter does not seem to have survived.
13. Hogg, *Collected Letters*, ed. Hughes, I, p. 145.
14. See James Hogg, *Memoir of the Author's Life* and *Familiar Anecdotes of Sir Walter Scott*, ed. Douglas S. Mack (Edinburgh: Scottish Academic Press, 1972), p. 45.
15. Hogg, *Collected Letters*, ed. Hughes, I, p. 326. See also Hogg, *Winter Evening Tales*, ed. Duncan, pp. xvi–xvii.
16. Hogg, *The Brownie of Bodsbeck*, ed. Douglas S. Mack (Edinburgh: Scottish Academic Press, 1976), p. 163.
17. *The Collected Essays, Journalism and Letters of George Orwell*, ed. Sonia Orwell and Ian Angus, 4 vols (London: Secker & Warburg, 1968), I, pp. 416, 417, 427–8.

Chapter 8 – McCracken-Flesher

1. *The Morning Chronicle*, 1 January 1832, quoted in Gillian Hughes, *James Hogg: A Life* (Edinburgh: Edinburgh University Press, 2007), p. 247.
2. Letter to Margaret Hogg, 17 February 1832, Hughes, *The Collected Letters*, vol. 3, pp. 35–9, see p. 36.
3. Allan Cunningham, 'Hogg,' *The Athenaeum* 313 (26 October 1833): pp. 720–1; see p. 720.
4. James Anthony Froude, *Thomas Carlyle. A History of the First Forty Years of His Life, 1795–1835*, 2 vols (New York: Charles Scribner's, 1897), vol. 2, p. 189 (hereafter, Froude).
5. Review, 'The Songs of James Hogg, the Ettrick Shepherd', *Athenaeum* (January 1831): pp. 6–7; see p. 7.
6. 'James Hogg, The Ettrick Shepherd', *Athenaeum* (1835), pp. 912–13 (see p. 912).
7. Sir Walter Scott to Lord Montagu, 1 July 1821, *The Letters of Sir Walter Scott*,

ENDNOTES

ed. H. J. C. Grierson, 12 vols (1934; rpt. New York: AMS, 1971), vol. 6, pp. 487–91; see p. 487 (hereafter Scott, *Letters*).

8. Benedict Anderson, *Imagined Communities: Reflections on the Origin and Spread of Nationalism*, rev. edn (London: Verso, 1991), 'Introduction'.

9. Douglas S. Mack recuperates the idea of Hogg as the common man and critiques the assumption that he was therefore naïve. See *Scottish Fiction and the British Empire* (Edinburgh: Edinburgh University Press, 2006), p. 32.

10. Tom Nairn, 'The Three Dreams of Scottish Nationalism', in Lindsay Paterson (ed.), *A Diverse Assembly: The Debate on a Scottish Parliament* (Edinburgh: Edinburgh University Press, 1998), pp. 31–9; see p. 36.

11. Frantz Fanon, *The Wretched of the Earth*, trans. Constance Farrington (New York: Grove Weidenfeld, 1991), pp. 210, 49.

12. See Craig Beveridge and Ronald Turnbull, *The Eclipse of Scottish Culture: Inferiorism and the Intellectuals* (Edinburgh: Polygon, 1989).

13. John Gibson Lockhart, *Peter's Letters to his Kinsfolk*, ed. William Ruddick (Edinburgh: Scottish Academic Press, 1977), pp. 44–5.

14. Homi K. Bhabha, 'DissemiNation: Time, Narrative, and the Margins of the Modern Nation', in his *Nation and Narration* (London: Routledge, 1990), pp. 291–322; especially pp. 297–302.

15. Valentina Bold, *James Hogg: A Bard of Nature's Making* (Bern: Peter Lang, 2007), pp. 64–9.

16. Ian Duncan, 'The Upright Corpse: Hogg, National Literature and the Uncanny', *Studies in Hogg and His World* 5 (1994), pp. 29–54; Murray Pittock, *Scottish and Irish Romanticism* (Oxford: Oxford University Press, 2008), p. 216.

17. James Hogg, *Memoir of the Author's Life and Familiar Anecdotes of Sir Walter Scott*, ed. Douglas S. Mack (Edinburgh: Scottish Academic Press, 1972), pp. 11–12.

18. Anon. [Dr. James Browne], *The "Life" of the Ettrick Shepherd Anatomised* (Edinburgh: William Hunter, 1832), p. 10.

19. James Hogg, *Familiar Anecdotes of Sir Walter Scott*, in *Anecdotes of Scott*, ed. Jill Rubenstein (Edinburgh: Edinburgh University Press, 1999), p. 59.

20. James Hogg, *The Queen's Wake*, 1813, ed. Douglas S. Mack (Edinburgh: Edinburgh University Press, 2004).

21. James Hogg, *Mador of the Moor*, 1816, ed. James E. Barcus (Edinburgh: Edinburgh University Press, 2005).

22. Louise Olga Fradenburg, *City, Marriage, Tournament* (Madison: University of Wisconsin Press, 1991).

23. In 1821, Scott had encouraged Hogg to attend George's coronation to that end. He did not go (Scott, *Letters*, vol. 6, pp. 487–91; see p. 487).

24. James Hogg, 'The Royal Jubilee', 1822, rpt. *Studies in Hogg and His World* 5 (1994), pp. 102–51 (see p. 111).

25. James Hogg, *The Three Perils of Man*, 1822, ed. Graham Tulloch and Judy King (Edinburgh: Edinburgh University Press, 2012).

26. James Hogg, *The Three Perils of Woman*, 1823, ed. David Groves, Antony Hasler, and Douglas S. Mack (Edinburgh: Edinburgh University Press, 1995).

27. James Hogg, *The Private Memoirs and Confessions of a Justified Sinner*, 1824, ed. P. D. Garside (Edinburgh: Edinburgh University Press, 2001).

28. *Athenaeum* (1835), p. 913.

29. *Athenaeum* (1833), p. 720.

30. George Goldie, 'Letter to a Friend; containing observations on the Memoir of James Hogg, the Ettrick Shepherd' (1821), 2nd edn (Edinburgh: George Abercromby Douglas, 1832).

31. 'Familiar Epistles to Christopher North, from an Old Friend with a New Face', *Blackwood's Edinburgh Magazine* 10 (August 1821: 2), pp. 43–52; see p. 43.

32. John Scott, 'The Mohock Magazine', *London Magazine* 2 (December 1820): pp. 666–85; see p. 668. See Patrick O'Leary, *Regency Editor: Life of John Scott* (Aberdeen: Aberdeen University Press, 1983).

33. David McCrone, *The Sociology of Nationalism: Tomorrow's Ancestors* (London: Routledge, 1998), p. 52. See also *Understanding Scotland: The Sociology of a Stateless Nation* (London: Routledge, 1992).

Chapter 9 – Mergenthal

1. James Hogg, 'The Renowned Adventures of Basil Lee', in James Hogg, *Winter Evening Tales. Collected Among the Cottagers of Scotland*, ed. Ian Duncan (Edinburgh: Edinburgh University Press, 2002), pp. 3–74.

2. See Duncan's note to 'Basil Lee', *Winter Evening Tales*, p. 548.

3. 'Basil Lee', p. 20.

4. One cannot help being reminded of Hogg's own response when he himself became embroiled in an 'affair of honour' in 1818: according to a letter by Scott to the Duke of Buccleuch, Hogg locked up the two seconds who attended on him on behalf of the Glasgow publisher John Douglas in his room and then sent for the police. See Ian Duncan, *Scott's Shadow. The Novel in Romantic Edinburgh* (Princeton: Princeton University Press, 2007), p. 150. See also Gillian Hughes, *James Hogg: A Life* (Edinburgh: Edinburgh University Press, 2007), pp. 149–50.

5. This final paragraph is followed by two stanzas from Hogg's own long poem *Mador of the Moor*.

6. 'Basil Lee', p. 73.

7. Ibid., p. 18.

8. James Hogg, *The Three Perils of Man. War, Women and Witchcraft*, ed. Douglas Gifford (Edinburgh: Scottish Academic Press, 1989).

9. James Hogg, *The Three Perils of Woman, or Love, Leasing, and Jealousy: A Series of Domestic Scottish Tales*, ed. Antony Hasler and Douglas S. Mack (Edinburgh: Edinburgh University Press, 2002).

10. See Graham Tulloch, 'Writing "by advice": *Ivanhoe* and *The Three Perils of Man*', *Studies in Hogg and his World* 15 (2004), pp. 32–52, here p. 41; Graham Tulloch, 'The Perilous Castle(s) of *The Three Perils of Man*', in Sharon Alker and Holly Faith Nelson (eds), *James Hogg and the Literary Marketplace: Scottish Romanticism and the Working-Class Author* (Farnham: Ashgate, 2009), pp. 157–74. My own reading of *Three Perils of Man* is also indebted to Penny Fielding, *Writing and Orality: Nationality, Culture, and Nineteenth-Century Scottish Fiction* (Oxford: Clarendon, 1996).

11. *Three Perils of Man*, p. 342.

12. On the national tale see Katie Trumpener, *Bardic Nationalism: The Romantic Novel and the British Empire* (Princeton: Princeton University Press, 1997). See also Anne McClintock, '"No Longer in a Future Heaven": Nationalism, Gender, and Race', in Geoff Eley and Ronald Grigory Suny (eds), *Becoming National: A Reader* (Oxford: Oxford University Press, 1996), pp. 260–84.

13. *Three Perils of Woman*, p. 224.

14. See Antony J. Hasler's introduction to the 2002 edition, in particular p. xxxiv. See also Antony J. Hasler, 'Reading the Land: James Hogg and the Highlands', in *Studies in Hogg and his World* 4 (1993), pp. 57–82. This reading of both *Perils* also draws upon Meiko O'Halloran, 'Treading the Borders of Fiction: Veracity, Identity, and Corporeality in *The Three Perils*', in *Studies in Hogg and his World* 12 (2001), pp. 40–55.

15. *Three Perils of Woman*, pp. 392 and 399, respectively.

16. For a concise summary of the critical discussion regarding Gatty's death-in-life state, see Richard D. Jackson, 'Gatty Bell's Illness in James Hogg's *The Three Perils of Woman*', in *Studies in Hogg and his World* 14 (2003), pp. 16–29. For a survey of Hogg's 'upright corpses' see Duncan, *Scott's Shadow*, pp. 183–214.

17. In his late tale 'On the Separate Existence of the Soul', Hogg's narrator explicitly speculates on the gender (grammatical and otherwise) of the soul: 'I wonder what can be the reason that people take it upon them to *her* and to *she* both their own souls and those of other people; yet both poets and philosophers uniformly do so. I cannot think it feasible that the souls of men can all become of the feminine gender, unless it could be made to appear that the souls of the women turned out to be of the other sex. This amalgamation might do pretty well, but then the principle is not to be borne out by the character.' See James Hogg, *Selected Stories and Sketches*, ed. Douglas S. Mack (Edinburgh: Scottish Academic Press, 1982), pp. 180–95, here pp. 184–5. See also, for a contemporary treatise on the topic, Thomas Huntingford, *Testimonies in Proof of the Separate Existence of the Soul in a State of Self-Consciousness Between Death and the Resurrection* (London: Rivington, 1829).

18. *Three Perils of Woman*, pp. 199 and 399, respectively.

19. Harold Garfinkel, *Studies in Ethnomethodology* (Englewood Cliffs: Prentice Hall, 1967), p. 118.

20. *Three Perils of Woman*, p. 29.

Chapter 10 – McCue

1. See 'Memoir of the Life of James Hogg', in James Hogg, *The Mountain Bard*, ed. Suzanne Gilbert (Edinburgh: Edinburgh University Press, 2007), pp. 9–10.

2. See Gillian Hughes, *James Hogg: A Life* (Edinburgh: Edinburgh University Press, 2007). See pp. 160, 245–8, and 270–1. See also Hogg's account of a performance of 'Donald M'Donald' in *Anecdotes of Scott*, ed. Jill Rubinstein (Edinburgh: Edinburgh University Press, 1999), pp. 23–4.

3. See H. B. de Groot, 'Musical Notation in the *Highland Journeys*: Did Hogg have perfect pitch?', in *Studies in Hogg and his World* 16 (2005), 127–30.

4. See Murray G. H. Pittock, 'James Hogg: Scottish Romanticism, Song and the Public Sphere', in Sharon Alker and Holly Faith Nelson (eds), *James Hogg and the Literary Marketplace: Scottish Romanticism and the Working-Class Author* (Farnham and Burlington: Ashgate, 2009), pp. 111–22.

5. See *The Mountain Bard*, ed. Gilbert, p. 7.

6. See M. G. Garden, *Memorials of James Hogg, The Ettrick Shepherd*, second edn (Paisley and London: Alexander Gardner, 1887), pp. 5, 13.

7. See Elaine Petrie, 'Hogg as Songwriter', in *Studies in Hogg and his World* 1 (1990), pp. 19–29.

8. Hogg's 1832 'Memoir' suggests that it was 1797 when he first heard about Burns. See James Hogg, 'Memoir of the Author's Life', in *Altrive Tales*, pp. 17–18. See references to Burns in Hughes's *James Hogg: A Life*. See also Kirsteen McCue, "Singing 'more old songs than ever ploughman could': The Songs of James Hogg and Robert Burns in the Musical Marketplace", in *James Hogg and the Literary Marketplace*, pp. 123–38.

9. See James Hogg, *Songs by The Ettrick Shepherd* (Edinburgh: Blackwood, 1831), p. 1. A full account of the textual and publishing history of 'Donald Macdonald' is given in James Hogg, *The Forest Minstrel*, ed. Peter Garside and Richard Jackson (Edinburgh: Edinburgh University Press, 2006), pp. 348–52. See also *The Mountain Bard*, ed. Gilbert, pp. 454–5. See also Peter Garside, 'The Origins and History of James Hogg's "Donald Macdonald"', *Scottish Studies Review* 7:2 (Autumn 2006), pp. 24–39.

10. See James Hogg, *Highland Journeys*, ed. H. B. de Groot (Edinburgh: Edinburgh University Press, 2010), pp. 7–8.

11. Ibid., p. 60.

12. Ibid., p. 167.

13. See Kirsteen McCue, 'From the Songs of *Albyn's Anthology* to *German Hebrew Melodies*: the Musical Adventures of James Hogg', in *Studies in Hogg and his World* 20 (2009), pp. 67–83.

14. See Hogg's letter to Walter Scott, 24 December [1803] in *The Collected Letters of James Hogg*, vol. 1 1800–1809, ed. Gillian Hughes et al. (Edinburgh:

Edinburgh University Press, 2004), pp. 38–41. Hogg suggests he has enough songs at this time to 'make above an hundred pages closs [sic] printed' (p. 39).

15. See *The Forest Minstrel*, ed. Garside and Jackson, pp. xxxix–l.
16. See *The Mountain Bard*, ed. Gilbert, p. 207.
17. Although *The Forest Minstrel* contained only lyrics or text in 1810, the new edition by Garside and Jackson has presented probable musical sources for the songs too, employing a wide range of contemporary musical sources, many of which Hogg would have known.
18. Here Hogg was contesting Scott's place as Border ballad collector in the *Minstrelsy of the Scottish Border*. See *The Mountain Bard*, ed. Gilbert, pp. xxvi–xxviii.
19. See James Hogg, *The Queen's Wake*, ed. Douglas S. Mack (Edinburgh: Edinburgh University Press, 2005), pp. xlviii–liii.
20. Hogg apparently had reservations about the quality of some of the songs and ballads and states in his 1821 'Memoir' that he thought *The Queen's Wake* was 'a very imperfect and unequal work': see *The Mountain Bard*, ed. Gilbert, p. 215.
21. See Hogg's 1832 'Memoir' in *Altrive Tales*, p. 24.
22. See Kirsteen McCue, '"The Skylark": the popularity of Hogg's 'Bird of the Wilderness"' (2009), on The James Hogg research website, at www.jameshogg.stir.ac.uk/ (accessed May 2010). See also Kirsteen McCue, 'From the Songs of *Albyn's Anthology* to *German Hebrew Melodies*, pp. 71–80.
23. For further information see: James Hogg, *Contributions to Musical Collections and Miscellaneous Songs*, ed. Kirsteen McCue (with Janette Currie) (Edinburgh: Edinburgh University Press, forthcoming). You can listen to this setting of the song at: www.jameshogg.stir.ac.uk/ (accessed May 2010).
24. See James Hogg, *Contributions to Musical Collections and Miscellaneous Songs*, ed. McCue (with Currie), forthcoming. For a broader introductory account of Hogg's contributions to contemporary musical collections see: Janette Currie and Kirsteen McCue, 'Editing the text and music of *Songs by the Ettrick Shepherd* (1831)', in *Scottish Studies Review*, vol. 8, no. 2 (November 2007), pp. 54–68.
25. See James Hogg, *Highland Journeys*, ed. de Groot, pp. 134, 176 and 184.
26. See James Hogg, *The Jacobite Relics of Scotland (First Series)* and *(Second Series)*, ed. Murray G. H. Pittock (Edinburgh: Edinburgh University Press, 2002 and 2003, respectively). See Murray G. H. Pittock, 'James Hogg and the Jacobite Song of Scotland', in *Studies in Hogg and his World* 14 (2003), pp. 73–87.
27. See Pittock, 'James Hogg and the Jacobite Song of Scotland', p. 75 and also *Jacobite Relics* (Second Series), ed. Pittock, pp. xvi–xvii.
28. See Pittock, 'James Hogg and the Jacobite Song of Scotland', p. 74.
29. Ibid., p. 77.

30. See *The Jacobite Relics of Scotland* (Second Series) ed. Pittock, pp. 160–2 (text); p. 355 (Hogg's note), p. 518 (editorial note).
31. See Currie and McCue, 'Editing the text and music of *Songs by the Ettrick Shepherd* (1831)' for more detailed information about these collections and their editors.
32. See James Hogg, *Contributions to Annuals and Gift-Books*, ed. Janette Currie and Gillian Hughes (Edinburgh: Edinburgh University Press, 2006), pp. 143–55. See also James Hogg, *Contributions to Blackwood's Edinburgh Magazine*, vol. 1, ed. Thomas Richardson (Edinburgh: Edinburgh University Press, 2008).
33. See *Letters*, vol. 2, pp. 380–1, 390–1, 400–1, and 404–7. These letters date from March to October 1830.
34. See *Letters*, vol. 2, p. 405. A *Queer Book*, including some smaller poems and ballads, appeared in exactly the same format and was in process only weeks after *Songs* was published. The two were considered companion volumes. See James Hogg, *A Queer Book*, ed. Peter Garside (Edinburgh: Edinburgh University Press, 1995). Hogg also suggested that *The Queen's Wake* might be reissued.
35. See Hogg's entry in Bryan N. S. Gooch and David S. Thatcher, *Musical Settings of British Romantic Literature*, vol. 2 (New York and London: Garland, 1982), pp. 787–809.
36. See James Hogg, 'Memoir of the Author's Life', in *Altrive Tales*, p. 18.
37. See 'Reminiscences of Former Days', in *Altrive Tales*, p. 55.

Chapter 11 – Wilson

1. Suzanne Gilbert (ed.), "Introduction" in James Hogg, *The Mountain Bard* (Edinburgh: Edinburgh University Press, 2007), p. xx.
2. James Hogg, *The Mountain Bard* (Edinburgh: Edinburgh University Press, 2007), p. 206.
3. Gillian Hughes, *James Hogg: A Life* (Edinburgh: Edinburgh University Press, 2007), pp. 101–4.
4. James Hogg, *The Queen's Wake*, ed. Douglas S. Mack (Edinburgh: Edinburgh University Press, 2005).
5. William Wordsworth, 'Preface' (1802), *Lyrical Ballads, and Other Poems 1797–1800*, ed. James Butler and Karen Green (Ithaca and London: Cornell University Press, 1992), p. 750.
6. James Hogg, *Altrive Tales*, ed. Gillian Hughes (Edinburgh: Edinburgh University Press, 2003), p. 68.
7. James Hogg, *Pilgrims of the Sun*, in *Midsummer Night Dreams and Related Poems*, ed. Jill Rubenstein, Gillian Hughes and Meiko O'Halloran (Edinburgh: Edinburgh University Press, 2008).
8. See Meiko O'Halloran, '"Circling the Pales of Heaven": Hogg and

Otherworld Journeys from Dante to Byron', in *Midsummer Night Dreams*, p. lxxviii.

9. See James Barcus, "Introduction," in Barcus (ed.), James Hogg, *Mador of the Moor* (Edinburgh: Edinburgh University Press, 2005), pp. xv–xviii, p. xxiii.

10. James Hogg, *The Spy*, ed. Gillian Hughes (Edinburgh: Edinburgh University Press, 2000), p. 398.

11. Susan Manning, 'James Hogg, *The Spy* (review)', *Studies in Hogg and His World*, 11 (2000), p. 135.

12. Suzanne Gilbert and Douglas S. Mack, 'Introduction', in Suzanne Gilbert and Douglas S. Mack (eds), James Hogg, *Queen Hynde* (Edinburgh: Edinburgh University Press, 1998), p. xi.

13. See Gilbert and Mack (eds), *Queen Hynde*, p. xv.

14. Gilbert and Mack, 'Introduction', *Queen Hynde*, p. xxx.

Chapter 12 – O'Halloran

1. *The Mountain Bard*, ed. Suzanne Gilbert (Edinburgh: Edinburgh University Press, 2007), p. 200. For Hogg's early playwriting, see the introduction to *The Bush Aboon Traquair and The Royal Jubilee*, ed. Douglas Mack (Edinburgh: Edinburgh University Press, 2008).

2. *Highland Journeys*, ed. H. B. de Groot (Edinburgh: Edinburgh University Press, 2010), pp. 21, 118.

3. 'Preface to Shakespeare', in *Johnson on Shakespeare*, ed. Arthur Sherbo, 2 vols (New Haven: Yale University Press, 1968), I, pp. 88, 89.

4. Michael Dobson, *The Making of the National Poet: Shakespeare, Adaptation and Authorship, 1660–1769* (Oxford: Clarendon, 1992), p. 8.

5. James C. Dibdin, *The Annals of the Edinburgh Stage* (Edinburgh: R. Cameron, 1888), p. 87.

6. For recent research which challenges many older perceptions about the vibrancy of Scottish theatre in this period, see Ian Brown, 'Public and Private Performance: 1650–1800', in Ian Brown (ed.), *The Edinburgh Companion to Scottish Drama* (Edinburgh: Edinburgh University Press, 2011), pp. 22–40.

7. *The Spy*, ed. Gillian Hughes (Edinburgh: Edinburgh University Press, 2000), p. 135.

8. Ibid., p. 135.

9. *Altrive Tales*, p. 28. See also Gillian Hughes, *James Hogg: A Life* (Edinburgh: Edinburgh University Press, 2007), pp. 86–7, and 'Hogg and Theatre', *Studies in Hogg and his World*, 15 (2004), pp. 53–66.

10. *The Spy*, p. 130.

11. Ibid., p. 130.

12. *Collected Letters of Samuel Taylor Coleridge*, ed. E. L. Griggs, 6 vols (Oxford: Oxford University Press, 1956–71), III, 437.

13. Hogg entrusted his play to John Grieve, William Laidlaw, Walter Scott,

William Roscoe, Bernard Barton, Capel Lofft. See Hughes, *James Hogg*, p. 119.

14. J. H. Craig of Douglas, *The Hunting of Badlewe, A Dramatic Tale* (Edinburgh and London, 1814), p. viii. Hereafter page references are given in parentheses.

15. See *Collected Letters of James Hogg*, ed. Gillian Hughes, 3 vols (Edinburgh: Edinburgh University Press, 2004–8), I, pp. 179, 182, 185.

16. For Hogg's earlier use of Holinshed's *Scottish Chronicle*, 2 vols (Arbroath: J. Findlay, 1805), see *The Queen's Wake*, pp. 178, 186, 442n, 445n.

17. *Badlewe*, IV, 2, p. 105.

18. Ibid., p. 107. *Hamlet*, IV, 7, l. 168.

19. *The Winter's Tale*, IV, 4, ll. 83, 92–3.

20. Karl Miller, *Electric Shepherd: A Likeness of James Hogg* (London: Faber, 2003), pp. 124–7.

21. *Altrive Tales*, p. 42.

22. *The Private Memoirs and Confessions of a Justified Sinner*, ed. John Carey (Oxford: Oxford University Press, 1969), p. 124.

23. *Westminster Review* (October 1824), 560–2, reproduced by Carey, pp. 256–8 (p. 258).

Chapter 13 – Plotz

1. Edgar Allen Poe, review of *Twice-Told Tales*, *Graham's Magazine*, 20 (1842), pp. 298–300. For Brander Matthews, Poe's principal acolyte, see Charles May (ed.) *The New Short Story Theories* (Athens: Ohio State University Press, 1984) and Mary Louise Pratt, 'The Long and the Short of It', *Poetics* 10 (1981), pp. 175–94. For similar views of the genre's key formal features and genealogy see Boris Eikhenbaum, 'O. Henry and the Theory of the Short Story' [1925], trans. I. R. Titunik, in L. Matejka (ed.), *Readings in Russian Poetics* (Cambridge, MA: MIT Press, 1971), pp. 227–70 (p. 234), and Dean Baldwin, 'The Tardy Evolution of the Short Story', *Studies in Short Fiction* 30 (1993), pp. 23–33 (p. 24).

2. Brander Matthews, *The Philosophy of the Short-story* (New York: Longmans, Green, 1901), p. 73.

3. Poe, p. 299.

4. Quoted in Tim Killick, *British Short Fiction in the Early Nineteenth Century: The Rise of the Tale* (Burlington: Ashgate, 2008) p. 14.

5. Killick, for example, argues that 'The relatively brief, self-contained prose fiction narrative that constitutes the modern idea of the short story does exist during the [early nineteenth century] but it is tied into a complex network of miscellaneous and comic extracts, single-volume tales, narrative essays and sketches, and other ephemeral and elastic modes of writing' (p. 19).

6. For the straightforward chronicle of early short fiction in English, see Barbara

Korte, *The Short Story in Britain: A Historical Sketch and an Anthology* (Tübingen: Francke, 2010). One helpful account of recent criticism that attempts to locate a long genealogy of the short story collection as a 'programmatically cosmopolitan form' is R. Johnson, R. Maxwell and K. Trumpener, '*The Arabian Nights*, Arab-European Literary Influence, and the Lineages of the Novel', *Modern Language Quarterly* 68:2 (2007), pp. 243–79.

7. Cf. Baldwin and Korte.

8. Gilles Deleuze and Felix Guattari, *Kafka: Towards a Minor Literature*, trans. D. Polan (Minneapolis: University of Minnesota Press, 1986 [1975]), pp. 17–27.

9. Robert Crawford, 'Bad Shepherd', *London Review of Books* (5 April 2010), pp. 28–9.

10. *The Listener* (28 March 1974).

11. David Cecil, 'Introduction', *Short Stories by Sir Walter Scott* (New York: Oxford University Press, 1934) p. ix.

12. Walter Scott, 'The Two Drovers', *Short Stories by Sir Walter Scott*, p. 259.

13. Franco Moretti, *The Way of the World; The Bildungsroman in European Culture*, trans. Alberto Sbragia (New York: Verso, 2000), p. 7.

14. James Hogg, 'An Old Soldier's Tale', *Winter Evening Tales*, ed. Ian Duncan (Edinburgh: Edinburgh University Press, 2004), pp. 98–107 (p. 107).

15. Douglas Mack, 'Aspects of the Supernatural in the Shorter Fiction of James Hogg', in Y. Valerie Tinkler-Villani and Peter Davidson (eds), *Exhibited by Candlelight* (Atlanta: Rodopi, 1995) pp. 129–35; Killick, p. 149.

16. Killick, p. 150.

17. James Hogg, 'An Old Soldier's Tale', p. 99.

18. The material in the paragraphs above is adapted from John Plotz, 'Review Essay: The Whole Hogg', *Novel: A Forum on Fiction* 43:2 (2010), pp. 320–5 (p. 323).

19. Maureen McLane, *Balladeering, Minstrelsy and the Making of British Romantic Poetry* (New York: Cambridge University Press, 2008), p. 182.

20. McLane, pp. 184–94.

21. James Hogg, 'Mr. Adamson of Laverhope', in James Hogg, *Shepherd's Calendar*, ed. Douglas Mack (Edinburgh: Edinburgh University Press, 2002), pp. 38–56 (p. 54).

22. Christopher Herbert, *Culture and Anomie: Ethnographic Imagination in the Nineteenth Century* (Chicago: University of Chicago Press, 1995) and James Buzard, *Disorienting Fiction: The Auto-Ethnographic Work of Nineteenth-Century British Novels* (Princeton: Princeton University Press, 2005).

23. Buzard, p. 34.

24. James Hogg, *The Spy*, ed. Gillian Hughes (Edinburgh: Edinburgh University Press, 2000), p. 230.

25. The material in the paragraphs above is also adapted from Plotz, 'The Whole Hogg', p. 324.

26. James Hogg, 'Singular Dream, From a Correspondent', *Winter Evening Tales*, pp. 159–65 (pp. 163, 164).
27. James Hogg, 'The Long Pack', *Winter Evening Tales*, pp. 130–40 (p. 134).
28. Hogg, 'The Long Pack', pp. 139, 140.
29. Cf. Bianca Theissen, 'Simultaneity: A Narrative Figure in Kleist', *MLN* 121 (2006), pp. 514–21.
30. Gillian Hughes, 'Introduction', in James Hogg, *Altrive Tales: Collected among the Peasantry of Scotland and from Foreign Adventurers By the Ettrick Shepherd*, ed. Hughes (Edinburgh: Edinburgh University Press, 2005), pp. xi–lxvii (p. xlix).
31. 'Footing' is Erving Goffman's term to describe a speaker's understanding of the social codes and local relationships that form the context within which a given utterance can be produced: *Forms of Talk* (Philadelphia: University of Pennsylvania Press, 1981), especially chapter 3, 'Footing', pp. 124–57.

Chapter 14 – Tulloch

1. James Hogg, 'Reminiscences of Former Days', in *Altrive Tales*, ed. Gillian Hughes (Edinburgh: Edinburgh University Press, 2003), p. 55.
2. James Hogg, *The Private Memoirs and Confessions of a Justified Sinner*, ed. P. D. Garside (Edinburgh: Edinburgh University Press, 2001), p. 175.
3. Ina Ferris, *The Romantic National Tale and the Question of Ireland* (Cambridge: Cambridge University Press, 2002), pp. 49–50.
4. Ian Duncan, *Scott's Shadow: The Novel in Romantic Edinburgh* (Princeton: Princeton University Press, 2007), pp. 70–8.
5. James Hogg, *The Three Perils of Man; or, War, Women and Witchcraft*, ed. Judy King and Graham Tulloch (Edinburgh: Edinburgh University Press, 2012), p. 43.
6. Hogg, *The Three Perils of Man*, p. 315.
7. 'Introduction' to *The Brownie of Bodsbeck*, in James Hogg, *Tales and Sketches by the Ettrick Shepherd*, 6 vols (Glasgow: Blackie and Son, 1836–7), I, p. 3.
8. Duncan, *Scott's Shadow*, p. 152.
9. P. D. Garside, 'Introduction', in Hogg, *Confessions of a Justified Sinner*, p. xiii.
10. Hogg, *The Three Perils of Man*, pp. 156–9, 187, 340.
11. Ian Duncan, 'Scotland and the Novel', in Richard Maxwell and Katie Trumpener (eds), *The Cambridge Companion to Fiction in the Romantic Period* (Cambridge: Cambridge University Press, 2008), p. 262.
12. Katie Trumpener, *Bardic Nationalism: The Romantic Novel and the British Empire* (Princeton: Princeton University Press, 1997), p. 111.
13. See, for example, Garside, 'Introduction', *Confessions of a Justified Sinner*, pp. xix–xx where Garside benefits, as he points out, from a long line of Hogg criticism.
14. Hogg, 'Reminiscences of Former Days', p. 55.

15. Hogg, *Confessions of a Justified Sinner*, p. 15. See also 'Notes', p. 217 and 'Historical and Geographical Note', pp. 200–5.

Chapter 15 – Fielding

1. James Hogg, *The Private Memoirs and Confessions of A Justified Sinner*, ed. Peter Garside (Edinburgh: Edinburgh University Press, 2001), p. 164. Further references appear in the text.
2. Susan Manning, *The Puritan-Provincial Vision: Scottish and American Literature in the Nineteenth Century* (Cambridge: Cambridge University Press, 1990), p. 83.
3. For helpful accounts of doubling in the novel see Barbara Bloedé, 'James Hogg's *The Private Memoirs and Confessions of a Justified Sinner*: The Genesis of the Double', *Etudes Anglaises* 26:2 (1973), pp. 174–86; Rosemary Jackson, *Fantasy: the Literature of Subversion* (London: Methuen, 1981), pp. 49–51 and 106–7; Karl Miller, *Doubles* (Oxford: Oxford University Press, 1985), pp. 1–20.
4. Penguin Freud Library, vol. 14: *Art and Literature* (Harmondsworth: Penguin, 1990), p. 357.
5. Eve Kosofsky Sedgwick, *Between Men: English Literature and Male Homosocial Desire* (New York: Columbia University Press, 1985), p. 106.
6. Ibid.
7. Ian Duncan, *Scott's Shadow: The Novel in Romantic Edinburgh* (Princeton: Princeton University Press, 2007), p. 213.
8. Nicholas Abraham and Maria Torok, *The Shell and the Kernel*, trans. Nicholas Rand (Chicago: Chicago University Press, 1994).
9. Scott Mackenzie, 'Confessions of a Gentrified Sinner: Secrets in Scott and Hogg', *Studies in Romanticism* 41:1 (2002), pp. 3–32 (p. 25).
10. Douglas S. Mack, *Scottish Fiction and the British Empire* (Edinburgh: Edinburgh University Press, 2006), pp. 159–66.
11. Murray Pittock, *Scottish and Irish Romanticism* (Oxford: Oxford University Press 2008), p. 217.
12. *The Scotsman* 24 (5 July 1817).
13. John MacQueen, *The Enlightenment and Scottish Literature*, vol. 2, *The Rise of the Historical Novel* (Edinburgh: Scottish Academic Press, 1989), pp. 245–51.
14. Cairns Craig, *Out of History: Narrative Paradigms in Scottish and English Culture* (Edinburgh: Edinburgh University Press, 1996), p. 76.
15. Ina Ferris, 'Scholarly Revivals: Gothic Fiction, Secret History, and Hogg's *Private Memoirs and Confessions of a Justified Sinner*', in *Recognising the Romantic Novel: New Histories of British Fiction, 1780–1830*, ed. Jillian Heydt-Stevenson and Charlotte Sussman (Liverpool, 2008), pp. 267–84 (pp. 280–1).
16. For example see Peter Garside, 'Printing *Confessions*', *Studies in Hogg and his World* 9 (1988), pp. 16–31.

17. Pierre Bourdieu, *The Field of Cultural Production: Essays on Art and Literature*, ed. Randal Johnson (Oxford: Polity Press, 1993), pp. 118–19.

18. David Groves, *James Hogg: The Growth of a Writer* (Edinburgh: Scottish Academic Press, 1988), p. 127.

19. Mark L. Schoenfield, 'Butchering James Hogg: Romantic Identity in the Magazine Market', in Mary A. Favret and Nicola J. Watson (eds), *At the Limits of Romanticism: Essays in Cultural, Feminist, and Materialist Criticism* (Bloomington: Indiana University Press, 1994), pp. 207–24 (p. 211).

20. Duncan, *Scott's Shadow*, p. 285.

21. Jacques Derrida, *Demeure: Fiction and Testimony*, trans. Elizabeth Rottenberg (Stanford: Stanford University Press, 2000), p. 43.

22. For Calvinism in the novel see Manning, *Puritan-Provincial*, pp. 80–4, and Crawford Gribben, 'James Hogg, Scottish Calvinism and literary theory', *Scottish Studies Review* 5:2 (2004), pp. 9–26.

23. Ian Duncan, 'Fanaticism and Civil Society: Hogg's Justified Sinner', *Novel: A Forum on Fiction* 42:2 (2009), pp. 343–8 (p. 344).

24. Meredith Evans. 'Persons Fall Apart: James Hogg's Transcendent Sinner', *Novel: A Forum on Fiction* 36:2 (2003), pp. 198–218 (p. 199).

Chapter 16 – Hughes

1. James Hogg, *The Private Memoirs and Confessions of a Justified Sinner*, ed. P. D. Garside (Edinburgh: Edinburgh University Press, 2001), pp. xi, lxxi, xcvi.

2. Emily Brontë, *Wuthering Heights*, ed. Ian Jack (Oxford: Oxford University Press, 1981), pp. 33, 82; 'A Scots Mummy', *Blackwood's Edinburgh Magazine*, 14 (August 1823), pp. 188–90; for Branwell's letter to the Blackwood firm of December 1835 see Margaret Oliphant, *Annals of a Publishing House: William Blackwood and his Sons*, 2 vols (Edinburgh and London: William Blackwood, 1897), II, pp. 177–9.

3. See Eric Massie, 'Robert Louis Stevenson and *The Private Memoirs and Confessions of a Justified Sinner*', *Studies in Hogg and his World*, 10 (1999), pp. 73–7.

4. See Andrew Lang, 'Our Fathers' and Joseph Conrad, 'The Heart of Darkness' in *Blackwood's Edinburgh Magazine* 165 (February 1899), pp. 165–6, 193–220 (online at www.conradfirst.net/view/image?id=22849).

5. For 'The Blast of the Book' and 'The Hammer of God' see G. K. Chesterton, *The Penguin Complete Father Brown* (Harmondsworth: Penguin Books, 1981), pp. 620–31 (p. 622) and 118–31 respectively.

6. Sir Arthur Conan Doyle, 'The Final Problem', in *The Memoirs of Sherlock Holmes* (Harmondsworth: Penguin Books, 1950, repr. 1981), pp. 236–55.

7. Hermann Hesse, *Demian*, trans. by W. J. Strachan (London: Panther, 1969, repr. 1978). (Thanks to Robert Calder for this suggestion.)

8. Karl Miller, *Doubles: Studies in Literary History* (Oxford: Oxford University

Press, 1985), p. 415; Vladimir Nabokov, *Despair* (London: Penguin Books, 2000), pp. 20, 144, 167–8.

9. Peter Guttridge, *Two to Tango* (London: Headline, 1998), p. 238.
10. James Hynes, *The Lecturer's Tale* (New York: Picador, 2001); James Lasdun, *The Horned Man* (London: Vintage, 2002).
11. *London Review of Books* (25 March 2010), p. 40.
12. Ian Rankin, *Exit Music* (London: Orion, 2007); *The Falls* (London: Orion, 2001), p. 202.
13. Ian Rankin, *The Black Book*, in *Three Great Novels: Rebus: The St Leonard's Years* (London: Orion, 2001), p. 328.
14. John Herdman, *Pagan's Pilgrimage* (Blackburn: Akros, 1978), p. 7.
15. Stuart Hood, *The Upper Hand* (Manchester: Carcanet Press, 1987), pp. 71, 25, 162, 182.
16. James Robertson, *The Testament of Gideon Mack* (London: Hamish Hamilton, 2006), pp. 361, 214, 36, 27.
17. Emma Tennant, *The Bad Sister* (London: Picador, 1979, repr. 1983), p. 138.
18. Sebastian Faulks, *Engleby* (London: Vintage, 2008).
19. Alice Munro, *The View from Castle Rock* (London: Chatto & Windus, 2006), p. 7.
20. *Friend of My Youth* (London: Vintage, 1996), pp. 20–1.
21. 'A Wilderness Station', in *Open Secrets* (London: Vintage, 1995), pp. 190–225 (pp. 191, 225).
22. Robertson Davies, *Murther & Walking Spirits* (London: Sinclair-Stevenson, 1991), p. 354.
23. For further information on Thomas Wilson's opera (unfortunately the recording is not currently available commercially) see www.thomaswilsoncomposer.co.uk.
24. *Confessions of a Justified Sinner* by James Hogg adapted by Mark Thomson was performed at Edinburgh's Royal Lyceum Theatre from 16 October to 7 November 2009 – for further information see the programme. Alexander Reid's version was broadcast on Radio 4 on 3 January 1983.

Further Reading

Hogg's works

The Stirling/South Carolina Research Edition of the Collected Works of James Hogg, published by Edinburgh University Press, has been in progress since 1995, under the general editorship of Douglas S. Mack and Gillian Hughes and (latterly) Suzanne Gilbert and Ian Duncan. At time of writing (September 2011) twenty-five of the projected thirty-nine volumes have appeared, with several titles available in paperback, including Peter Garside's edition of *The Private Memoirs and Confessions of a Justified Sinner* (2002). Several other versions of the *Justified Sinner* are currently in print, including those edited by Ian Duncan (Oxford University Press, 2010), Adrian Hunter (Broadview, 2001) and Karl Miller (Penguin, 2006).

Life and Letters

Hughes, Gillian (ed.), *The Collected Letters of James Hogg* (3 vols; Edinburgh: Edinburgh University Press, 2005, 2006, 2008).

Hughes, Gillian, *James Hogg: A Life* (Edinburgh: Edinburgh University Press, 2007).

Miller, Karl, *Electric Shepherd: A Likeness of James Hogg* (London: Faber, 2003).

Criticism: Book-length Studies of Hogg

Alker, Sharon and Holly Faith Nelson (eds), *James Hogg and the Literary Marketplace* (Farnham: Ashgate, 2009).

Bold, Valentina, *James Hogg: A Bard of Nature's Making* (Oxford: Peter Lang, 2007).

Gifford, Douglas, *James Hogg* (Edinburgh: Ramsay Head, 1976).

Groves, David, *James Hogg: The Growth of a Writer* (Edinburgh: Scottish Academic Press, 1988).

Mergenthal, Silvia, *James Hogg, Selbstbild und Bild: zur Rezeption des 'Ettrick Shepherd'* (Frankfurt-am-Main and New York: Peter Lang, 1990).

Simpson, Louis A. M., *James Hogg: A Critical Study* (New York: St Martin's Press, 1962).

Criticism: Monographs featuring Significant Discussion of Hogg

Craig, Cairns, *Out of History: Narrative Paradigms in Scottish and English Culture* (Edinburgh: Edinburgh University Press, 1996).

Craig, David, *Scottish Literature and the Scottish People, 1680–1833* (London: Chatto & Windus, 1961).

Duncan, Ian, *Scott's Shadow: The Novel in Romantic Edinburgh* (Princeton: Princeton University Press, 2007).

Fang, Karen, *Romantic Writing and the Empire of Signs: Periodical Culture and Post-Napoleonic Authorship* (Charlottesville and London: University of Virginia Press, 2010).

Fielding, Penny, *Writing and Orality: Nationality, Culture, and Nineteenth-Century Scottish Fiction* (Oxford: Clarendon Press, 1996).

Fielding, Penny, *Scotland and the Fictions of Geography: North Britain 1760–1830* (Cambridge: Cambridge University Press, 2008).

Harris, Jason Marc, *Folklore and the Fantastic in Nineteenth-Century British Fiction* (Aldershot: Ashgate, 2008).

Kelly, Gary, *English Fiction of the Romantic Period, 1789–1830* (London: Longmans, 1989).

Killick, Tim, *British Short Fiction in the Early Nineteenth Century: The Rise of the Tale* (Burlington: Ashgate, 2008).

Mack, Douglas S., *Scottish Fiction and the British Empire* (Edinburgh: Edinburgh University Press, 2006).

MacQueen, John, *The Enlightenment and Scottish Literature, Vol. 2: The Rise of the Historical Novel* (Edinburgh: Scottish Academic Press, 1989).

Manning, Susan, *The Puritan-Provincial Vision: Scottish and American Literature in the Nineteenth Century* (Cambridge: Cambridge University Press, 1990).

Maxwell, Richard, *The Historical Novel in Europe, 1650–1950* (Cambridge: Cambridge University Press, 2009).

McLane, Maureen N., *Balladeering, Minstrelsy, and the Making of British Romantic Poetry* (Cambridge: Cambridge University Press, 2008).

Miller, Karl, *Doubles: Studies in Literary History* (Oxford: Oxford University Press, 1985).

Pittock, Murray, *Poetry and Jacobite Politics in Eighteenth-Century Britain and Ireland* (Cambridge: Cambridge University Press, 1994).

Pittock, Murray, *Scottish and Irish Romanticism* (Oxford: Oxford University Press, 2008).

Robertson, Fiona, *Legitimate Histories: Scott, Gothic and the Authorities of Fiction* (Oxford: Oxford University Press, 1994).

Russett, Margaret, *Fictions and Fakes: Forging Romantic Authenticity, 1760–1845* (Cambridge: Cambridge University Press, 2006).

Schoenfield, Mark, *British Periodicals and Romantic Identity: The Literary 'Lower Empire'* (Houndsmills: Palgrave Macmillan, 2008).

Sedgwick, Eve Kosofsky, *Between Men: English Literature and Male Homosocial Desire* (New York: Columbia University Press, 1985).

Shields, Juliet, *Sentimental Literature and Anglo-Scottish Identity, 1745–1820* (Cambridge: Cambridge University Press, 2010).

Simpson, Erik, *Literary Minstrelsy, 1770–1830: Minstrels and Improvisers in British, Irish, and American Literature* (Houndmills: Palgrave Macmillan, 2008).

Trumpener, Katie, *Bardic Nationalism: The Romantic Novel and the British Empire* (Princeton: Princeton University Press, 1997).

Watson, Nicola, *Revolution and the Form of the British Novel, 1790–1805: Intercepted Letters, Interrupted Seductions* (New York: Oxford University Press, 1994).

Criticism: Selected Essays

Studies in Hogg and his World (hereafter *SHW*), the journal of the James Hogg Society, edited by Gillian Hughes (1990–2010) and H. B. de Groot (2011–), is an indispensable resource for scholars and students. Some essays of broad interest, in *SHW* and elsewhere, include:

Alexander, J. H., 'Hogg in the *Noctes Ambrosianae*.' *SHW* 4 (1993), pp. 37–47.

Alker, Sharon and Holly Faith Nelson, '"Ghastly in the Moonlight": Wordsworth, Hogg, and the Anguish of War', *SHW* 15 (2004), pp. 76–89.

Barrell, John, 'Putting down the Rising', in Leith Davis, Ian Duncan and Janet Sorensen (eds), *Scotland and the Borders of Romanticism* (Cambridge: Cambridge University Press, 2004), pp. 130–8.

Beveridge, Allan, 'James Hogg and Abnormal Psychology: Some Background Notes', *SHW* 2 (1991), pp. 91–4.

Bloedé, Barbara, 'James Hogg's *Private Memoirs and Confessions of a Justified Sinner:* The Genesis of the Double', *Etudes Anglaises* 26:2 (1973), pp. 174–86.

Bold, Valentina, 'The Magic Lantern: Hogg and Science', *SHW* 7 (1996), pp. 5–17.

Campbell, Ian, 'James Hogg and the Bible', in *The Bible and Scottish Literature*, ed. David F. Wright (Edinburgh, 1988), pp. 94–109.

Crawford, Thomas, 'James Hogg: The Play of Region and Nation', in *The History of Scottish Literature: Volume 3, Nineteenth Century*, ed. Douglas Gifford (Aberdeen: Aberdeen University Press, 1988), pp. 89–105.

de Groot, H. B., 'The Imperilled Reader in *The Three Perils of Man*', *SHW* 1 (1990), pp. 114–25.

Duncan, Ian, 'Sympathy, Physiognomy, and Scottish Romantic Fiction', in Jill Heydt-Stevenson and Charlotte Sussman (eds), *Recognizing the Romantic*

Novel: New Histories of British Fiction, 1780–1830 (Liverpool: Liverpool University Press, 2008), pp. 249–69.

Duncan, Ian, 'Fanaticism and Civil Society: Hogg's Justified Sinner', *Novel: A Forum on Fiction* 42:2 (2009), pp. 343–8.

Evans, Meredith, 'Persons Fall Apart: James Hogg's Transcendent Sinner', *Novel: A Forum on Fiction* 36:2 (2003), pp. 198–218.

Ferris, Ina, 'Scholarly Revivals: Gothic Fiction, Secret History, and Hogg's *Private Memoirs and Confessions of a Justified Sinner*', in Jillian Heydt-Stevenson and Charlotte Sussman (eds), *Recognizing the Romantic Novel: New Histories of British Fiction, 1780–1830* (Liverpool: Liverpool University Press, 2008), pp. 267–84.

Fielding, Penny, 'Burial Letters: Death and Dreaming in "Cousin Mattie"', *SHW* 16 (2005), pp. 5–19.

Garside, Peter, 'Three Perils in Publishing: Hogg and the Popular Novel', *SHW* 2 (1991), pp. 45–63.

Garside, Peter, 'Hogg and the Blackwoodian Novel', *SHW* 15 (2004), pp. 5–20.

Garside, Peter, and Gillian Hughes, 'James Hogg's "Tales and Sketches" and the Glasgow Number Trade', *Cardiff Corvey: Reading the Romantic Text* 14 (Summer 2005). At: www.romtext.cf.ac.uk/articles/cc14_n02.html.

Goldsmith, Jason N., 'Hogging the Limelight: *The Queen's Wake* and the Rise of Celebrity Authorship', *SHW* 16 (2005), pp. 52–60.

Gribben, Crawford, 'James Hogg, Scottish Calvinism and Literary Theory', *Scottish Studies Review* 5:2 (2004), pp. 9–26.

Groves, David, 'James Hogg's *Confessions* and *The Three Perils of Woman* and the Edinburgh Prostitution Scandal of 1823', *The Wordsworth Circle* 18 (1987), pp. 127–31.

Hasler, Antony J., 'Reading the Land: James Hogg and the Highlands', *SHW* 4 (1993), pp. 57–82.

Hughes, Gillian, 'James Hogg and Edinburgh's Triumph over Napoleon', *Scottish Studies Review* 4:1 (2003), pp. 98–111.

Hughes, Gillian, 'Hogg, Gillies, and German Romanticism', *SHW* 14 (2003), pp. 62–72.

Hughes, Gillian, 'Hogg, Wallace, and Waterloo', *SHW* 18 (2007), pp. 24–33.

Inglis, Katherine, '"My Ingenious Answer to that Most Exquisite Question": Perception and Testimony in *Winter Evening Tales*', *SHW* 17 (2006), pp. 81–95.

Inglis, Katherine, 'Maternity, Madness and Mechanization: The Ghastly Automaton in James Hogg's *The Three Perils of Woman*', in Deirdre Coleman and Hilary Fraser (eds), *Minds, Bodies, Machines: 1770–1930* (Houndmills: Palgrave Macmillan, 2011), pp. 61–82.

Jackson, Richard D., 'Gatty Bell's Illness in James Hogg's *The Three Perils of Woman*', *SHW* 14 (2003), pp. 16–29.

Mack, Douglas S., 'Lights and Shadows of Scottish Life: James Hogg's *The Three Perils of Woman*', in Horst W. Drescher and Joachim Schwend (eds), *Studies in Scottish Fiction: Nineteenth Century* (Frankfurt-am-Mainz, Bern and New York: Publications of the Scottish Studies Centre of the Universitat Mainz 3, 1985), pp. 15–27.

Mack, Douglas S., 'Aspects of the Supernatural in the Shorter Fiction of James Hogg', in Valeria Tinkler-Villani and Peter Davidson (eds), *Exhibited by Candlelight: Sources in the Gothic Tradition* (Atlanta: Rodopi, 1995), pp. 129–35.

Mackenzie, Scott, 'Confessions of a Gentrified Sinner: Secrets in Scott and Hogg', *Studies in Romanticism* 41:1 (2002), pp. 3–32.

MacLachlan, Robin, 'Scott and Hogg: Friendship and Literary Influence', in J. H. Alexander and David Hewitt (eds), *Scott and his Influence* (Aberdeen: Association for Scottish Literary Studies, 1983), pp. 331–40.

MacLachlan, Robin, 'Hogg and the Art of Brand Management', *SHW* 14 (2003), pp. 5–15.

Manning, Susan, 'That Exhumation Scene Again: Transatlantic Hogg', *SHW* 16 (2005), pp. 86–111.

McCracken-Flesher, Caroline, '"The great disturber of the age": James Hogg at the King's Visit, 1822', *SHW* 9 (1998), pp. 64–83.

McCracken-Flesher, Caroline, 'The Fourth Peril of James Hogg: Walter Scott and the Demonology of Minstrelsy', *SHW* 11 (2000), pp. 39–55.

McCue, Kirsteen, 'From the Songs of *Albyn's Anthology* to *German Hebrew Melodies*: The Musical Adventures of James Hogg', *SHW* 20 (2009), pp. 67–83.

Mergenthal, Silvia, 'James Hogg and his "Best Benefactor": Two Versions of Hogg's Anecdotes of Scott', *SHW* 4 (1993), pp. 26–36.

O'Halloran, Meiko, 'Treading the Borders of Fiction: Veracity, Identity, and Corporeality in *The Three Perils*', *SHW* 12 (2001), pp. 40–55.

Petrie, Elaine, 'Hogg as Songwriter', *SHW* 1 (1990), pp. 19–29.

Pittock, Murray, 'James Hogg and the Jacobite Song of Scotland', *SHW* 14 (2003) pp. 73–87.

Polsgrove, Carol, 'They Made it Pay: British Short-Fiction Writers, 1820–1840', *Studies in Short Fiction* 11 (1974), pp. 417–21.

Redekop, Magdalene, 'Beyond Closure: Buried Alive with Hogg's *Justified Sinner*', *ELH* 52: 1 (1985), pp. 159–84.

Rubenstein, Jill, 'Varieties of Explanation in *The Shepherd's Calendar*', *SHW* 4 (1993), pp. 1–11.

Schoenfield, Mark, 'Butchering James Hogg: Romantic Identity in the Magazine Market', in Mary A. Favret and Nicola Watson (eds), *At the Limits of Romanticism: Essays in Cultural, Feminist, and Materialist Criticism* (Bloomington: Indiana University Press, 1994), pp. 207–24.

Shepherd, W. G., 'Fat Flesh: The Poetic Theme of *The Three Perils of Man*', *SHW* 3 (1992), pp. 1–9.

Sutherland, Helen, 'James Hogg: A Shepherd's Role in the Scottish Enlightenment', *SHW* 19 (2008), pp. 5–20.

Tulloch, Graham, 'Writing "By Advice": *Ivanhoe* and *The Three Perils of Man*', *SHW* 15 (2004), pp. 32–52.

Tulloch, Graham, 'Hogg in the 1890s', *SHW* 17 (2006), pp. 19–35.

Webb, Samantha, 'Inappropriating the Literary: James Hogg's *Poetic Mirror* Parodies of Scott and Wordsworth', *SHW* 13 (2002), pp. 16–35.

Weber, Carolyn, 'Delighting in the Indissoluble Mixture: The Motley Romanticism of James Hogg', *SHW* 17 (2006), pp. 49–62.

Web

The James Hogg Research Website (www.jameshogg.stir.ac.uk/about.php) provides a full listing of early American publications of Hogg texts, early sheet publications of Hogg's songs, digitised reproductions of Hogg's song-sheets, the texts of the songs, and a hitherto unrecorded short story ('Death at Sea'), as well as downloadable recordings of selected Hogg songs.

Notes on Contributors

Sharon Alker is Associate Professor of English at Whitman College. She is co-editor of *James Hogg and the Literary Marketplace* (2009) and has also published, often with Holly Faith Nelson, on the works of Daniel Defoe, Margaret Cavendish, William Lithgow, Maria Edgeworth and others. More recently, she is co-editor of the forthcoming collection *Transatlantic Burns* (2012).

Valentina Bold is Reader in Literature and Ethnology at the University of Glasgow, Dumfries, where she is currently developing the Solway Centre for Environment and Culture. Publications include *James Hogg: A Bard of Nature's Making* (2007), *Smeddum: A Lewis Grassic Gibbon Anthology* (2001), and an edition of Burns's *The Merry Muses of Caledonia* (2009).

H. B. de Groot taught at the University of Toronto from 1965 until mandatory retirement in 2004, but has since then returned to part-time teaching. He is the editor of the *Highland Journeys* volume in the Stirling/South Carolina edition of the Collected Works of James Hogg, published in 2010. He also edits the periodical *Studies in Hogg and his World*.

Ian Duncan is Florence Green Bixby Professor of English at the University of California, Berkeley. His books include *Scott's Shadow: The Novel in Romantic Edinburgh* (2007), *Modern Romance and Transformations of the Novel* (1992), *Scotland and the Borders of Romanticism* (co-editor, 2004), and the new Oxford World's Classics edition of *The Private Memoirs and Confessions of a Justified Sinner* (2010). He is a General Editor of the Collected Works of James Hogg, for which he edited *Winter Evening Tales* (2002).

Penny Fielding teaches English and Scottish Literature at the University of Edinburgh, where she is co-director of the project for Scottish Writing in the Nineteenth Century (SWINC). Her books include *Scotland and the Fictions of Geography: North Britain 1760–1830* (2008), *Writing and Orality: Nationality,*

Culture and Nineteenth-Century Scottish Fiction (1996), and the Edinburgh Edition of Scott's *The Monastery* (2001).

Peter Garside is Honorary Professorial Fellow at the University of Edinburgh. He has helped provide a number of bibliographical resources relating to British fiction of the Romantic period, including *The English Novel, 1770–1829* (2000), and has also edited a number of novels belonging to this period, among them Hogg's *Private Memoirs and Confessions of a Justified Sinner* (2001) and Scott's *Waverley* (2007).

Suzanne Gilbert is Senior Lecturer in English at the University of Stirling. She is a General Editor of the Stirling/South Carolina Research Edition of the Collected Works of James Hogg, for which she has edited *The Mountain Bard* (2007) and *Scottish Pastorals* (2012), and co-edited *Queen Hynde* (1998); and a co-editor of the forthcoming *Edinburgh Companion to Scottish Traditional Literatures*. Other publications include articles on eighteenth- and nineteenth-century Scottish literature, ballads, and chapbooks.

Gillian Hughes is the author of *James Hogg: A Life* (2007), and has edited or co-edited several volumes in the Stirling/South Carolina Edition of his works, including the three-volume *Collected Letters of James Hogg* (2004–8). She was the founding editor of *Studies in Hogg and his World* and is currently working towards a new Hogg bibliography.

Douglas S. Mack, late Professor of English at the University of Stirling, led the modern recovery of Hogg's reputation. The founding General Editor of the Stirling/South Carolina Research Edition of the Collected Works of James Hogg, he edited several volumes in the series, as well as the Edinburgh Edition of Scott's *Tale of Old Mortality*. In addition to articles on Hogg, Scott, and Scottish literature, he is the author of a monograph, *Scottish Fiction and the British Empire* (2006).

Caroline McCracken-Flesher is Professor of English at the University of Wyoming. Her publications include *Possible Scotlands: Walter Scott and the Story of Tomorrow* (2005) and *The Doctor Dissected: A Cultural Anatomy of Burke and Hare* (2011). She is the editor of volumes of critical essays on the Scottish Parliament (2008) and Scottish science fiction (2011), as well as the forthcoming *Approaches to Teaching the Works of Robert Louis Stevenson* (2012).

Kirsteen McCue is Head of Scottish literature and co-director of the Centre for Robert Burns Studies at the University of Glasgow. She has published on Romantic song culture and is the editor of James Hogg's *Songs by the Ettrick*

Shepherd and his *Contributions to Musical Collections and Miscellaneous Songs* for the Collected Works of James Hogg. She will edit Robert Burns's songs for George Thomson for the new Oxford Collected Works of Robert Burns.

Silvia Mergenthal is a Professor of English literature and literary theory at the University of Konstanz, where she also coordinates the university's Gender Studies programme. She has published extensively on English and Scottish Romanticism, and is also interested, more generally, in constructions of identity at the interface of gender, ethnicity, and class.

Holly Faith Nelson is Professor and Chair of English at Trinity Western University in Langley, British Columbia. She has published widely on the literature of the long eighteenth century, with a focus on works by Scottish authors as well as on the treatment of the Scot in literature. She has recently co-edited *James Hogg and the Literary Marketplace: Scottish Romanticism and the Working Class Author* (2009) and *Robert Burns and Transatlantic Culture* (2012).

Meiko O'Halloran is a Lecturer in Romantic Literature at Newcastle University. Her publications include two essays for volumes of the Stirling/South Carolina Collected Works of James Hogg, *The Queen's Wake* (2004) and *Midsummer Night Dreams* (2008). She is currently completing a monograph on Hogg.

John Plotz is Professor of Victorian literature at Brandeis University. He is the author of *The Crowd: British Literature and Public Politics* (2000) and *Portable Property: Victorian Culture on the Move* (2008); his current project is 'Semi-Detached: The Aesthetics of Partial Absorption'. He is a Guggenheim Foundation Fellow and a residential Fellow of the Radcliffe Institute for Advanced Study in 2011–12.

Graham Tulloch is Professor of English at Flinders University and has edited novels by Scott and Hogg, including *Ivanhoe* (1998) and *The Three Perils of Man* (2011). He is the author of various books and articles on Scottish literature and language, including *The Language of Walter Scott* (1980).

Fiona Wilson teaches at Sarah Lawrence College. A poet and scholar, she works on British Romanticism and Scottish literature. She has contributed essays to the Edinburgh Companions to *Contemporary Scottish Poetry* and *Contemporary Scottish Literature*, and to the forthcoming *Approaches to Teaching Robert Louis Stevenson*. She is currently writing a book on Byron and Scotland.

Index